The Black Presence

in the Era of

the American Revolution

1770-1800

The Black Presence in the Era
of the American Revolution
1770-1800

SIDNEY KAPLAN

NATIONAL PORTRAIT GALLERY

SMITHSONIAN INSTITUTION   CITY OF WASHINGTON   1973

Published by the NEW YORK GRAPHIC SOCIETY LTD.

in association with the SMITHSONIAN INSTITUTION PRESS

EXHIBITION STAFF

BEVERLY JONES COX, Coordinator of Exhibitions
JOSEPH MICHAEL CARRIGAN, Designer of Exhibition Installation

International Standard Book Number 0-8212-0541-2 (cloth)
International Standard Book Number 0-8212-0541-5 (paper)
Library of Congress Card Catalog Number 73-79335
Smthsonian Institution Press Number 4831

First published 1973 by the New York Graphic Society Ltd.,
140 Greenwich Avenue, Greenwich, Connecticut 06830,
in association with the Smithsonian Institution Press

Manufactured in the United States of America
by Vinmar Lithographing Company
Designed by Elizabeth Sur

Frontispiece: The Battle of Bunker Hill
by James Mitan (1776-1822)
after John Trumbull

CONTENTS

FOREWORD

An exhibition on *The Black Presence in the Era of the American Revolution 1770-1800,* presented by a museum called the National Portrait Gallery, is by its very nature a precarious—and worthwhile—enterprise. Among the many hundreds of portraits painted during this period, the faces of Afro-Americans are very rare. For this reason, the authentic few that have survived are all the more crucial to the construction of a true iconography of the Revolution.

While portraits are, of course, the first business of the National Portrait Gallery, the Gallery's ultimate aim is to tell the whole history of this country in terms of the individuals who made that history. Too often, the images of black men and women, eminent or otherwise, in this period have not come down to us. Sometimes a portrait in words on the frayed pages of original documents has had to serve in lieu of a pictorial likeness. For example, although there is no genuine portrait of that magnificent black Bostonian, Prince Hall, we can savor the quality of the man in the eloquence of his speeches and letters. Not all Afro-Americans were of Prince Hall's stature. We will never know what the four courageous slaves who signed a petition to the general court of Massachusetts in April of 1773 looked like, but the words of their admonition—"We expect great things from men who have made such a noble stand against the designs of their *fellow-men* to enslave them"—give us a pretty good notion of what manner of men they must have been. As noted in the text, "their portraits are vivid in the language of their pleas."

Where reliable likenesses exist, such as those of William Lee, James Armistead Lafayette, and Agrippa Hull, who served Generals Washington, Lafayette, and Kosciuszko, by supplementing their portraits with documentary evidence of their activities and characters, we are able to arrive at a fuller understanding of the *dramatis personae* of the epoch. (Only half of the more than two hundred items shown in the exhibition and listed in the catalog at the end of this book are reproduced in these pages.)

Among the black clergy of this period we are fortunate in having a number of good portraits, and one great one, that of Absalom Jones by Raphaelle Peale. If this painting (which narrowly escaped oblivion) stirs us because of the sure power with which the artist limned the strength and dignity of his sitter, we are no less grateful to look upon the small pastel-and-chalk likeness of his compatriot, Richard Allen, done about the time both men, dragged from their knees at St. George's Methodist Church in Philadelphia, set out to found a church where they could pray in peace. Also represented among the clergy are two portraits of Lemuel Haynes, but, alas, none of John Marrant, whose magnetic words are all that we have left to conjure up what must have been a moving presence.

Thankful as we are that we have any portraits at all of figures like Benjamin Banneker and Paul Cuffe, Phillis Wheatley and Olaudah Equiano, whose gifts and powers loomed so large in the Revolutionary Era, we must nevertheless regret that these portraits do not match in quality the achievements of their subjects. Now and then, as in the case of Banneker, there exists a portrait in the words of his time which fleshes out the image, telling us not only what the man looked like but what he was like: "His ample forehead, white hair, and reverent deportment, gave him a venerable appearance, as he leaned on the long staff (which he always carried with him) in contemplation. . . . The countenance of Banneker had a most benign and thoughtful expression. . . . His figure was perfectly erect, showing no inclination to stoop as he advanced in years." Indeed, one person who knew the black astronomer thought "the statue of Franklin at the Library in Philadelphia the perfect likeness of him."

I should note that the present exhibition and this book are but a part of the undertaking as initially conceived. The original idea—to record in portrait, document, and artifact the black achievement in America over a span of two centuries—was a comprehensive enterprise, tentatively titled, *The Afro-American: Portraits of Men and Women of Mark from the Revolution to the Second World War.*

To initiate this project, I asked Dr. Sidney Kaplan, who collaborated with me on the exhibition, *The Portrayal of the Negro in American Painting, 1710-1963,* held at Bowdoin College almost ten years ago, to take a leave from his professorial post at the University of Massachusetts and come to Washington. Dr. Kaplan, who for almost thirty years has been a student of the black presence in American history, literature, and art, teaches in the English Department and the W. E. B. DuBois Department of Afro-American Studies at his university. In 1949, he was awarded a Bancroft Prize by the *Journal of Negro History;* in 1969 he co-edited the well-known anthology, *Black and White in American Culture;* and he is at present a consulting editor of the papers of W. E. B. DuBois, now being published by the University of Massachusetts Press.

A distinguished Advisory Committee consisting of several historians and critics, a journalist, a poet, and an artist, generously agreed to lend their knowledge to the project. I am deeply grateful to Romare H. Bearden, Ernest Kaiser, Dorothy Porter, Dudley Randall, Benjamin Quarles, Chuck Stone, Darwin T. Turner, and Charles H. Wesley.

It became increasingly clear, after a year and a half of intensive research at the National Portrait Gallery, that the sheer abundance of vital materials being gathered to illustrate two centuries of Afro-American history could not be encompassed within a single exhibition. It therefore seemed right to divide the exhibition into three parts, the first to deal with the Revolutionary Era. In his acknowledgments and text, Dr. Kaplan has expressed our gratitude for the help given by those members of the Advisory Committee whose scholarship in the Revolutionary period has been of great value to this undertaking.

MARVIN SADIK, Director
National Portrait Gallery, Smithsonian Institution

LENDERS TO THE EXHIBITION

Albany Institute of History and Art
Allegheny College Library, Meadville, Pennsylvania
American Antiquarian Society
American Philosophical Society
Amherst College Library
The Library of the Boston Athenaeum
The Bostonian Society
Bowdoin College Library, Brunswick, Maine
Buten Museum of Wedgewood, Merion, Pennsylvania
William L. Clements Library, The University of Michigan, Ann Arbor
College of Charleston Library
The Connecticut Historical Society
Connecticut State Library
Cornell University Library
Duke University Library
Enoch Pratt Free Library, Baltimore, Maryland
Free Library of Philadelphia
Georgetown University Library, Washington, D.C.
Historical Society of Montgomery County, Norristown, Pennsylvania
Historical Society of Pennsylvania
Howard University Library, Washington, D.C.
Lafayette College, Easton, Pennsylvania
Library Company of Philadelphia
Library of Congress
Maryland Historical Society
Massachusetts Historical Society
The Metropolitan Museum of Art
Mother Bethel African Methodist Episcopal Church, Philadelphia
Williston Memorial Library, Mount Holyoke College, South Hadley,
    Massachusetts
Museum of the City of New York
National Archives and Records Service
National Gallery of Art, Rosenwald Collection
The National Museum of History and Technology, Divisions of
    Numismatics and Military History, Smithsonian Institution
New Bedford Free Public Library
New Bedford Whaling Museum

ACKNOWLEDGMENTS

This volume could not have come into existence without the earlier labors of a few historians whose books pioneered the subject: most notably, Benjamin Quarles' *The Negro in the American Revolution,* indispensable for its masterly orchestration of the black military presence during the birthing-time of the Nation; William C. Nell's *The Colored Patriots of the American Revolution,* which over a century ago posed many of the basic questions; Laura E. Wilkes' early pamphlet on *Missing Pages in American History;* Dorothy Porter's bibliographical compilations, as well as her recent anthology of *Early American Negro Writing, 1760-1837;* Carter G. Woodson's *The History of the Negro Church* and *The Negro in Our History;* Charles H. Wesley's *Richard Allen;* and Herbert Aptheker's *A Documentary History of the Negro People in the United States.* In addition, scores of articles, notes, and passages from monographs—such as Rayford W. Logan's *Diplomatic Relations of the United States with Haiti*—have furnished clues and insights into the lives and deeds of the black Revolutionary generation. The pictorial and documentary materials included in the exhibition and treated in the text are carefully sourced in the descriptive catalog at the end of this volume, and an annotated copy of the manuscript has been placed for reference in the library of the National Portrait Gallery.

I am indebted to Beverly Jones Cox of the National Portrait Gallery for her knowledgeable and devoted assistance over a long period; to Joann Lewis, formerly of the Smithsonian Office of Exhibits, for calling to my attention the gravestone replicas which were made under her direction; to Richard E. Ahlborn of The National Museum of History and Technology for allowing me to consult his department's photographic archives; to Louise Daniel Hutchinson, Coordinator of Research for Anacostia Studies; to "Spike" Harris, indefatigable collector of Afro-Americana; to Milton Kaplan, Curator of Historical Prints at the Library of Congress; and to Richard Pruitt and Judith S. King.

Finally, without the expert collaboration of Emma Nogrady Kaplan, who was granted a leave from her post in the Smith College Library and worked with me in the capital, this book would not have seen the light of day.

SIDNEY KAPLAN
University of Massachusetts

Mounting an exhibition which includes such a large number of documents is particularly difficult because of the understandable reluctance of prospective lenders to part with these fragile, and, in many instances, unique pieces. The participating institutions and individuals have, nevertheless, shown a remarkable generosity in allowing this material to travel, and, for this, we are sincerely grateful.

Among those who have lent considerable assistance to this undertaking, special thanks are owed the following: Mr. Leo Flaherty, Curator, Archives Division, Commonwealth of Massachusetts; Mr. Robert A. Lauze, Director, Division of Records Management and Archives, The State of New Hampshire; Dr. Louis H. Manarin, State Archivist, Virginia State Library; Mr. William Runge, Curator of Rare Books, University of Virginia Library; Mr. James C. Brown, Archives Technician, National Archives; and especially Mrs. Dorothy Porter, Curator of the Moorland-Spingarn Collection, Howard University Library. For their patient response to repeated requests and aid in tracking down elusive material, we are also indebted to Mr. John D. Cushing and Miss Winifred Collins of the Massachusetts Historical Society, and Mr. John C. Dann, Curator of Manuscripts, Clements Library, University of Michigan. Mr. Herbert Sanborn, Exhibits Officer, and Mr. Leonard Faber, Visual Information Specialist, have spent much time and effort in expediting the loan process with the Library of Congress. The Reverend Joseph L. Joiner of the Mother Bethel African Methodist Episcopal Church Philadelphia, and Mr. F. Leonard Williams, chairman of the church's historical commission, were exceptionally generous in allowing us to borrow the original pulpit of their church carved by Richard Allen. We are grateful, too, for the willingness of the Bunker Hill Monument Association to lend us the rifle of Peter Salem which unfortunately was stolen from their museum during the interim and is still missing.

In several instances, we have been dependent upon reproductions of original documents, and we should like to thank Mr. George Cushing for his many photographs of material located in Massachusetts; Mr. R. E. Mobley, Director of Audiovisual Center, Savannah State College, for his photograph of the stained-glass window of the Reverend Andrew Bryan; and Mr. W. Franklin Gooding, Clerk, Circuit Court of Fairfax, Virginia, for permission to reproduce excerpts from the will of George Washington.

We are deeply appreciative of the efforts of the staff of the National Portrait Gallery, particularly Mrs. Joyce Chisley of the National Portrait Gallery–National Collection of Fine Arts Library; Mr. Jon Freshour, Registrar; Miss Suzanne Jenkins, Assistant Registrar; Mr. Eugene Mantie, Staff Photographer; and Miss Velda Warner, Mr. Elmer Snyder, and Mr. Duncan Macpherson of the Exhibition staff.

BEVERLY J. COX
Coordinator of Exhibitions

The Black Presence in the Era of the American Revolution 1770-1800

1. Liberty Displaying the Arts and Sciences. Samuel Jennings, 1792. Library Company of Philadelphia.

2

The celebration of a Revolution, especially one that promised liberty and justice for all, may provide an opportune moment for a fresh view of one feature of the event that for two centuries has been absent from the official rhetoric of the Fourth of July. It is the aim of this book, and its array of pictures and documents of the time, to restore to the national memory an historic fact that has been long suppressed or forgotten—the living presence of black men and women during the thirty years that stretched from the martyrdom of Crispus Attucks in the Boston Massacre of 1770 to the conspiracy of Gabriel Prosser in Virginia at the turn of the century.

In 1855, when William C. Nell, the pioneer black historian and abolitionist, published his *Colored Patriots of the American Revolution,* it was his friend, Harriet Beecher Stowe, who wrote the introduction to the volume [figure 2]. In considering the services of the black soldiers and sailors who had fought for the independence of the new Nation, she observed: "We are to reflect upon them as far more magnanimous," because they served "a nation which did not acknowledge them as citizens and equals, and in whose interests and prosperity they had less at stake. It was not for their own land they fought, not even for a land which had adopted them, but for a land which had enslaved them, and whose laws, even in freedom, oftener oppressed than protected. Bravery, under such circumstances, has a peculiar beauty and merit."

Not all were Patriots. As Benjamin Quarles points out in his study of *The Negro in the American Revolution,* the role of the black soldier in the Revolutionary War

can best be understood by realizing that his major loyalty was not to a place nor a people, but to a principle. Insofar as he had freedom of choice, he was likely to join the side that made him the quickest and best offer in terms of those "unalienable rights" of which Mr. Jefferson had spoken. Whoever invoked the image of liberty, be he American or British, could count on a ready response from the blacks.

Thus Thomas Peters of Virginia, for one, accepted Lord Dunmore's promise of freedom, joined the British army, sailed with the king's fleet to Nova Scotia, and ultimately returned to Africa to play a part as founding father of Sierra Leone. That for blacks the Revolution was incomplete would be clear enough at an early stage. "This Fourth of July is *yours,* not *mine,*" cried Frederick Douglass to the whites in his audience at Corinthian Hall in Rochester nine years before the Civil War.

Long nourished—or starved—on a stale textbook version of the Revolution that pictured a few million whites split into Patriots and Tories; while half a million slaves toiled quietly and loyally in the fields—a notion not entirely lacking in Samuel Jennings' anti-slavery painting of 1792, the first of its kind by an American artist [figure 1]—for some of us the sheer existence of a black Revolutionary generation may come as news from a buried past.

Since that fateful day in the summer of 1619 when twenty kidnapped Africans dragged their feet onto American soil, the Nation's slaves had never rested in their chains. Emerging now from the enforced anonymity of

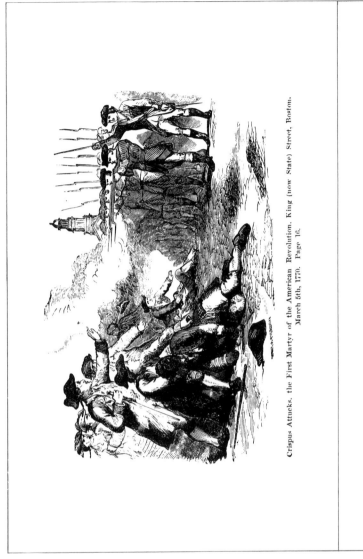

THE

COLORED PATRIOTS

OF THE

AMERICAN REVOLUTION,

WITH SKETCHES OF SEVERAL

DISTINGUISHED COLORED PERSONS:

TO WHICH IS ADDED A BRIEF SURVEY OF THE

Condition and Prospects of Colored Americans.

BY WM. C. NELL.

WITH AN INTRODUCTION BY
HARRIET BEECHER STOWE.

BOSTON:
PUBLISHED BY ROBERT F. WALLCUT.
1855.

Crispus Attucks, the First Martyr of the American Revolution, King (now State) Street, Boston. March 5th, 1770. Page 16.

2. *The Colored Patriots of the American Revolution*. William C. Nell, 1855. Library of Congress.

a century and a half of bondage—moved no doubt by slogans of liberty that filled the air—an advance guard of blacks, distinguished by the "peculiar beauty and merit" of their struggle for freedom and dignity, endowed with a variety of gifts and powers, forced an entrance onto the stage of American history as movers and shapers. Here are a few of their portraits and deeds in pictures and words—as soldier and sailor, founder of the black church, fighter for equality, organizer of school, lodge, and society; as scientist, writer, poet, artist, captain, physician, frontiersman, and rebel.

PART I ☞

Preludes

to

the

Declaration

The BLOODY MASSACRE perpetrated in King —┤— Street BOSTON on March 5th 1770 by a party of the 29th REGT.

Engrav'd Printed & Sold by PAUL REVERE BOSTON

BUTCHER'S HALL

Unhappy BOSTON! see thy Sons deplore,
Thy hallow'd Walks besmear'd with guiltless Gore.
While faithless P—n and his savage Bands,
With murd'rous Rancour stretch their bloody Hands;
Like fierce Barbarians grinning o'er their Prey,
Approve the Carnage, and enjoy the Day.

If scalding drops from Rage from Anguish Wrung,
If speechless Sorrows lab'ring for a Tongue,
Or if a weeping World can ought appease
The plaintive Ghosts of Victims such as these;
The Patriot's copious Tears for each are shed,
A glorious Tribute which embalms the Dead.

But know, FATE summons to that awful Goal,
Where JUSTICE strips the Murd'rer of his Soul:
Should venal C—ts the scandal of the Land,
Snatch the relentless Villain from her Hand,
Keen Execrations on this Plate inscrib'd,
Shall reach a JUDGE who never can be brib'd.

The unhappy Sufferers were Mess[rs]. SAM[L] GRAY, SAM[L] MAVERICK, JAM[S] CALDWELL, CRISPUS ATTUCKS & PAT[K] CARR
Killed. Six wounded; two of them (CHRIST[R] MONK & JOHN CLARK) Mortally

3. "The Bloody Massacre Perpetuated in King Street . . . Boston, 5 March 1770. . . ."
Paul Revere. Line engraving. National Gallery of Art, Rosenwald Collection.

CRISPUS ATTUCKS AND THE

BOSTON MASSACRE

During the fall of 1750, a quarter of a century before the Declaration of Independence, a Massachusetts slave by the name of Crispus struck a revolutionary blow for his own liberty. The *Boston Gazette* [figure 4] on the second of October told the story: "Ran away from his Master *William Brown of Framingham* . . . a Molatto Fellow, about 27 Years of age, named *Crispas* [sic] 6 feet two Inches high, short curl'd Hair, his Knees nearer together than common: had on a light colour'd Bearskin Coat. . . ." Deacon Brown offered ten pounds as a reward, but Crispus was never taken. He next appears in the record, twenty years later, as Crispus Attucks, who strikes a revolutionary blow for American liberty—the first martyr of the American Revolution.

The tale of the Boston Massacre, depicted by Paul Revere in his famous broadside [figure 3] has often been told. For a year and a half the King had quartered his truculent redcoats upon the outraged citizens of Boston to enforce by cutlass and bayonet obnoxious laws passed in London without their consent. On the fifth of March 1770, grievances, long simmering, came to a boil. A week later the *Gazette* reported the affair.

Monday evening . . . Several Soldiers of the 29th Regiment were abusive in the Street, with their Cutlasses, striking a Number of Persons: About 9 o'Clock some young Lads . . . met three Soldiers, two of them with drawn Cutlasses . . . who stop'd the Lads, and made a stroke at them, which they returned, having Sticks in their Hands; one of the Lads was wounded in the Arm; presently 10 or 12 Soldiers came from the Barracks with their Cutlasses drawn . . . a Scuffle ensued, some seeing the naked Swords flourishing ran and set the Bells a ringing: This collected the People, who at length made the Soldiers retire to their Barracks. . . .

Some of "the People" then walked to the Custom House on King Street where they chided the lone sentinel, charging him with mauling a boy with the butt of his gun. Snowballs and pieces of ice flew through the air. With the sentinel crying for help, Captain Thomas Preston and a squad of eight ran to his aid, "formed in an half Circle," and "loaded and pointed their Guns breast-high to the People."

It was now that another group of citizens, apparently led by a tall, robust man with a dark face, appeared on the scene. There "came down a number from *Jackson's* corner," testified Andrew, a slave, at the subsequent trial, "huzzaing and crying, Damn them, they dare not fire, we are not afraid of them; one of these people, a stout man with a long

4. William Brown of Framingham, Massachusetts, advertises for his runaway slave "Crispas," *Boston Gazette*, October 2, 1750.

7

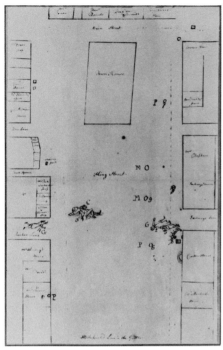

5. Diagram of the Boston Massacre. Paul Revere, 1770. From original in Boston Public Library, Mellen Chamberlain Autograph Collection.

cordwood stick, threw himself in, and made a blow at the officer . . . cried kill the dogs, knock them over; this was the general cry. . . ." Pressed to identify the "stout man," Andrew replied that it was "the Molatto who was shot." Five martyrs fell that night: Samuel Gray, ropemaker; James Caldwell, mate; Samuel Maverick, apprentice joiner; Patrick Carr, an Irishman; and the "stout man," the first to die, "named Attucks, who was born in Framingham, but lately belonging to New-Providence [Bahamas], and was here in order to go for North-Carolina, killed on the Spot, two Balls entering his Breast" [figure 5]. On Thursday, the corpse of Attucks was taken from Faneuil Hall, "all the Bells were ordered to toll a solemn Peal," and the five were interred in a common grave.

Thus, Crispus Attucks passed into history. Little is known of his personal life. In local lore his father was an African, his mother an Indian, probably a descendant of John Attucks, a converted Christian, who was executed for treason in 1676 because he sided with his own people during King Philip's War. The word "attuck" in the language of the Natick Indians means "deer." As a slave in Framingham, Crispus was known as a good judge of cattle, buying and selling on his own. He probably also worked as a seaman on coastal vessels. It is possible that he had arrived in Boston on a Nantucket whaleship.

At the trial of the king's officers, the fallen Attucks was very much alive. The evidence given in court, the newspaper reports, the earliest tradition, all single him out, in praise or blame, as the shaper of the event. For John Adams, one of the lawyers for the crown and later to be our second president, it was all blame: Attucks was one of "a mob"—"a motley rabble of saucy boys, negroes and molattoes, Irish teagues and outlandish jack-tarrs." Here is Adams in his final plea.

This Attucks . . . appears to have undertaken to be the hero of the night; and to lead this army with banners, to form them in the first place in Dock square, and march them up to King street with their clubs . . . this man with his party cried, do not be afraid of them . . . to have this reinforcement coming down under the command of a stout mulatto fellow, whose very looks was enough to terrify any person, what had not the soldiers then to fear? He had hardiness enough to fall in upon them, and with one hand took hold of a bayonet, and with the other knocked the man down: this was the behavior of Attucks . . . a Caar from Ireland, and an Attucks from Framingham, happening to be here, shall sally out upon their thoughtless enterprises, at the head of such a rabble of negroes, &c., as they can collect together. . . .

Curiously enough, some three years later, Adams seems to have had second thoughts on the matter. In an entry in his diary on a Monday in July 1773, [figure 6], there is a letter to Governor Thomas Hutchinson, possibly intended for the press.

Sir

You will hear from Us with Astonishment. You ought to hear from Us with Horror. You are chargeable before God and Man, with out Blood.—

The Soldiers were but passive Instruments, were Machines, neither moral nor voluntary Agents in our Destruction more than the leaden Pelletts, with which we were wounded.—You was a free Agent. You acted, cooly, deliberately, with all that premeditated Malice, not against Us in Particular but against the People in general, which in the Sight of the law is an ingredient in the Composition of Murder. You will hear from Us hereafter.

The signature, in Adams' own hand, is "Chrispus Attucks."

On March 5, 1858, black abolitionists in Boston inaugurated a Crispus Attucks Day. A "festival" was held in Faneuil Hall. As Wendell Phillips approached the rostrum, he noticed an exhibit of revolutionary relics including a cup owned by Attucks, an engraving of Emanuel Leutze's

9

Washington Crossing the Delaware with black Prince Whipple at the stroke oar, and the silk flag that John Hancock had presented to Boston's black company, the Bucks of America. "Emerson said the first gun heard round the world was that of Lexington," declared Phillips.

Who set the example of guns? Who taught the British soldier that he might be defeated? Who first dared look into his eyes? Those five men! The 5th of March was the baptism of blood. . . . I place, therefore, this Crispus Attucks in the foremost rank of the men that dared. When we talk of courage, he rises, with his dark face, in the clothes of the laborer, his head uncovered, his arm raised above him defying bayonets . . . when the proper symbols are placed around the base of the statue of Washington, one corner will be filled by the colored man defying the British muskets.

AFTERMATH OF ATTUCKS:

PORTRAITS IN PETITIONS

The blood of Attucks nourished the tree of liberty, in Jefferson's phrase, in two ways. Five years later, when protest gave way to arms, the name of the man who first had "dared" was still green in the memory of the minutemen—black and white—who took their stand at Lexington and Bunker Hill. More immediately, the spirit of Attucks spurred the slaves of Massachusetts now openly to organize and petition the government of their white masters—to fling the shame of slavery into the faces of those who cried "Liberty or Death." Five of these petitions of the years 1773 and 1774, echo the American patriot and orator James Otis' cries for the rights of man with a new intensity, and deserve to be enshrined among the treasures of our literature. The mood is one of exasperation, even anger, although the phraseology is sometimes cautious. Freedom is their impassioned theme.

On January 6, 1773, to Governor Hutchinson and the general court came "the humble Petition of many Slaves, living in the Town of Boston, and other Towns in the Province . . . who have had every Day of their Lives imbittered with this most intollerable Reflection, That, let their Behaviour be what it will, nor their Children to all Generations, shall ever be able to do, or to possess and enjoy any Thing, no not even *Life itself*, but in a Manner as the *Beasts that perish*. We have no Property! We have no Wives! No Children! We have no City! No Country! . . ." The signature, ironically, is "Felix."

Three months later, a printed leaflet in the form of a letter to the delegates of the towns in the House of Representatives was circulated by four slaves—Peter Bestes, Sambo Freeman, Chester Joie, and Felix Holbrook (the same Felix?) —"in behalf of our fellow slaves in this province. and by order of their Committee" [figure 7]. The letter begins with a taunt: "We expect great things from men who have made such a noble stand against the designs of their *fellow-men* to enslave them" and continues with a suggestion: now, at least, allow the "Africans . . . one day in a week to work for themselves, to enable them to earn money" so that they can buy their freedom. Even so, there is no future in America: we will "leave the province . . . as soon as we can, from our joynt labours procure money to transport ourselves to some part of the Coast of *Africa*, where we propose a settlement." (Long before Sierra Leone and Liberia, Martin Delany and Marcus Garvey.) The House tabled the petition. When the four slaves appealed to the governor, he said that he could not assist them.

In June, another petition was sent to Hutchinson and the general

SIR,

THE efforts made by the legiflative of this province in their laft feffions to free themfelves from flavery, gave us, who are in that deplorable ftate, a high degree of fatisfacton. We expect great things from men who have made fuch a noble ftand againft the defigns of their *fellow-men* to enflave them. We cannot but wifh and hope Sir, that you will have the fame grand object, we mean civil and religious liberty, in view in your next feffion. The divine fpirit of *freedom*, feems to fire every humane breaft on this continent, except fuch as are bribed to affift in executing the execrable plan.

WE are very fenfible that it would be highly detrimental to our prefent mafters, if we were allowed to demand all that of *right* belongs to us for paft fervices ; this we difclaim. Even the *Spaniards*, who have not thofe fublime ideas of freedom that Englifh men have, are confcious that they have no right to all the fervices of their fellowmen, we mean the *Africans*, whom they have purchafed with their money ; therefore they allow them one day in a week to work for themfelve, to enable them to earn money to purchafe the refidue of their time, which they have a right to demand in fuch portions as they are able to pay for (a due appraizment of their fervices being firft made, which always ftands at the purchafe money.) We do not pretend to dictate to you Sir, or to the honorable Affembly, of which you are a member : We acknowledge our obligations to you for what you have already done, but as the people of this province feem to be actuated by the principles of equity and juftice, we cannot but expect your houfe will again take our deplorable cafe into ferious confideration, and give us that ample relief which, *as men*, we have a natural right to.

BUT fince the wife and righteous governor of the univerfe, has permitted our fellow men to make us flaves, we bow in fubmiffion to him, and determine to behave in fuch a manner, as that w may have reafon to expect the divine approbation of, and affiftance in, our peaceable nd lawful attempts to gain our freedom.

WE are willing to fubmit to fuch regulations and laws, as may be made relative to us, until we leave the province, which we determine to do as foon as we can from our joynt labours procure money to tranfport ourfelves to fome part of the coaft of *Africa*, where we propofe a fettlement. We are very defirous that you fhould have inftructions relative to us, from your town, therefore we pray you to communicate this letter to them, and afk this favor for us.

In behalf of our fellow flaves in this province,
And by order of their Committee.

PETER BESTES,
SAMBO FREEMAN,
FELIX HOLBROOK,
CHESTER JOIE.

For the REPRESENTATIVE of the town of *Thompson*

7. Circular letter "in behalf of our fellow slaves in this province, and by order of their Committee." April 20, 1773. The New-York Historical Society.

court, "in behalf all thous who by divine Permission are held in a state of slavery, within the bowels of a free Country." The fragment that survives has the flavor of the Declaration of Independence: "Your Petitioners apprehend they have in comon with other men a naturel right to be free and without molestation to injoy such property as they may acquire by their industry, or by any other means not detrimental to their fellow men. . . ."

A year later, May 25, 1774, there came still another petition to the new Governor Thomas Gage and the general court from "a Grate Number of Blackes of the Province . . . held in a state of Slavery within a free and christian Country." This document cannot be greatly shortened without damage; here is most of it verbatim:

Your Petitioners apprehind we have in common with all other men a naturel right to our freedoms without Being depriv'd of them by our fellow men as we are a freeborn Pepel and have never forfeited this Blessing by aney compact or agreement whatever. But we were unjustly dragged by the cruel hand of power from our dearest frinds and sum of us stolen from the bosoms of our tender Parents and from a Populous Pleasant and plentiful country and Brought hither to be made slaves for Life in a Christian land. Thus we are deprived of every thing that hath a tendency to make life even tolerable, the endearing ties of husband and wife we are strangers to. . . . Our children are also taken from us by force and sent maney miles from us. . . . Thus our Lives are imbittered. . . . There is a great number of us sencear . . . members of the Church of Christ how can the master and the slave be said to fulfil that command Live in love let Brotherly Love contuner and abound Beare yea onenothers Bordenes. How can the master be said to Beare my Borden when he Beares me down which the . . . chanes of slavery. . . . Nither can we reap an equal benefet from the laws of the Land which doth not justifi but condemns Slavery or if there had bin aney Law to hold us in Bondage . . . ther never was aney to inslave our children for life when Born in a free Countrey. We therefore Bage your Excellency and Honours will . . . cause an act of the legislative to be pessed that we may obtain our Natural right our freedoms and our children be set at lebety at the yeare of twenty one. . . .

Finally, in June the same petition was submitted once more, this time with a significant addition: "give and grant to us some part of the unimproved land, belonging to the province, for a settlement, that each of us may there quietly sit down under his own fig tree" and enjoy "the fruits of his labour." Once more, the court voted to let the question "subside."

Who were these eloquent and courageous black men in bondage who composed these documents? We have a few names, but no faces. Their portraits are vivid in the language of their pleas.

It is clear that their indignation did not "subside." At the end of that summer, Abigail Adams wrote to her husband John: "There has been in town a conspiracy of the negroes. At present it is kept pretty private, and was discovered by one who endeavored to dissuade them from it. . . . They conducted in this way . . . to draw up a petition to the Governor, telling him they would fight for him provided he would arm them, and engage to liberate them if he conquered." Had she read the earlier petitions? "I wish most sincerely," she concluded, "there was not a slave in the province; it always appeared a most iniquitous scheme to me to fight ourselves for what we are daily robbing and plundering from those who have as good a right to freedom as we have."

THE SHOT HEARD ROUND THE WORLD:

LEXINGTON AND CONCORD,

BUNKER HILL, AND GREAT BRIDGE

Mrs. Adam's alarm mirrored the anger of Boston's slaves at the hypocrisy of white legislators who gave lip service to liberty where blacks were concerned. True enough, following the lead of James Otis in the 1760s, a few bold spokesmen for the rights of man, like the Reverend Isaac Skillman in his oration of 1772 "upon the Beauties of Liberty," had included the black man in their cries for justice. A week before, Bunker Hill slaves in the counties of Worcester and Bristol had petitioned the Committee of Correspondence "to assist them in obtaining their freedom." Shortly thereafter, white delegates to a county convention in Worcester declared that they abhorred "the enslaving of any of the human race;" whenever "a door opened they would strive for" the emancipation of the negroes." But the indifference of assemblies and governors to the repeated appeals of the slave petitioners rankled deeply. Speculating on how the British might exploit black exasperation, General Thomas Gage in June 1775, five months before Lord Dunmore's call for a regiment of freed slaves in Virginia, had formulated a similar plan: "Things are now come to that Crisis, that we must avail ourselves of every resource, even to raise the Negros, in our cause."

It is clear that the blacks of Boston and its environs, newly awakened to a sense of their own unity and stirred by the promise of a new dawn of liberty for all, found themselves at a fork in the road. Which way to freedom? When the embattled farmers fired the shot heard round the world, it is probable that in New England most blacks saw their destiny, if only dimly, in the triumph of a democratic revolution that might somehow, in the shakeup of things, give substance to its slogans. Thus, even though at the start they were barred from the ranks by legislators and generals, black slaves and freemen insisted on taking part in the struggle.

When Patriots in arms gathered at Lexington and Concord on the nineteenth of April 1775 to confront the redcoats from Boston, black minutemen with flintlocks were among them. Early on the ground was the Lexington slave "Prince Easterbrooks, A Negro Man," as he is described in the list of the wounded, who had enlisted in Captain John Parker's company, the first to get into the fight [figure 8]. He would serve in almost every major campaign of the war. From Framingham—the town that Crispus Attucks had fled—came another slave, Peter Salem, private in

15

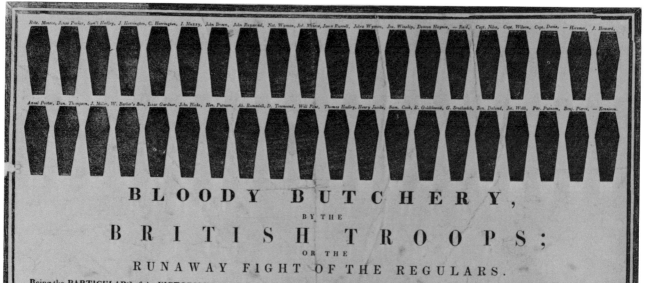

Robt. Monroe, Jonas Parker, Sam'l Hadley, J. Harrington, C. Harrington, I. Muzzy, John Brown, John Raymond, Nat. Wyman, Jed. Munroe, Jason Russell, Jabez Wyman, Jos. Winship, Deacon Haynes, — Reed, Capt. Niles, Capt. Wilson, Capt. Davis, — Hosmer, J. Howard.

Axal Porter, Dan. Thompson, J. Miller, W. Barber's Son, Isaac Gardiner, John Hicks, Hen. Putnam, Ab. Ramsdell, D. Townsend, Will Flint, Thomas Hadley, Henry Jacobs, Sam. Cook, E. Goldthwait, G. Southwick, Ben. Daland, Jos. Webb, Per. Putnam, Benj. Pierce, — Kennison.

BLOODY BUTCHERY,

BY THE

BRITISH TROOPS;

OR THE

RUNAWAY FIGHT OF THE REGULARS.

Being the PARTICULARS of the VICTORIOUS BATTLE fought at and near CONCORD, situated Twenty Miles from Boston, in the Province of the Massachusetts-Bay, between Two Thousand Regular Troops, belonging to His Britannic Majesty, and a few Hundred Provincial Troops, belonging to the Province of Massachusetts-Bay, which lasted from sunrise until sunset, on the 19th of April, 1775, when it was decided greatly in favor of the latter. These particulars are published in this cheap form, at the request of the friends of the deceased WORTHIES, who died gloriously fighting in the CAUSE OF LIBERTY and their COUNTRY, and it is their sincere desire that every Householder in the country, who are sincere well-wishers to America, may be possessed of the same, either to frame and glass, or otherwise to preserve in their houses, not only as a Token of Gratitude to the memory of the Deceased Forty Persons, but as a perpetual memorial of that important event, on which, perhaps, may depend the future Freedom and Greatness of the Commonwealth of America. To which is annexed a Funeral Elegy on those who were slain in the Battle.

8. "A Bloody Butchery. . . ." Broadside commemorating the fight at Menotomy, April 19, 1775. Massachusetts Historical Society.

9. "Return of Captain Benjamin Lock's Company in the 37th Regiment of Foot. . . ." listing three blacks, among whom was Cuff Whitemore. Massachusetts Archives.

Captain Simon Edgel's company; from Braintree, Pompy, private in Captain Seth Turner's company; from Brookline, Prince, slave of Joshua Boylston, in Captain Thomas White's company; and from parts unknown, one Pomp Blackman, later in the Continental Line. Cato Stedman and Cato Boardman had joined Captain Samuel Thatcher's company in Cambridge. Young Cuff Whitemore and Cato Wood, both in Captain Benjamin Locke's company from Arlington, had signed on "as soldiers in the Massachusetts Service for the Preservation of the Liberties of America" [figure 9]. The last four smelled their first powder as they harassed the British at Lincoln. On the last lap of the British retreat back into Boston, Lieutenant Mackenzie of the Royal Welsh Fusileers observed that a Negro "was wounded near the houses close to the Neck, out of which the Rebels fired to the last."

Two months later at the bloody Battle of Bunker Hill, among the score or so of black soldiers who held their fire until they could see the whites of the enemy's eyes, were Cuff Whitemore and Peter Salem, again in the thick of the fray. According to Samuel Swett, the earliest chronicler of the battle, "Whittemore fought bravely in the redoubt. He had a ball through his hat . . . fought to the last, and when compelled to retreat, though wounded . . . he seized the sword [of a British officer] slain in the redoubt . . . which in a few days he unromantically sold. He served faithfully through the war, with many hair-breadth 'scapes from sword and pestilence."

Peter Salem, although not the only black hero of Bunker Hill, is the best known, probably because the painter, John Trumbull, imaginatively reconstructing the event, put him on canvas, where he grasps the musket still preserved at the Bunker Hill Monument in Charlestown [figure 10]. Trumbull witnessed the fireworks from Roxbury across the harbor and possibly met Salem within the next few days, but he painted his picture in London in 1786 and probably worked from a black model in his

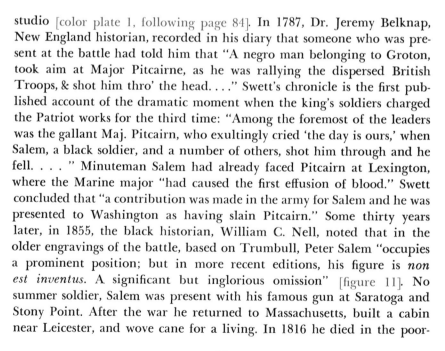

10. French Charleville musket of the type used by the American army during the Revolution. National Museum of History and Technology, Division of Military History, Smithsonian Institution.

studio [color plate 1, following page 84]. In 1787, Dr. Jeremy Belknap, New England historian, recorded in his diary that someone who was present at the battle had told him that "A negro man belonging to Groton, took aim at Major Pitcairne, as he was rallying the dispersed British Troops, & shot him thro' the head. . . ." Swett's chronicle is the first published account of the dramatic moment when the king's soldiers charged the Patriot works for the third time: "Among the foremost of the leaders was the gallant Maj. Pitcairn, who exultingly cried 'the day is ours,' when Salem, a black soldier, and a number of others, shot him through and he fell. . . . " Minuteman Salem had already faced Pitcairn at Lexington, where the Marine major "had caused the first effusion of blood." Swett concluded that "a contribution was made in the army for Salem and he was presented to Washington as having slain Pitcairn." Some thirty years later, in 1855, the black historian, William C. Nell, noted that in the older engravings of the battle, based on Trumbull, Peter Salem "occupies a prominent position; but in more recent editions, his figure is *non est inventus*. A significant but inglorious omission" [figure 11]. No summer soldier, Salem was present with his famous gun at Saratoga and Stony Point. After the war he returned to Massachusetts, built a cabin near Leicester, and wove cane for a living. In 1816 he died in the poor-

11. The Battle of Bunker Hill. James Mitan after John Trumbull. Engraving, 1801. The Metropolitan Museum of Art.

house in Framingham, whose citizens in 1882 erected a monument to his memory.

Also at Bunker Hill that June day in 1775 were Barzillai Lew of Chelmsford and Salem Poor of Andover. Lew, a veteran of the French and Indian War, thirty-two years old, six feet high, enlisted in Captain John Ford's company of the 27th Massachusetts Regiment. He marched to Ticonderoga and served in the army a full seven years as front-line soldier, fifer, and drummer. A legend has come down that he "organized for guerilla warfare at a later period of the struggle a band of Negro men, all in one family, known as Lew's men." But where is there a depiction of "The Spirit of '76" that shows a black fifer or drummer?

Most celebrated of the black soldiers who fought at Bunker Hill was twenty-eight-year-old Salem Poor, freeman and church member, who left his wife behind to enlist in the militia company captained by Benjamin Ames. For his valor and intrepidity—he was perhaps responsible for picking off another important redcoat, Lieutenant Colonel James Abercrombie—fourteen officers who had been on the field that day, including Colonel William Prescott, a few weeks later submitted a petition to the general court of Massachusetts, suggesting that the Continental Congress itself bestow "The Reward due to so great and Distinguisht a Caracter."

The Subscribers begg leave to Report to your Honble. House (Which Wee do in justice to the Caracter of so Brave a Man) that under Our

19

Own observation, Wee declare that A Negro Man Called Salem Poor of Col. Fryes Regiment. Capt. Ames. Company in the late Battle at Charleston, behaved like an Experienced Officer, as Well as an Excellent Soldier, to Set forth Particulars of his Conduct would be Tedious, Wee Would Only begg leave to say in the Person of this sd. Negro Centers a Brave & gallant Soldier—

There is no record that a "Reward" was ever given to Salem Poor, who went on to serve at Valley Forge and White Plains.

At Lexington, Concord, and Bunker Hill, a year before the Declaration of Independence, black soldiers and white fired the first shots of the Revolution in the North. Not long after, black soldiers and white—on both sides—would fire the first shots in the South. At the Battle of the Great Bridge near Norfolk, Virginia, during the winter of 1775, a detachment of Lord Dunmore's army, including black soldiers of his Ethiopian Regiment, sallied out of their island fort, crossed a bridge over the Elizabeth River, drove back the Patriot guards with heavy fire, and attacked Colonel William Woodford's Second Virginia Regiment waiting in the breastworks. Woodford, who had employed a black spy to dupe the redcoats into thinking that his defense was weak, was ready for the assault.

20

The fight was short and furious—the British retreated into their fort.

Among the stubborn guards at the bridge was a black freeman from Portsmouth by the name of William Flora. Captain Thomas Nash, who was wounded during the engagement, later wrote down his memory of the day.

Flora, a colored man, was the last sentinel that came into the breast work . . . he did not leave his post until he had fired several times. Billy had to cross a plank to get to the breast work, and had fairly passed over it when he was seen to turn back, and deliberately take up the plank after him, amidst a shower of musket balls. He . . . fired eight times.

Thirty years later, in 1806, when William Flora—by this time a prosperous businessman and property owner who had bought the freedom of his slave wife and children—applied for a land grant, his old commander testified that he had served "in the Continental line untill the seige of York . . . and was held in high esteem as a soldier" [figure 12]. Virginia granted the black veteran one hundred acres in gratitude for his Revolutionary service.

A local historian who knew Flora well in his later years recalled that the old man had "volunteered to act as a marine under Commodore Decatur" in the second war against England: "He was true patriot to the last. I recollect that when the troops of Norfolk and Portsmouth were under arms . . . in consequence of the cowardly attack on the frigate *Chesapeake* by the British ship *Leopard,* Billy Flora made his appearance with his gun on his shoulder . . . observing that he had brought with him the same musket which he had fought with at the Great Bridge."

THE DECLARATION OF INDEPENDENCE

"We hold these truths to be self-evident, that all men are created equal, that they are endowed by their Creator with certain unalienable Rights, that among these are Life, Liberty and the pursuit of Happiness." When on July 4, 1776, "the Representatives of the united States of America, in General Congress," proclaimed this revolutionary doctrine to the world, what might have been the reactions of the black people of the new Nation —of Salem Poor and William Flora, for example?

Did "all men" include African Americans? Where in this manifesto of quality was the word "slave" to be found? Searching every line for an acknowledgment of the tyranny of white racism in the colonies, all that these two black heroes might discover was an indictment of George III: "He has excited domestic insurrections amongst us," a reference to the British generals who had offered liberty, with a gun, to the slaves of patriots, "and has endeavoured to bring on the inhabitants of our frontiers, the merciless Indian savages." Was the Tory ex-Governor Thomas Hutchinson correct when he pointed out the clash between a theory of equality for "all men" and the reality of depriving "more than a hundred thousand Africans of their rights to liberty"? And if Salem Poor and William Flora knew that the Congress in fact had repudiated Jefferson's denunciation of the slave trade—the clause that John Adams called the "vehement phillipic against Negro slavery"—would this knowledge have transformed the Declaration [figure 13] into something they could, in good conscience defend? Yet, examine the problem from another angle. Conceding that the Delaration had in fact not abolished slavery in the year 1776, might not its noble phrases hold forth the promise of a future society with liberty for all? And shouldn't blacks fight for that promise?

There is little doubt that such questions troubled the minds of slaves and freemen as they tried to figure their stake in the new Nation. Enlisting in the Patriot cause on land and sea, they would continue to affix their names and marks to agonized petitions that echo and re-echo the language of the Declaration, demanding "Life, Liberty, and the pursuit of Happiness" for black Americans as well as white.

Thus, in Massachusetts, six months after the Declaration, once again the petition of "A Great Number of Blackes detained in a State of Slavery in the Bowels of a free & Christian Country" [figure 14] asserted their "Natural and Unaliable Right to that freedom which the Grat Parent of the Unavers hath Bestowed equalley on all menkind" and admonished the general court:

[Following] the Lawdable Example of the Good People of these States your petitononers have Long and Patiently waited the Evnt of petition

A Declaration by the Representatives of the UNITED STATES OF AMERICA, in General Congress assembled.

When in the course of human events it becomes necessary for one people to dissolve the political bands which have connected them with another, and to ~~[crossed out]~~ assume among the powers of the earth the separate and equal station to which the laws of nature & of nature's god entitle them, a decent respect to the opinions of mankind requires that they should declare the causes which impel them to the separation.

We hold these truths to be self-evident; that all men are created equal, that they are endowed by their creator with equal ~~[crossed out]~~ rights; that ~~[crossed out]~~ inherent & inalienable, among these are the preservation of life & liberty, & the pursuit of happiness; that to secure these ends, governments are instituted among men, deriving their just powers from the consent of the governed; that whenever any form of government becomes destructive of these ends, it is the right of the people to alter or to abolish it, & to institute new government, laying it's foundation on such principles & organising it's powers in such form, as to them shall seem most likely to effect their safety & happiness. prudence indeed will dictate that governments long established should not be changed for light & transient causes: and accordingly all experience hath shewn that mankind are more disposed to suffer while evils are sufferable than to right themselves by abolishing the forms to which they are accustomed. but when a long train of abuses & usurpations [begun at a distinguished period & pursuing invariably the same object, evinces a design to subject reduce them under absolute Despotism, it is their right, it is their duty, to throw off such government & to provide new guards for their future security. such has been the patient sufferance of these colonies; & such is now the necessity which constrains them to expunge their former systems of government. the history of the present king of Great Britain is a history of unremitting injuries and usurpations, among which appears no solitary fact to contradict the uniform tenor of the rest, but all have in direct object the establishment of an absolute tyranny over these states. to prove this, let facts be submitted to a candid world, for the truth of which we pledge a faith yet unsullied by falsehood.]

13. Draft of the Declaration of Independence written by Thomas Jefferson including a passage, later deleted, on the slave trade. Library of Congress.

he has refused his assent to laws the most wholesome and necessary for the pub-
- lic good:

he has forbidden his governors to pass laws of immediate & pressing importance,
    unless suspended in their operation till his assent should be obtained;
    and when so suspended, he has utterly neglected utterly to attend to them.

he has refused to pass other laws for the accomodation of large districts of people
    unless those people would relinquish the right of representation in the legislature, a right
    instimable to them, & formidable to tyrants only:

he has dissolved Represent -ative houses repeatedly & continually, for
    opposing with manly firmness his invasions on the rights of the people:

when dissolved, he has refused for a long space of time, time after such dissolutions, to cause others to be elected;
whereby the legislative powers, incapable of annihilation, have returned to
    the people at large for their exercise, the state remaining in the mean time
    exposed to all the dangers of invasion from without & convulsions within:

he has endeavored to prevent the population of these states; for that purpose
    obstructing the laws for naturalization of foreigners; refusing to pass others
    to encourage their migrations hither, & raising the conditions of new ap-
    -propriations of lands:

he has suffered the administration of justice totally to cease in some of these
    states, refusing his assent to laws for establishing judiciary powers:

he has made [our] judges dependant on his will alone, for the tenure of their offices,
    the + & payment
    and amount of their salaries:

he has erected a multitude of new offices [by a self-assumed power,] & sent hi-
    -ther swarms of officers to harrass our people & eat out their substance:

he has kept among us in times of peace, standing armies [& ships of war;] without the consent of our legislature

he has affected to render the military, independent of & superior to the civil power:

he has combined with others to subject us to a jurisdiction foreign to our constitu-
    -tions and unacknoleged by our laws; giving his assent to their pretended acts of
    & legislation, for quartering large bodies of armed troops among us;

        for protecting them by a mock-trial from punishment for any murders
            which
            they should commit on the inhabitants of these states;

        for cutting off our trade with all parts of the world;

        for imposing taxes on us without our consent;
                    in many cases
        for depriving us of the benefits of trial by jury;

        for transporting us beyond seas to be tried for pretended offences:
        for abolishing the free system of English laws in a neighboring province, establishing therein an arbitrary government,
            and enlarging it's boundaries so as to render it at once an example & fit instrument for introducing the same
            into these colonies:

+ Dr. Franklin

+ & mr Adams

†abolishing our most valuable ~~important~~ Laws

for taking away our charters & altering fundamentally the forms of our governments

for suspending our own legislatures & declaring themselves invested with power to

legislate for us in all cases whatsoever:

he has abdicated government here, [by declaring us out of his protection & waging war against us withdrawing his governors, & declaring us out

of his allegiance & protection:]

he has plundered our seas, ravaged our coasts, burnt our towns & destroyed the

lives of our people:

he is at this time transporting large armies of Scotch and other foreign mercenaries to compleat

the works of death, desolation & tyranny already begun with circumstances

of cruelty & perfidy, scarcely paralleled in the most barbarous ages, & totally unworthy the head of a civilized nation:

he has endeavored to bring on the inhabitants of our frontiers the merciless Indian

savages, whose known rule of warfare is an undistinguished destruction of

all ages, sexes, & conditions [of existence:]

[he has incited treasonable insurrections of our fellow ~~citizens~~, with the

allurements of forfeiture & confiscation of our property:

he has waged cruel war against human nature itself, violating it's most sa-

-cred rights of life & liberty in the persons of a distant people who never of-

fended him, captivating & carrying them into slavery in another hemisphere,

or to incur miserable death in their transportation thither. the

piratical warfare, the opprobrium of infidel powers, is the warfare of the

Christian king of Great Britain. determined to keep open a market

where MEN should be bought & sold he has prostituted his negative

for suppressing every legislative attempt to prohibit or to restrain this

execrable commerce: and that this assemblage of horrors might want no fact

of distinguished die, he is now exciting those very people to rise in arms

among us, and to purchase that liberty of which he has deprived them,

by murdering the people upon whom he also obtruded them: thus paying

off former crimes committed against the liberties of one people, with crimes

which he urges them to commit against the lives of another.]

in every stage of these oppressions" we have petitioned for redress in the most humble

terms"; our repeated petitions have been answered only by repeated injuries". a prince

whose character is thus marked by every act which may define a tyrant", is unfit

to be the ruler of a people [who mean to be free. future ages will scarce believe'

that the hardiness of one man", adventured within the short compass of twelve years

only, to build a foundation so broad & undisguised for tyranny

over a people fostered & fixed in principles

of freedom.]

Nor have we been wanting in attentions to our British brethren. we have warned them from time to time of attempts by their legislature to extend *an unwarrantable* a jurisdiction over [these our states] we have reminded them of the circumstances of our emigration & settlement here, no one of which could warrant so strange a pretension: that these were effected at the expence of our own blood & treasure, unassisted by the wealth or the strength of Great Britain: that in constituting indeed our several forms of government, we had adopted one common king, thereby laying a foundation for perpetual league & amity with them: but that submission to their ~~~~~~ credited: and we ~~ appealed to their native justice & magnanimity, [as well as to the ties *& we have conjured them* of our common kindred to disavow these usurpations which [were likely to] interrupt *would inevitably* our *connection &* correspondence ~~~~~~. they too have been deaf to the voice of justice & of consanguinity, [*we must therefore* & when occasions have been given them by the regular course of their laws, of removing from their councils the disturbers of our harmony, they have by their free election re-established them in power. at this very time too they are permitting their chief magistrate to send over not only soldiers of our common *troops to us* blood, but Scotch & foreign mercenaries to invade & ~~~~~~~~~. these facts have ~~~~~ the last stab to agonizing affection, and manly spirit bids us to renounce for ever these unfeeling brethren. we must endeavor to forget our former love for them, and to hold them as we hold the rest of mankind, enemies in war, in peace friends. we might have been a free & a great people together; but a communication of grandeur & of freedom it seems is below their dignity. be it so, since they will have it: the road to ~~~~~ happiness *& to glory* is open to us too; we will ~~~~~ it *apart from them,* ~~~~~~~~~~ and acquiesce in the necessity which de-nounces our ~~~~ eternal [eternal] separation! *and hold them as we hold the rest of mankind enemies in war, in peace friends*

We therefore the representatives of the United States of America in General Congress assembled, *appealing to the supreme judge of the world for the rectitude of our intentions,* do, in the name & by authority of the good people of these [states,] *colonies* reject & renounce all allegiance & subjection to the kings of Great Britain & all others who may hereafter claim by, through, or under them; & utterly dissolve & break off all political connection which may ~~~ heretofore *have* subsisted between us & the people or parliament of Great Britain; and finally we do assert and declare these colonies to be free and independant states, and that as free & independant states they shall hereafter have *full* power to levy war, conclude peace, contract alliances, establish commerce, & to do all other acts and things which independant states may of right do. And for the support of this declaration] we mutually pledge to each other our lives, our fortunes, & our sacred honour.

a different place pointing to another
+ Dr. Franklin

after petition . . . they Cannot but express their Astonishment that It have Never Bin Considered that Every Principle from which America has Acted in the Cours of their Unhappy Dificultes with Great Briton Pleads Stronger than A thousand arguments . . . [that] they may be Restored to the Enjoyments of that which is the Naturel Right of all men. . . .

Eight Boston blacks, most of them freemen, signed this petition: Prince Hall, organizer of the African Lodge of Freemasons; Lancaster Hill; Peter Best; Bristol Slenzer; Jack Pierpont; Nero Funelo; Newport Sumner; and Job Lock.

In Connecticut, during the spring of 1779, a freedom-seeking petition [figure 15] of "the Negroes in the Towns of Stratford and Fairfield," signed by Prime and Prince, queried the Hartford meeting of the general assembly as to "whether it is consistent with the present Claims, of the united States, to hold so many Thousands, of the Race of Adam, our Common Father, in perpetual Slavery." Is it not a "flagrant Injustice" that those "nobly contending, in the Cause of Liberty" deny that "Reason & Revelation join to declare, that we are the creatures of that God, who made of one Blood, and Kindred, all the Nations of the Earth"?

In Portsmouth, New Hampshire, during the fall of the same year, nineteen "natives of Africa"—"born free,"—including Prince Whipple, who in 1776 had crossed the Delaware in the same boat with Washington, implored the council and House, sitting in Exeter, to restore their freedom "for the sake of justice, humanity, and the rights of mankind," arguing that "the God of nature gave them life and freedom, upon the terms of the most perfect equality with other men; That freedom is an inherent right of the human species, not to be surrendered but by consent, for the sake of social life; That private or public tyranny and slavery are alike detestable to minds conscious of the equal dignity of human nature. . . ." A Declaration of Independence—for whom? The arguments of these black petitions will reverberate through the era of the Revolution, and beyond.

To the Honorable Council & House of Representatives for the State of Massachusetts-Bay, in General Court assembled January 13th 1777 —

The Petition of a great number of Negroes who are detained in a state of Slavery, in the Bowels of a free & Christian Country — Humbly sheweth

That your Petitioners apprehend that they have, in common with all other Men, a natural & unalienable right to that freedom, which the great Parent of the Universe hath bestowed equally on all Mankind & which they have never forfeited by any compact or agreement whatever — But they were unjustly dragged, by the cruel hand of Power, from their dearest friends & some of them even torn from the embraces of their tender Parents — From a populous, pleasant & plentiful country — & in Violation of the Laws of Nature & of Nations & in defiance of all the tender feelings of humanity, brought hither to be sold like Beasts of Burthen, & like them condemned to slavery for Life — Among a People professing the mild Religion of Jesus, a People not insensible of the sweets of rational freedom — Nor without spirit to resent the unjust endeavours of others, to reduce them to a state of Bondage & Subjection — Your Honors need not to be informed that a Life of Slavery like that of your Petitioners, deprived of every social privilege, of every thing requisite to render Life even tolerable, is far worse than Nonexistence — In imitation of the laudable example of the good People of these States, your Petitioners have long & patiently waited the event of Petition after Petition by them presented to the Legislative Body of this State, & can not but with grief reflect that their success has been but too similar — They can not but express their astonishment that it has never been considered that every principle from which America has acted in the course of their unhappy difficulties with Great-Britain, pleads stronger than a thousand arguments in favor of your Petitioners — They therefore humbly beseech your Honors, to give this Petition its due weight & consideration & cause an act of the Legislature to be passed whereby they may be restored to the enjoyment of that freedom which is the natural right of all Men — & their Children (who were born in this Land of Liberty) may not be held as slaves after they arrive at the age of twenty one Years — So may the Inhabitants of this State (no longer chargeable with the inconsistency of acting, themselves, the part which they condemn & oppose in others) be prospered in their present glorious struggle for Liberty, & have those blessings secured to them ... And your Petitioners ...

Lancaster Hill
Peter Bess
Brister Slenfen
Prince Hall
Jack Pierpont
Nero Funelo
Newport Sumner
Job Lock

14. Petition of "A Great Number of Negroes," January 13, 1777. Massachusetts Archives.

to your Honours serious Consideration, whether it is Consistent, with the present Claims, of the united States, to hold so many Thousands, of the Race of Adam, our Common Father, in perpetual Slavery; can human Nature endure the Shocking Idea? can your Honours, any longer Suffer, this great Evil to prevail, under your Government? we entreat your Honours, let no Considerations of Publick Inconvenience, deter your Honours, from interposing in Behalf of your Petitioners; who ask for nothing, but what we are fully persuaded, is ours to Claim. we beseech your Honours, to weigh this matter, in the Scale of Justice, and in your great Wisdom and Goodness, apply such Remedy, as the Evil does require; and let your Petitioners, rejoice with your Honours, in the Participation, with your Honours, of that inestimable Blessing, __Freedom__ and your Humble Petitioners, as in Duty bound shall Ever pray &c.

Dated in Fairfield the 11th Day of May A D 1779 —

Signed in Presence of

Jonath Sturges.

PRIME a Negro Man
Servant to mr Saml Sturge of Fairfield

his
Prime + a Negro man
Mark
Servant of Capt Stephen Jennings
of Fairfield
in Behalf of themselves and
the other Petitioners

15. Excerpt from "Petition of Prime, Prince, and others . . ., May 1779. Connecticut State Library.

29

PART II ☞

Bearers

of

Arms:

Patriot

and

Tory

On the eve of the Revolution, there were two-and-one-half million Americans in the rebellious colonies. Of these, half a million were black, a few free, the rest slaves. It has been estimated that during the seven years of war some 5,000 blacks served on the patriot side. The black soldier was, in fact, eager to fight on two fronts—for his own freedom as well as for the freedom of his country. Therefore, when white governors and generals, running short of manpower in the army and navy or white masters chary of risking their necks on the battlefield, promised the slave his freedom if he joined the ranks, he was more than willing to shoulder a musket in behalf of his own and American independence.

It was not easy for slave owners, worried by the threat of sabotage and revolt, to arm their chattels, and two southern states resisted the idea to the end. As Lorenzo J. Greene once pointed out, the half-million blacks in the country might have been assessed by both Patriots and Tories as crucial in the balance of military power. But in July of 1775, when Washington arrived in Massachusetts to take command of the American forces, one of his earliest orders barred "Negroes" and "vagabonds" from being recruited into the army. Many months passed before the general and Congress saw the light. Three years later, Adjutant General Alexander Scannell reported the names of over 750 black soldiers on the rolls of fourteen brigades of the Continental Army. During the summer of 1781, the Baron Ludwig Von Closen, viewing the army at White Plains, noted in his journal: "A quarter of them were negroes, merry, confident, and sturdy."

There were, of course, many blacks who fought with the Tories. The British, always short of men in spite of their 30,000 German mercenaries, saw clearly from the start the role that black power might play in the struggle ahead. When slaves abandoned their Patriot masters in response to the blandishments of Lord Dunmore and Sir Henry Clinton, the decision to join the British was for them, as for their brothers on the opposite side, a blow struck against American slavery and for their own independence. It is possible that tens of thousands of slaves in South Carolina and Georgia went over to the British. Some blacks fled into the swamps and the forests or conspired to fight their own battle for freedom. By the war's end, 14,000 black men, women, and children, some still bound to fleeing Tory masters, some now free and ready to begin new lives in new places, had been evacuated by the British from Savannah, Charleston, and New York, and transported to Florida, Nova Scotia, Jamaica, and later, to Africa.

The black soldier and sailor of the Revolution, whether he fought for Congress or king, served in a variety of ways—as infantryman, artilleryman, scout, guide, spy, guard, courier, waggoner, orderly, cook, waiter, able seaman, privateersman, and military laborer of all sorts. In a few cases, blacks formed their own units.

How many were killed or wounded, we can only guess. Some were heroes. Not long after they had fallen most of them were forgotten. The white memory of things recorded in print and paint usually left them out.

A TRIO WITH THE GENERALS:

WILLIAM LEE,

JAMES ARMISTEAD LAFAYETTE,

AGRIPPA HULL

In the year 1768 George Washington bought a slave by the name of William from Mary Lee. Seven years later, when Washington took command of the Continental Army, William Lee journeyed with him to Massachusetts and continued at the general's side as servant and orderly through thick and thin to the close of the war [figure 16]. In his portrait of Washington at West Point, painted by John Trumbull in London in 1780, the artist shows young William, in a turban, holding the bridle of the general's horse [figure 17]. The fighting over, he returned to Virginia with Washington to serve the Mount Vernon household for the next twenty years. It is as a factotum of the Washington family—George and Martha with their grandchildren—that Edward Savage portrayed the black veteran in 1796 [figure 18]. The genre of both these paintings, white master and black servant—a traditional one for the white artist—perhaps conceals the deep feeling that Washington had for his Revolutionary comrade. When William in 1784 asked the general if he could bring to Mount Vernon his wife, Margaret Thomas, a free woman of Philadelphia, Washington reluctantly agreed to do so: "I cannot refuse his request . . . as he has lived with me so long and followed my fortunes through the War with fidility."

Washington's soul-searching about the rightness of slavery is well known. There was "not a man living," he wrote to two friends in 1786, who wished more sincerely than he "to see some plan adopted by which slavery may be abolished by law." When he died in 1799, his will provided that upon Martha's death all of his slaves should be liberated, but "to my Mulatto man William [calling himself William Lee] I give immediate freedom. . . . I allow him an annuity of thirty dollars during his natural life . . . and this I give him as a testimony of my sense of his attachment to me, and for his faithful services during the Revolutionary War" [figure 19].

In June 1804 on a visit to Mount Vernon, the artist Charles Willson Peale, who would later paint a vivid portrait of the black Muslim Yarrow Mamout, sought out the aged William Lee, whom he found in an outbuilding, crippled, cobbling shoes. The two sat down together and talked about old times and how to live a long, healthy life.

16. Le Général Washington. Noel Le Mire after Jean-Baptiste Le Paon. Engraving, not dated. Library of Congress.

17. George Washington. John Trumbull, 1780. The
Metropolitan Museum of Art.

18. The Washington Family. Edward Savage. Engraving, 1798. Mr. and Mrs. John T.
Pierce, Alexandria, Virginia.

34

the aged and infirm; — seeing that a regular and permanent fund be established for their support so long as there are
subjects requiring it; — not trusting to
the uncertain provision to be made by
individuals. — And to my Mulatto
man William (calling himself William
Lee) I give immediate freedom; or if
he should prefer it (on account of the
accidents which have befallen him, and
which have rendered him incapable of
walking or of any active employment)
to remain in the situation he now is,
it shall be optional in him to do so: In
either case however, I allow him an
annuity of thirty dollars during his
natural life, which shall be independent of the victuals & cloaths he has
been accustomed to receive, if he chuses
the last alternative; but in full, with
his freedom, if he prefers the first; —
I give him as a testimony of my sense
of his attachment to me, and for his
faithful services during the Revolutionary War. —

Item. To the Trustees (Governors, or by whatsoever other name they may be designated)
of the Academy in the Town of Alexandria, I give and bequeath, in Trust,
four thousand dollars, or in other
words twenty of the shares which I

19. Excerpt from the will of George Washington dealing with his slave, William Lee.
Fairfax County Courthouse, Virginia.

35

In March 1781 Washington rushed General Lafayette to Virginia in an effort to stop Cornwallis. Shortly thereafter, a slave by the name of James, in New Kent County, asked his master, William Armistead, for permission to enlist under the French major general. That spring and summer, Lafayette felt a crucial necessity to recruit black troops. He called for four hundred laborers and wagoners, and wrote frantically to Washington: "Nothing but a treaty of alliance with the Negroes can find us dragoon Horses . . . it is by this means the enemy have so formidable a Cavalry." As a master spy, James gave yeoman service. After the surrender at Yorktown, when Cornwallis visited Lafayette's headquarters, he was amazed to see there the black man he had believed to be *his* spy [figure 20].

The war over, in November 1784 James met Lafayette in Richmond. In his own hand, the Frenchman wrote a testimonial which he handed to James, certifying that the ex-spy had rendered "services to me while I had the honour to command in this state. His intelligence from the enemy's camp were industriously collected and more faithfully delivered. He perfectly acquitted himself with some important commissions I gave him and appears to me entitled to every reward his situation can admit of" [figure 21]. It is barely possible that James, whose "situation" was still that of slave, by his very presence played a certain part in clarifying the thinking of the marquis about race and slavery. It was about this time that Lafayette began to develop the outlook that would move him in 1783 to propose to Washington a plan "which might greatly benefit the black part of mankind. Let us unite in purchasing a small estate where we may try the experiment to free the Negroes and use them only as tenants." Five years later in Paris, this led to his fervent sponsorship of the Society of the Friends of the Blacks.

During the autumn of 1786 the General Assembly of Virginia, echoing Lafayette's words—"at the peril of his life found means to frequent the British camp, and thereby faithfully executed important commissions entrusted to him by the marquis"—emancipated James, ordering that his master be compensated at the going auction-block figure. When thirty-odd years later the freeman, "now poor and unable to help himself," petitioned for relief, the state gave him sixty dollars and finally placed him on the regular pension list.

In the year 1824, Lafayette, on a triumphal return visit to America, came to Richmond. The black veteran, who for a long time had called himself James Lafayette, and the French nobleman who had survived *his* revolution, greeted each other. The scene can be imagined the more vividly because it was probably during this year that the artist John B. Martin, whose portrait of Chief Justice John Marshall hangs in the Supreme Court, painted the aging James Lafayette in a military coat [color plate 2, following page 84].

During the summer of 1844, Francis Parkman spent a few days in Stockbridge, a town in western Massachusetts. On July 7, he recorded in

20. Marquis de Lafayette at Yorktown. Jean-Baptiste Le Paon, 1783. Lafayette College, Easton, Pennsylvania.

This is to certify that the Bearer by the Name of James Has done Essential Services to me While I had the Honour to command in this State. His Intelligences from the Enemy's Camp were Industriously Collected and most faithfully Delivered He perfectly Acquitted Himself With Some Important Commissions I Gave him and Appears to me Entitled to Every Reward his Situation Can Admit of. Done Under My Hand, Richmond November 21st 1784 / Lafayette

his journal: "The old Negro . . . had been a soldier in W's army. He had four children in the churchyard, he said with a solemn countenance, but 'these are my children' he added, stretching his cane over a host of little boys. 'Ah, how much we are consarned to fetch them up well and virtuous' etc. He was very philosophical and every remark carried the old patriarch into lengthy orations on virtue and temperance. He looked on himself as father to all Stockbridge." The old patriarch was a black veteran who, sixty years before his conversation with the noted historian, had served as orderly to the noble Pole, General Tadeusz Kosciuszko. To this day, Agrippa Hull is a legendary figure in the Berkshire town where his portrait complete with cane, in the historical room of the library, broods over the memorabilia of the past [color plate 3, following page 84].

Agrippa Hull was born free in Northampton in 1759. At age six—so the story goes—a black man by the name of Joab, former servant to Jonathan Edwards, brought him to Stockbridge. On May 1, 1777, the eighteen-year-old youth—"5 ft. 7 in.; complexion, black; hair, wool"— enlisted for the duration as a private in the brigade of General John Paterson of the Massachusetts Line. For two years he served with Paterson, and then for another four years and two months as orderly for Paterson's friend, the Polish patriot, in spheres of action ranging from Saratoga to Eutaw Springs. In South Carolina, assigned to assist the surgeons, Hull always remembered with horror the bloody amputations. In July of 1783 at West Point, he received his discharge, signed by George Washington.

Back home in Stockbridge he farmed a small plot, did odd jobs, acted as butler for the local gentry and major domo at weddings, married a fugitive slave, adopted as a daughter another fugitive, and became the village seer. In 1797 when Kosciuszko visited the United States, Hull traveled to New York. There was an affectionate reunion; no doubt both smiled as they recalled the time the general surprised the orderly dressed in his commander's uniform in the midst of a party Agrippa had thrown for his black friends. It was on this visit that Kosciuszko, a lover of liberty, was awarded a gift of land in Ohio and directed that it be sold to found a school for blacks.

In 1828, when Hull was seeking to have his soldier's pension mailed directly to his home, his friend, Charles Sedgwick, wrote to the official in charge: "I enclose his discharge & take the liberty to request that it may be returned—and also to mention as an interesting fact in regard to this man that I have obtained his permission to send it with great difficulty, he declaring that he had rather forego the pension than lose the discharge" [figure 22].

Agrippa Hull "had a fund of humor and mother-wit," recalled the novelist, Catharine Maria Sedgwick, "and was a sort of Sancho Panza in the village, always trimming other men's follies with a keen perception, and the biting wit of wisdom." Electa Jones, historian of the town, shortly after Agrippa's death at eighty-nine, remembered him as having "no cringing servility" in his makeup, always feeling "himself every whit a man." An anecdote she tells gives the measure of his character: "Once, when servant to a man who was haughty and overbearing, both Agrippa and his master attended the same church, to listen to a discourse from a distinguished mulatto preacher [Lemuel Haynes?] . . . the gentleman said to Agrippa, 'Well how do you like nigger preaching?' 'Sir,' he promptly retorted, 'he was half black and half white; I liked *my* half, how did you like *yours*?' "

Sir. I perceive by an advertisement of yours in Niles' Register that the Pensioners of the U.S. claiming under the Law of 1828 can (if allowed) have their money transmitted to them at the place of their residence. I am reluctant to impose any unnecessary burden upon yr department, but am induced by the wish to serve one of the most respectable survivors of the Revy army a colored man to avail myself of the privilege there offered & to request that his money may be transmitted to him at Stockbridge by mail (an order if convenient on some Bank in Boston or N. York) — I inclose his discharge & take the liberty to request that it may be returned — and also to mention as an interesting fact in regard to this man ~ he declaring that he had rather forego the pension than lose the discharge. —

Lenox June 12. 1828.

I am Sir, with great respect
& Obt Sert
Chas. Sedgwick

Hon Mr Rush. —

Hon. W. Rush) If it is agreeable to the rules of your department I should esteem it a favr that if the amt of my pension (provided it be obtained) could be remitted to me now & hereafter as it may fall due at Stockbridge thro the P. Office — & by means of a draft on Boston or N York. —

I have the honor to be
with great respect
yr Obt Sert:

Lenox
Jun. 12. 1828.

Agrippa Hull.

22. Letter from Charles Sedgwick and Agrippa Hull to acting Secretary of State Richard Rush, June 12, 1828. National Archives.

A MUSTER OF BRAVE SOLDIERS

AND SAILORS

After the fireworks were over on July 4, 1847, John Greenleaf Whittier, poet laureate of anti-slavery, was moved to right an historic wrong. The result was a lead editorial in the *National Era* on "The Black Men of the Revolution of 1776 and War of 1812." "The return of the Festival of our National Independence," Whittier began, "has called our attention to a matter which has been very carefully kept out of sight by orators and toast-drinkers. We allude to the participation of colored men in the great struggle for Freedom." As a pacifist Quaker, he had no desire "to eulogize the shedders of blood, even in a cause of acknowledged justice," but

when we see a whole nation doing honor to the memories of one class of its defenders, to the total neglect of another class, who had the misfortune to be of darker complexion, we cannot forego the satisfaction of inviting notice to certain historical facts, which for the last half century have been quietly elbowed aside. . . . Of the services and sufferings of the colored soldiers of the Revolution, no attempt has, to our knowledge been made to preserve a record. They have had no historian. With here and there an exception, they all passed away, and only some faint tradition of their campaigns under Washington, and Greene, and Lafayette, and of their cruisings under Decatur and Barry, lingers among their descendants. Yet enough is known to show that the free colored men of the United States bore their full proportion of the sacrifices and trials of the Revolutionary war.

☛The faces of William Lee, Agrippa Hull, and James Lafayette have come down to us in paint because they were closely and valuably linked with famous generals. Such portraits are rare. The thousands of black rank-and-file who fought on the Patriot side—who marched, sailed, spied, piloted, scouted—remain almost invisible, often nameless, except as we can feebly try to reconstruct their reality from a few, sometimes grudging, words scattered here and there in the meager (where black is concerned) records of the time. As Benjamin Quarles puts it, "The typical Negro soldier was a private, consigned as if by caste, to the rank and file. Even more than other privates, he tended to lack identity. Often he bore no specific name. . . ."

When, in March of 1781, Maryland needed ships, a tidewater Patriot replied to the plea of the council that he would send "his schooner

Cheerfully," but with "a Negro Skipper, as no whit man would go." We would like to know more about this fearless black skipper even as we understand more clearly why General Washington, two years earlier, had written to Major Henry Lee: "I have granted a Warrant for the 1000 Dolls. promised the Negro pilots. . . ."

In John Marshall's *Life of Washington* there is a description of an episode towards the end of the Battle of Cowpens in South Carolina, in which General Daniel Morgan, outnumbered, routed the British dragoons under Tarleton. Lieutenant Colonel William Washington, leader of the Patriot cavalry and a relative of General Washington, was about to be cut down by a British sword, "when a waiter, too small to wield a sword, saved him by wounding the officer with a ball from a pistol." In 1845 William Ranney painted the scene, perhaps out of Marshall, perhaps from tradition [figure 24]. The Continental Congress awarded General Morgan a gold placque for his triumph at Cowpens—we do not even know the name of the brave black lad rendered so vigorously by the imagination of the artist.

Sometimes the record has the laconic eloquence of an epitaph: "Zechery Prince now ded, Recd his freedom"—so reads a brief line on a payroll of Simsbury, Connecticut, troops in the spring of 1779 [figure 25]. In the

24. The Battle of Cowpens.
William Ranney, 1845.
Mr. Frederick Donhauser,
Stony Point, Alaska.

log of the ship-of-war *Ranger,* at anchor in Charleston harbor on February 25, 1780, there is this entry: "at 10 this Night a Negro Called Cesar Hodgsdon died." But who *was* Zechery Prince? And who *was* Cesar Hodgsdon? We grope for the man and have to be content with a phrase. Here is a cluster of vignettes, short and long, randomly assembled, which, read together as a collective profile, might furnish a sketchy portrait of a sizable group of black soldiers and seamen of the Revolution.

Harry and Cupid: The armed schooner *Liberty* in the navy of Virginia, commanded by Captain James Barron—afterward Commodore Barron, senior officer of the United States Navy—fought twenty sharp actions during the war. When, in his old age, the Commodore put down his memories of the *Liberty,* he wrote of the
courageous patriots who had served on board of her during the war. Amongst these, I take pleasure in stating there were several coloured men, who, I think, in justice to their merits should not be forgotten. Harry (a slave, belonging to Captain John Cooper) was distinguished for his zeal and daring; Cupid (a slave of Mr. William Ballard) stood forth on all occasions as the champion of liberty, and discharged all his duties with a fidelity that made him a favorite of all the officers.

25. Excerpt from the payroll of Simsbury, Connecticut, April 10, 1779; "Zechery Prince, now Ded, Rec'd His Freedom." Connecticut State Library.

43

Jupiter: On a fading scrap of paper, miraculously preserved, a Virginia colonel by the name of George Muter certifies, on March 29, 1781, that "Jupiter (negro) saved four guns during the time the enemy were in Richmond, which he afterwards delivered to me & for which he has received no reward" [figure 26].

Antigua: In March 1783 a slave by this name was lauded by the General Assembly of South Carolina for his skill in "procuring information of the enemy's movements and designs." He "always executed the commissions with which he was entrusted with diligence and fidelity, and obtained very considerable and important information, from within the enemy's lines, frequently at the risk of his life." To reward him, the assembly liberated his "wife named Hagar, and her child." Presumably, Antigua remained a slave.

Prince Whipple: There are two well-known paintings that depict Washington's crossing of the Delaware on that wintry Christmas Eve in 1776. The earlier of the two, a huge canvas, was painted by Thomas Sully in 1819 for the state of South Carolina. It shows the general astride a mettlesome white horse on a snowy riverbank attended by four mounted men, three of them white officers, the fourth a young black soldier [figure 27]. The other picture—more familiar, painted by Emanuel Gottlieb Leutze in 1851, shows Washington standing in a rowboat

44

27. Washington's Passage of the Delaware. Thomas Sully, 1819. Museum of Fine Arts,
Boston.

28. Washington Crossing the Delaware. Paul Girardet after Emanuel Leutze. Engraving,
not dated. The New York Public Library.

moving through the ice [figure 28]. One of the oarsmen is black. According to a tradition there seems no reason to question(and first put into print by William C. Nell in 1851) the black trooper who crossed the river with Washington and who is thus depicted by Sully and Leutze, is Prince Whipple, "body-guard to Gen. Whipple, of New Hampshire, who was Aid to General Washington." Nell recounts something of Whipple's life.

Prince Whipple was born at Amabou, Africa, of comparatively wealthy parents. When about ten years of age, he was sent by them, in company with a cousin, to America, to be educated. An elder brother had returned four years before, and his parents were anxious that their child should receive the same benefits. The captain who brought the two boys over proved a treacherous villain, and carried them to Baltimore, where he exposed them for sale, and they were both purchased by Portsmouth men, Prince falling to Gen. Whipple. He was emancipated during the war, was much esteemed, and was once entrusted by the General with a large sum of money to carry from Salem to Portsmouth. He was attacked on the road, near Newburyport, by two ruffians; one he struck with a loaded whip, the other he shot. . . . Prince was beloved by all who knew him. He was the "Caleb Quotem" of Portsmouth, where he died at the age of thirty-two, leaving a widow and children.

James Forten: Friend of Richard Allen, Absalom Jones, Paul Cuffe, and William Lloyd Garrison, this founding father of abolitionism [figure 29] was born free in Philadelphia in 1766, where he briefly attended the school of the anti-slavery Quaker, Anthony Benezet. When he was fifteen he enlisted as a powder boy on the *Royal Louis,* a privateer commanded by Stephen Decatur, Senior, with a crew of two hundred, twenty of whom were black. Its first action was a bloody affair for both sides, but the English brig-of-war struck its colors. On the next cruise, the heavily armed English frigate *Amphyon,* supported by two other warships, forced Decatur to surrender. It was a bad moment for young Forten. Black prisoners were rarely exchanged; usually the British sold them in the West Indies.

But Forten was lucky. On board the *Amphyon* the captain's son, a lad of the same age, took a fancy to him, was astounded at his skill at marbles, and persuaded his father to offer Forten the life of an aristocrat in England. "No, No!" Forten said he replied, "I am here a prisoner for the liberties of my country; I never, never, shall prove a traitor to her interests!" Instead of the West Indies, he was shipped off to the prison ship *Jersey,* anchored off Long Island. "Thus," he later observed, "did a game of marbles save me from a life of West Indian servitude."

Aboard the *Jersey,* he sometimes doubted his luck as the days slowly passed. A thousand prisoners crowded her foul hold; ten thousand died miserably during the war in the rotten old hulk. William Nell records a noble deed, later attested by its benficiary: "An officer . . . was about to be exchanged for a British prisoner, when the thoughtful mind of Forten conceived the idea of an easy escape for himself in the officer's chest; but

29. Unidentified gentleman, possibly James Forten. Unidentified artist. The Historical Society of Pennsylvania.

. . . a fellow-prisoner, a youth, his junior in years . . . was thought of.
. . . The offer was accepted, and Forten had the satisfaction of assisting
in taking down the 'chest of old clothes' . . . from the side of the prison
ship." The rescued youth grew up to become a captain in the navy.

After seven months in the floating hell, he was released in a general
exchange of prisoners and walked home to Philadelphia.

James Forten would go on to a long and distinguished career. During
the next half century, he would make his mark on the times as inventor,
manufacturer, philanthropist, and organizer of protest. He was always
fond of recalling his youth. In 1833, nearing sixty, he·said: "My great-
grandfather was brought to this country as a slave from Africa. My grandfather obtained his own freedom. My father never wore the yoke. He
rendered valuable service to his country in the war of our Revolution;
and I, though then a boy, was a drummer in that war. I was taken prisoner, and was made to suffer not a little on board the *Jersey* prison-ship."

Oliver Cromwell: When this black veteran reached his hundredth year
during the spring of 1852, the *Burlington* [New Jersey] *Gazette* carried
the following story.

The attention of many of our citizens has, doubtless, been arrested by
the appearance of an old colored man, who might have been seen, sitting
in front of his residence, in East Union Street, respectfully raising his hat
to those who might be passing by. His attenuated frame, his silvered
head, his feeble movements, combine to prove that he was very aged; and
yet, comparatively few are aware that he is among the survivors of the gallant army who fought for the liberties of our country "in the days which
tried men's souls."

On Monday last, we stopped to speak to him, and asked him how old
he was. He asked the day of the month, and . . . replied with trembling
lips, "I am very old—I am a hundred years old today."

His name is Oliver Cromwell. . . .   He enlisted in a company commanded by Capt. Lowery, attached to the Second New Jersey Regiment,
under the command of Col. Israel Shreve. He was at the battles of Trenton, Princeton, Brandywine, Monmouth, and Yorktown, at which latter
place, he told us, he saw the last man killed. Although his faculties are
failing, yet he relates many interesting reminiscences of the Revolution.
He was with the army at the retreat of the Delaware, on the memorable
crossing of the 25th of December, 1776, and relates the story of the battles
of the succeeding days with enthusiasm. He gives the details of the march
from Trenton to Princeton, and told us, with much humor, that they
"knocked the British about lively" at the latter place. . . .
Cromwell, who had been "brought up a farmer," joined up in his early
twenties and served for six years and nine months under the immediate
command of Washington. His discharge [figure 30], said Dr. James
McCune Smith, the eminent New York abolitionist, "at the close of the
war, was in Washington's own hand-writing, of which he was very proud,
often speaking of it." When Cromwell died in January 1853, he had seen
his grandchildren to the third generation.

30. Honorable discharge of Oliver Cromwell, June 5, 1783. National Archives.

George Latchom: In 1781 the British landed at Henry's Point in Virginia where they were met by the militia under Colonel John Cropper. In this engagement, George Latchom, still a slave, played a heroic role. The colonel's biographer has preserved the details.

During the fight the militia retreated, leaving Cropper and a negro named George Latchom, who were in advance of the rest, engaged actively with the invaders. These two kept up the firing, until the foe were within a few rods of them, when they were compelled to fall back. Cropper had to retreat through a sunken, boggy marsh, in which he stuck fast up to the waist in soft mud, the enemy at the time being so close as to prepare to bayonet him.

At this critical juncture the faithful colored man fired and killed the foremost man, and seized hold of Cropper and dragged him by main strength out of the mud, and taking him on his back, carried him safely to dry land. This required great strength upon his part, Cropper weighing in the neighborhood of two hundred pounds.

Cropper thereupon bought Latchom from his owner, set him free, and "befriended him in every way he could, as an evidence of his gratitude, till Latchom's death."

Edward Hector: At the Battle of Brandywine in September 1777 this black artilleryman was thirty-three years old, a private in Captain Hercules Courtney's company, Third Pennsylvania Artillery of the Continental Line. He died in 1834, a nonagenerian. Two Norristown newspapers printed his obituary:

Edward Hector, a colored man and a veteran of the Revolution. Obscurity in life and oblivion in death, is too often the lot of the worthy—they pass away, and no "storied stone" perpetuates the remembrance of their noble actions. . . . During the war of the revolution, his conduct, on one memorable occasion, exhibited an example of patriotism and bravery which deserves to be recorded. At the battle of Brandywine he had charge of an ammunition wagon, attached to Col. Proctor's regiment, and when the American army was obliged to retreat, an order was given . . . to abandon them to the enemy. . . . The heroic reply of the deceased was uttered in the true spirit of the revolution: "The enemy shall not have my team; I will save my horses, or perish myself!" He instantly started on his way, and as he proceeded, amid the confusion of the surrounding scene, he calmly gathered up . . . a few stand of arms which had been left on the field by the retreating soldiers, and safely retired with wagon, team and all, in the face of the victorious foe. Some years ago a few benevolent individuals endeavored to procure him a pension, but without success. The Legislature of Pennsylvania, however, at the last session, granted him a donation of $40.00, which was all the gratuity he ever received for his Revolutionary services. . . .

Enough to bury Edward Hector.

Lambert Latham and Jordan Freeman: On Groton Heights, across the Thames from New London, the state of Connecticut in 1830 erected a granite shaft "in memory of the brave patriots who fell in the massacre at Fort Griswold near this spot on the 6th of September, A. D. 1781, when the British under the command of the traitor Benedict Arnold, burnt the towns of New London & Groton." On that shaft, inscribed on a marble tablet, are the names of the eighty-four Patriots slain that day; at the top is the name of Lieutenant Colonel William Ledyard, their commander; at the bottom, segregated by the label "Colored men," are the names of Sambo Latham and Jordan Freeman. On the day the shaft was dedicated a black man in the crowd, William Anderson of New London, recollecting what "two veterans who were present at the battle" had told him of the bloody event, reflected somewhat bitterly on the inscription: "One of these men was the brother of my grandmother, by the name of Lambert, but called Lambo,—since chiselled on the marble monument by the *American classic appelation of 'Sambo.'* "

Lambert worked for a farmer named Latham and when the alarm came they were out in a field taking care of the cattle. The assault by the British was a deadly one: "Finally, the little garrison was overcome, and, on the entrance of the enemy, the British officer inquired, 'Who commands this fort?' The gallant Ledyard replied, 'I once did; you do now,'—at the same time handing his sword, which was immediately run through his body to the hilt. . . . Lambert, being near Col. Ledyard when he was. slain, retaliated upon the officer by thrusting his bayonet through his body. Lambert, in return, received from the enemy *thirty-three bayonet* wounds, and thus fell, nobly avenging the death of his commander." According to a tradition in the Latham family, "Lambo fought manfully by his master's side up to the time he was slain. In the hottest of the conflict he stood near his master, loading and discharging his musket with great rapidity, even after he had been severely wounded in one of his hands."

On that same day, an eyewitness recalled, the British commander of the assault, Major Montgomery, as he scaled a wall of the fort, "was killed by spears in the hands of Captain Shapley and a black man named Jordan Freeman," who was Colonel Ledyard's orderly.

Jack Sisson: The derring-do capture of British Major General Richard Prescott at his headquarters near Newport, Rhode Island, in July 1777 by a patriot team of commandos soon got into song and ballad. In the annals of the time, the black volunteer who played an important part in this caper goes by several names—Jack or Tack Sisson, Guy Watson, and Prince. Lieutenant Colonel Barton, states the earliest newspaper report of the event, "selected and engaged about forty men to go with him on a secret expedition, by water in five batteaus . . . he told them his design, acknowledged it was hazardous . . . if any of them were unwilling to engage in the enterprize, they were then at full liberty to decline it. . . . On putting the matter to their choice, they unanimously resolved to go with him, and told him to lead them on to honor. They then set off with muffled oars on a dark night. . . ." With Sisson as one of the boat steerers, they "pased the enemy's forts," slipped through his "ships of war," and landed near Prescott's headquarters. "The col. went foremost, with a stout active Negro, close behind him, and another at a small distance. . . ." Barton and Sisson made short work of the single sentinel at the door. With "the rest of the men surrounding the house, the Negro, with his head, at the second stroke, forced a passage into it, and [into] the general's chamber . . . the colonel calling the general by name, told him he was a prisoner, he replied he knew it, and rising from his bed desired time to put on his clothes. The colonel told him to put on his breeches. . . ."

Legend has it that not long after Prescott's exchange for the American general, Charles Lee, he was dining aboard the admiral's ship off Newport and called for a song by a Yankee lad, a prisoner, thirteen years old. The ballad he sang was allegedly composed by a Newport sailor.

> A tawny son of Afric's race
>   Them through the ravine led,
> And entering then the Overing House,
>   They found him in his bed.
>
> But to get in they had no means
>   Except poor Cuffee's head,
> Who beat the door down then rush'd in,
>   And seized him in his bed.
>
> "Stop! let me put my breeches on,"
>   The general then did pray:
> "Your breeches, massa, I will take,
>   For dress we cannot stay."

Catherine Williams, the biographer of Colonel Barton, wrote down a dozen years after Sisson's death her memory of him in his last years. Through her genteel racism one can glimpse the old veteran.

A black servant of the Colonel . . . a faithful attendant and shrewd fellow, and one who, in his own opinion at least, formed a very important personage in the expedition . . . he continued to regret to the day of his death that his name had never appeared in any account of the transaction. After the capture of Prescott, Guy was made a drummer. . . . He was remarkably small. . . . On all public days he usually made his appearance on the parade ground, dressed in complete uniform, and his appearance was a perfect holiday to all the little urchins about street, who would immediately crowd around, to listen to his stories, and hear him in his cracked voice sing the old ballad, beginning "Brave Barton!"

The *Providence Gazette* of November 3, 1821, published his obituary: "In Plymouth (Mass.) . . . a negro man, aged about 78 years. He was one of the forty brave volunteers. . . ."

Quaco: During the British occupation of Newport, Quaco's Tory master sold him to a colonel in the king's army. Quaco fled to the Patriot line with valuable information. In January 1782, the General Assembly

51

of Rhode Island, in recognition that "the information he then gave, render[ed] great and essential service to this state and the public in general," declared him "a freeman."

Saul Matthews: As spy and guide, this slave proved himself of inestimable value. In 1781, Josiah Parker, colonel of the Virginia militia, said that he "deserved the applause of his country." Luther P. Jackson, historian of the black soldier in Revolutionary Virginia, has sketched Saul's career at the front.

This slave of Thomas Matthews "shouldered his musket" and went over to the American side in the early months of the war . . . in 1781 during the campaign of the British in the vicinity of Portsmouth, Saul, at the risk of his life, was sent into the British garrison. . . . He brought back military secrets of such value to Colonel Parker that on the same night, serving as a guide, he led a party of Americans to the British garrison. . . . On another occasion in 1781, when Saul's master and many other Virginians had fled into the adjoining state of North Carolina, he was sent by them to Norfolk to secure similar intelligence concerning the movements and plans of the British troops. For his services as a spy and a soldier such distinguished army officers as Baron von Steuben, Lafayette, Peter Muhlenberg, and General Nathaniel Greene praised him to the highest.

After the war Saul's master changed, but he continued to labor as a slave. In 1792 he petitioned the Virginia legislature for his freedom and in November of that year, "in consideration of many very essential services rendered to this Commonwealth during the late war," he was granted his "full liberty."

Austin Dabney: The Battle of Kettle Creek early in 1779 was "the hardest ever fought in Georgia." Dabney, an artilleryman who had been given his freedom in order to serve in his master's place, fought in this battle in Colonel Elijah Clark's corp. "No soldier under Clark," wrote a former governor of Georgia in 1855, "was braver, or did better service during the revolutionary struggle." Shot in the thigh, Dabney was rescued and nursed back to health by a white soldier named Harris. In gratitude, he worked for the Harris family; out of his own pocket, he sent his rescuer's eldest son through college and then arranged for his legal training.

Although Dabney was a pensioner, because he was black he was denied a chance in the lottery for land open to Revolutionary veterans in 1819. When the legislature finally granted him 112 acres for his "bravery and fortitude" in "several engagements and actions," a group of whites in Madison County protested the award, claiming "it was an indignity to white men, for a mulatto to be put upon an equality with them in the distribution of the public land."

Austin Dabney existed gingerly, a friend of a few upper class white veterans of the Revolution. "He owned fine horses, attended the racecourse, entered the list for the stake. . . ." In his old age, in "the evening after the adjournment of the court in Danielsville, he usually went into the room occupied by the judges and the lawyers, where, taking a low seat, he listened to what was said, or himself told of the struggles between the Whigs and the Tories in upper Georgia and South Carolina. His memory was retentive, his understanding good, and he described what he knew well."

Caesar Tarrant: For four years, Caesar, a slave in the Tarrant family of Hampton, Virginia, served in the state's navy as a pilot on the armed *Patriot*, steering the vessel in its most important engagement south of the Virginia capes. During the whole action, he "behaved gallantly." Other black seamen on the *Patriot* were David Baker, Jack Knight, Mark Starlins, Pluto, and Cuffee. Tarrant was aboard the *Patriot* when she captured the *Fanny* on the way to Boston with supplies for the British.

In 1789 the Virginia legislature, because he had "entered very early into the service of his country, and continued to pilot the armed vessels of this state during the late war," set Caesar Tarrant free. During the next half-dozen years, the ex-slave and veteran bought several pieces of property in Hampton, and in 1796, when he died, willed houses and lots to his "loving wife." Thirty-five years later, the government granted to his daughter, Nancy, 2,666 acres of land in Ohio in recognition of her father's crucial part in the operations of the Virginia navy.

Titus: Not exactly a brave sailor, but an interesting person. Hundreds of black seamen served on Patriot privateers. Titus, of Salem, Massachusetts, served as a business agent for the privateers, and did well at it according to the entry of August 13, 1781, in the diary of William Pynchon.

Fair and cool. News that Mrs. Fairfield's son died in the prison ship at New York. Three more privateers are taken. . . . Mrs. Cabot makes her will; in it gives Titus, her negro, £40 and his freedom in case he shall continue in her service henceforth till her death. Titus cares not, as he gets money apace, being one of the agents for some of the privateersmen, and wears cloth shoes, ruffled shirts, silk breeches and stockings, and dances minuets at Commencement; it is said he has made more profits as agent than Mr. Ansil Alcock. . . .

Minny: The short and simple annals of the brave—and black. Scene: Convention of Delegates of Virginia. Saturday, June 15, 1776. Business: "A petition of Lucretia Pritchett . . . setting forth that in a late atatck on a piratical [British] tender in Rappahannock river, Minny, a negro man . . . voluntarily entered himself on board a vessel commanded by Mr. Hugh Walker, and being used to the water, and a good pilot, bravely and successfully exerted himself against the enemy, until he was unfortunately killed, whereby the estate of the said Joseph Pritchett was deprived of a valuable slave. . . since the said slave was lost by means of a meritorious act, in defence of the country, she [asks to be reimbursed] the value thereof. Two weeks later, the Virginia delegates awarded Lucretia Pritchett one hundred dollars for the death of her slave, Minny.

"Captain" Mark Starlins: Another reminiscence of Commodore James Barron in his old age is all there is to furnish a glimpse into the life of the black Virginia pilot, Mark Starlins, who called himself "Captain." The Commodore remembered "a very singular and meritorious character in the person of an African, who had been brought over to this country when he was young, and soon evinced a remarkable attachment to it; he was brought up as a pilot, and proved a skilful one, and a devoted patriot," who sometimes "allowed his patriotism to get the better of his judgment." The "noble African," wrote Barron, "lived and died a slave soon after the peace, and just before a law was passed that gave freedom to all those devoted men of colour who had so zealously volunteered their services in the patriotic cause." Starlins was held in high estimation "by all worthy citizens, and, more particularly, by all the navy officers of the State."

THREE BLACK UNITS

There were two all-black units in the Continental Army and a third which voyaged from Haiti with the French. Colonel Christopher Greene's First Rhode Island Regiment distinguished itself for efficiency and gallantry throughout the war—perhaps the war would have ended sooner if its example had been heeded. About the Bucks of America, a Massachusetts company, little is known except that John Hancock chose it for special honor. The Black Brigade of Saint Domingue, Haiti, in this day of Pan-African aspiration, needs to be better known.

The Black Regiment of Rhode Island came into being because that state was not able to supply its quota of white troops to the Continental Line—and because blacks wanted to fight for their own freedom [figure 31]. The rationale of the decision to create this unit is of some interest. Since history had supplied "frequent precedents of the wisest, the freest, and bravest nations having liberated their slaves, and enlisted them as soldiers to fight in defence of their country," and since the British had "taken possession of the capital, and of a greater part" of the state, it was simply "impossible . . . to furnish recruits. . . ." So, voted Rhode Island's legislature in February 1778, any slave volunteering for the new battalions would be declared "absolutely free" and entitled to the wages and bounties of a regular soldier.

Colonel Christopher Greene, with Washington's blessing, hurried north from Valley Forge and before the spring was over he had begun to train the black soldiers who made up this extraordinary unit. The test of fire for the Black Regiment came all too soon in the Battle of Rhode Island, which General Lafayette called "the best fought action of the war." General John Sullivan, with six brigades, confronted a powerful force of British and Hessian troops. The Black Regiment—with its core of ninety-five ex-slaves and thirty freedmen, most of them raw recruits—assigned to what turned out to be one of the hottest sectors of the American right wing, was the special target of repeated Hessian charges. But here the Germans "experienced a more obstinate resistance than they had expected," noted an on-the-spot observer. "They found large bodies of troops behind the work and at its sides, chiefly wild looking men in their shirt sleeves, and among them many negroes." "It was in repelling these furious onsets," wrote a Rhode Island historian in 1860, "that the newly raised black regiment, under Col. Greene, distinguished itself by deeds of desperate valor. Posted behind a thicket in the valley, they three times drove back the Hessians who charged repeatedly down the hill to dislodge them." The day after the battle, the Hessian colonel "applied to exchange his command and go to New York, because he dared not lead his regiment again to battle, lest his men shoot him for

55

31. "Return of Freemen Inlisted during the War in First Rhode Island Battalion Commanded by Col. G. Greene." The Rhode Island Historical Society.

having caused them so much loss." On the day after the battle, General Sullivan announced that "by the best Information the Commander-in-Chief thinks that the Regiment will be intituled [sic] to a proper share of the Honours of the day."

This was the Black Regiment's first action—but not its last. One of the few American units that enlisted for the entire war, it proved itself again at Red Bank, Points Bridge, and Yorktown. "In the attack made upon the American lines, near Croton river, on the 13th of May, 1781," wrote William C. Nell, "Colonel Greene, the commander of the regiment, was cut down and mortally wounded: but the sabres of the enemy only reached him through the bodies of his faithful guard of blacks, who hovered over him to protect him, *and every one of whom was killed.*"

Traveling in Connecticut in 1781, the Marquis de Chastellux noted in his journal on January fifth: "At the ferry-crossing I met with a detachment of the Rhode Island regiment. . . . The majority of the enlisted men are Negroes or mulattoes; but they are strong, robust men, and those I saw made a very good appearance." When the victorious American army passed in review at Yorktown during the following July, Baron von Closen, an aide-de-camp to General Rochambeau remarked that "Three-quarters of the Rhode Island regiment consists of Negroes, and that regiment is the most neatly dressed, the best under arms, and the most precise in its maneuvres."

About all that is now known of Boston's all-black unit was recorded in 1855 by the pioneer black historian William C. Nell.

At the close of the Revolutionary War, John Hancock presented the colored company, called 'the Bucks of America,' with an appropriate banner, bearing his initials, as a tribute to their courage and devotion throughout the struggle. The 'Bucks,' under the command of Colonel Middleton, were invited to a collation in a neighboring town, and, *en route* were requested to halt in front of the Hancock Mansion, in Beacon street, where the Governor and his son united in the above presentation.

Three years later, at that same meeting from the rostrum of which Wendell Phillips praised Crispus Attucks as the man who "dared," an exhibit of "interesting relics and mementoes of the olden time" included the banner of the black company as well as "a flag presented to an association of colored men, called the 'Protectors,' who guarded the property of Boston merchants" during the revolution. Sitting in the audience was "Mrs. Kay, daughter of the Ensign who received the banner" from Hancock. During the Civil War, Nell presented the banner [figure 32] to the Massachusetts Historical Society, whose proceedings for 1862 describe it as "a silk flag, bearing the device of a Pine-tree and a Buck, with the initials 'J. H.' and 'G. W.' over a scroll, on which appear the words, 'The Bucks of America.' "

Lydia Maria Child has left us a sketch of Colonel Middleton, the black commander of the company, whom she knew well in his hale old age when he played the violin and still retained his skill as a "horse-breaker." She tells a story in which the old soldier displayed his revolutionary fire in "subduing" some "mettlesome colts." The occasion was an anniversary of the abolition of the slave trade, celebrated annually by the blacks of Boston.

It became a frolic with the white boys to deride them on this day, and finally . . . to drive them . . . from the Common. The colored people became greatly incensed by this mockery of their festival, and rumor reached us . . . that they were determined to resist the whites, and were going armed with this intention. . . . Soon, terrified children and women ran down Belknap street, pursued by white boys, who enjoyed their fright. The sounds of battle approached; clubs and brickbats were flying in [all] directions. At this crisis, Col. Middleton opened his door, armed with a loaded musket, and, in a loud voice, shrieked death to the first white who should approach. Hundreds of human beings, white and

32. The Bucks of America. Silk flag.
Massachusetts Historical Society.

black, were pouring down the street. . . . Col. Middleton's voice could
be heard above every other, urging his party to turn and resist to the last.
His appearance was terrific, his musket was levelled, ready to sacrifice the
first white man that came within its range. The colored party, shamed by
his reproaches, and fired by his example, rallied. . . .

The names of the Bucks of America, with one exception, their visages,
their exploits of "courage and devotion," so far are lost to history.
What remains is the bright banner.

☞ The Volunteer Chasseurs in another black outfit, from far-off Haiti—
a brigade of the seaborne French expedition that supported General
Lincoln in Georgia during the autumn of 1779—fought first in our
Revolution and then went on to lead the struggle for nationhood in their

own country, the second to achieve independence from Europe in the New World.

The aim of the Franco-American army was to evict the British from Savannah. In early September, a French fleet of thirty-three sail, under the command of the Comte d'Estaing, anchored off the Georgia coast and discharged its troops. As reported in the *Paris Gazette*, there were 2,979 "Europeans" and 545 "Colored: Volunteer Chasseurs, Mulattoes, and Negroes, newly raised at St. Domingo," the latter called the Fontages Legion after its French commander.

Among the colored volunteers in the American cause were young men destined to become famous in the Haitian revolution—among them were Andre Rigaud and Louis Jacques Beauvais, noncoms at Savannah; Martial Besse, a general under the Versailles Convention; Jean-Baptiste Mars Belley [figure 33], deputy to the convention; and Henri Christophe [figure 34], future king. Many tales are told of 12-year-old Christophe at Savannah—that he volunteered as a freeborn infantryman, that he was orderly to a French naval officer, and that he had been a slave and earned his freedom by his service in the Black Brigade.

To dislodge the well-entrenched enemy, Lincoln and d'Estaing decided to attack. But the British fought well, aided, it must be said, by thousands of slaves gathered from the countryside to build redoubts, mount cannon, and serve as guides. Georgian Patriots, however, fearful of slave revolt, always refused to give their bondsmen guns in exchange for liberty. As the French and Americans, raked by heavy fire, pulled back in retreat, the British, determined to wipe them out, charged. It was now that the Black Brigade, stationed as a reserve in the rear guard, showed its mettle by preventing the annihilation of the allied force. Count Casimir Pulaski, at the head of the cavalry, fell in this action. Martial Besse and Henri Christophe returned to Saint Domingue with slight wounds.

There is an ironic sequel. Eighteen years later when General Besse visited the United States on official business, he disembarked at Charleston, "dressed in the uniform of his grade," and was forced by the authorities to put up a bond as required by the law of South Carolina for all incoming blacks. It was only after the French consul in Charleston protested that General Besse was a representative of his government, and that, moreover, he had been wounded at the siege of Savannah, that the bond was remitted.

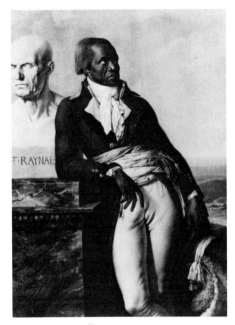

33. Jean-Baptiste Belley. Anne Louis Girodet de Roucy-Trioson, 1797. Musée National du Château de Versailles.

34. Henri Christophe. Richard Evans, ca. 1818. Formerly in the collection of the late Sir Bruce S. Ingram, London; present whereabouts unknown.

59

IN THE SERVICE OF THE KING

"The anecdote of the slave of Gen. Sullivan, of New Hampshire, is well known," Nell wrote in 1855. "When his master told him that they were on the point of starting for the army, to fight for liberty, he shrewdly suggested, that it would be a great satisfaction to know that he was indeed going to fight for *his* liberty. Struck with the reasonableness and justice of this suggestion, Gen. S. at once gave him his freedom." The general was an unusual person, but the anecdote suggests why some two hundred slaves volunteered to join Greene's First Rhode Island Reigment in the cause of American independence, while four times that number in Virginia fled their Patriot masters to join Lord Dunmore's Ethiopian Regiment in the king's cause. For slaves, the idea of freedom, body and soul, was more important than tea or taxes. In a war between white Patriot and white Tory, both upholders of the abominable institution, the question for Africans, enslaved in America for a century and a half, was clear enough: In which camp was there a better future for black freedom? The question was a simple one; the answer, always framed in terms of freedom was often complex and perilous, dependent on place, time, and opportunity, and on the way one could size up promises made by whites, Whig and Tory, desperately in need of black manpower for their own purposes. All slaves did not make the same choice, and there were some who sought their own path in flight or revolt.

In late April 1775, as Salem Poor was making his way to Bunker Hill, a group of Virginia blacks sought out the royal governor and offered to fight for the crown. Lord Dunmore was not yet ready, although for six months he had pondered the idea, feeling that "all the Slaves" were "on the side of Government." In mid-November a detachment of Dunmore's troops with black privates among them whipped the colonial militia at Kemp's Landing and slaves captured one of the Patriot colonels. The time and place were right—on November seventh at the scene of the victory, Dunmore proclaimed "all indented Servants, Negroes, or others, [appertaining to Rebels] free, that are able and willing to bear Arms" in the king's cause [figure 35].

As the *Virginia Gazette* appealed to the slaves with frantic arguments to cling to their kind masters—"Be not then, ye negroes, tempted by his proclamation to ruin your selves"—Patrick Henry, assailed the proclamation as "fatal to the publick Safety," and counseled "early and unremitting Attention to the Government of the Slaves." A broadside to the plantations strongly advised that "Constant, and well directed Patrols" were "indispensably necessary" to prevent the runaways from flocking to the royal standard. Meanwhile, blacks piloted Dunmore's

60

amphibian guerrilla forays, helped man his crews, and foraged widely to keep him in food. Within a week, five hundred bondmen had answered his call. He gave them guns "as fast as they came in." By the first of December nearly three hundred blacks in uniform, with the words "Liberty to Slaves" inscribed across their breasts, were members of "Lord Dunmore's Ethiopian Regiment."

For the patriotic slave masters of Virginia and points south, the "Ethiopian Regiment" was a terrifying version of the old nightmare of black revolt. In mid-December, the Virginia Convention published its answering proclamation: pardon to runaways who returned to their masters; a warning to the "seduced" that the penalty for slave insurrection was death without benefit of clergy [figure 36]. It should be noted that four months earlier the royal governor of South Carolina had reported to Lord Dartmouth the execution of Jerry, a black pilot and fisherman of Charlestown: "under colour of Law, they hanged & burned, an unfortunate wretch, a Free Negroe of considerable property, one of the most valuable & useful men in his way, in the Province, on suspicion of instigating an Insurrection. . . ." The convention also decreed that slaves taken in arms would be sold in the West Indies—this from patriots who indicted his majesty for supporting the slave trade. But the fugitives, perhaps a thousand strong, all too willing to strike a blow for their own freedom, were not to be bribed or frightened.

Yet the Tory operation "Liberty to Slaves" was only a partial success. It was not that the blacks could not understand the hollowness of Dunmore's libertarian pretenses—he offered freedom only to the slaves of rebels and helped Tory masters to retrieve their runaways—or that he had blocked the colony's effort to halt the slave trade. On the ninth of December at the Battle of Great Bridge—the Lexington of the South—the British force of six hundred, nearly half black, was thrown back by Woodford's Second Virginia Regiment. Dunmore then retreated to his ships with his troops and there continued to train his black soldiers in the use of small arms. Then, smallpox began to decimate the Ethiopian Regiment. By spring's end only "150 effective Negro men" were left. Had not the fever killed off "an incredible number of our people, especially blacks," reported Dunmore in June, the Ethiopian Regiment might have grown to two thousand. In August the harrassed British fleet was forced to abandon the Virginia coast. Seven ships sailing northward had aboard some three hundred black soldiers who would fight on other fields.

But Dunmore's defeat did not alter basic British policy. Two years later, in June 1778, Pennsylvania Tory Joseph Galloway, formulating grand strategy for the Earl of Dartmouth, in a report on the "Strength of America in Respect to Her Number of fighting Men," reiterated the Virginia governor's early appraisal:

The Negroes are truly intestine Enemies, and must in proportion to their Numbers subtract from the Strength of the Colony where they are, because they are Slaves, and desirous of recovering their freedom, and are ever ready to embrace an opportunity of doing it, and therefore it is

35. Proclamation of John Murray, Earl of Dunmore, November 7, 1775. Tracy W. McGregor Library, University of Virginia.

1775

By His Excellency the Right Honorable JOHN Earl of DUNMORE, His MAJESTY's Lieutenant and Governor General of the Colony and Dominion of VIRGINIA, and Vice Admiral of the sa , &c.

A PROCLAMATION.

AS I have ever entertained Hopes, that an Accommodation might have taken Place between GREAT-BRITAIN and this Colony, without being compelled by my Duty to this most disagreeable but now absolutely necessary Step, rendered so by a Body of armed Men unlawfully assembled, firing on His MAJESTY's Tenders, and the formation of an Army, and that Army now on their March to attack His Majesty's Troops and destroy the well disposed Subjects of this Colony. To defeat such treasonable Purposes, and that all such Traitors, and their Abettors, may be brought to Justice, and that the Peace, and good Order of this Colony may be again restored, which the ordinary Course of the Civil Law is unable to effect; I have thought fit to issue this my Proclamation, hereby declaring, that until the aforesaid good Purposes can be obtained, I do in Virtue of the Power and Authority to ME given, by His Majesty, determine to execute Martial Law, and cause the same to be executed throughout this Colony: and to the end that Peace and good Order may the sooner be restored, I do require every Person capable of bearing Arms, to resort to His MAJESTY's STANDARD, or be looked upon as Traitors to His MAJESTY's Crown and Government, and thereby become liable to the Penalty the Law inflicts upon such Offences; such as forfeiture of Life, confiscation of Lands, &c. &c. And I do hereby further declare all indented Servants, Negroes, or others, (appertaining to Rebels,) free that are able and willing to bear Arms, they joining His MAJESTY's Troops as soon as may be, for the more speedily reducing this Colony to a proper Sense of their Duty, to His MAJESTY's Crown and Dignity. I do further order, and require, all His MAJESTY's Leige Subjects, to retain their Quitrents, or any other Taxes due or that may become due, in their own Custody, till such Time as Peace may be again restored to this at present most unhappy Country, or demanded of them for their former salutary Purposes, by Officers properly authorised to receive the same.

GIVEN under my Hand on board the Ship WILLIAM, off Norfolk, the 7th Day of NOVEMBER, in the SIXTEENTH Year of His MAJESTY's Reign.

DUNMORE.

(GOD save the KING.)

62

VIRGINIA, *Dec.* 14, 1775.

By the REPRESENTATIVES *of the* PEOPLE *of the Colony and Dominion of* VIRGINIA, *assembled in* GENERAL CONVENTION.

A DECLARATION.

WHEREAS lord Dunmore, by his proclamation, dated on board the ship William, off Norfolk, the 7th day of November 1775, hath offered freedom to such able-bodied slaves as are willing to join him, and take up arms, against the good people of this colony, giving thereby encouragement to a general insurrection, which may induce a necessity of inflicting the severest punishments upon those unhappy people, already deluded by his base and insidious arts; and whereas, by an act of the General Assembly now in force in this colony, it is enacted, that all negro or other slaves, conspiring to rebel or make insurrection, shall suffer death, and be excluded all benefit of clergy: We think it proper to declare, that all slaves who have been, or shall be seduced, by his lordship's proclamation, or other arts, to desert their masters' service, and take up arms against the inhabitants of this colony, shall be liable to such punishment as shall hereafter be directed by the General Convention. And to the end that all such, who have taken this unlawful and wicked step, may return in safety to their duty, and escape the punishment due to their crimes, we hereby promise pardon to them, they surrendering themselves to col. William Woodford, or any other commander of our troops, and not appearing in arms after the publication hereof. And we do further earnestly recommend it to all humane and benevolent persons in this colony to explain and make known this our offer of mercy to those unfortunate people.

EDMUND PENDLETON, president.

36. A declaration of policy by the Virginia General Convention in response to Dunmore's Proclamation, December 14, 1775. John Carter Brown Library.

but just, in determining on the strength of America, to deduct their Number of fighting Men, which is 150,000. . . . And let it be further added, that in the Class of fighting Men among the Negroes, there are no men of property, none whose Attachments would render them averse to the bearing of Arms against the Rebellion—and that more fighting Men might be raised among them, upon proper Encouragement, than among the whites, though they amount to three times their Number.

The judgment of Dunmore and Galloway was reaffirmed a year later when Sir Henry Clinton, commander-in-chief of the king's forces, proclaimed from his Westchester headquarters that he would guarantee to any slave coming over to the British his full freedom and choice of military assignment. "Their property [slaves] we need not seek," echoed John Andre, the ill-fated English spy, "it flies to us and famine follows." One of these items of property, "Duncan a Negro belonging to Mr. Dill a Carpenter in Charlestown," Andre told Sir Henry, "run away from thence last night by going up Cooper River . . . whence he got a Canoe" and brought crucial intelligence of the situation inside the besieged city

Anguished Patriots agreed. Observed a pseudonymous Antibiastes in a broadside of 1777 urging the Americans to liberate their black servicemen: "Our non-emancipated soldiers are almost irresistibly tempted to desert to our foes, who never fail to employ them against us" [figure 37].

63

1777

OBSERVATIONS on the SLAVES and the INDENTED SERVANTS, inlisted in the Army, and in the Navy of the United States.

THE Resolve of Congress, for prohibiting the importation of Slaves, demonstrates the consistent zeal of our rulers in the cause of mankind. They have endeavoured, as early and as extensively as it then was in their power, to reform our morals, by checking the progress of the general depravation, which, sooner or later, proves the ruin of the countries, where domestic slavery is introduced.

From the liberal spirit of that resolve, which, soon after, was most cheerfully supported by their constituents, it is natural to infer that, had not the necessity of repelling the hostilities of powerful invaders so deeply engaged the attention of the several legislative bodies of our Union, laws would, long since, have been made, with every precaution, which our safety might have dictated, for facilitating emancipations. Many Slaves, however, too many perhaps, are incautiously allowed to fight under our banners. They share in the dangers and glory of the efforts made by us, the freeborn members of the United States, to enjoy, undisturbed, the common rights of human nature; and THEY remain SLAVES!

The exquisite sensibility, the enlightened equity of a free people, cannot suffer them to be ungrateful.---To stand indebted for the recovery of the least portion of our rights, to a race of men, whose unhappy lot must be to continue in a state of the most dishonourable degradation, would be too painful, too humiliating.---Have we not ourselves taught those men, on the most rational principles, and with all the energy which our feelings could give us, to execrate that state as unnatural, and contrary to the laws of GOD? Would public faith had been pledged to the Slaves, before they were permitted to fight in our cause, that their own liberty was one of the recompences, which they were to receive, for their courage and fidelity! It would have been a restitution, not a recompence, though policy, to conceal our blushes, should have suggested a name for it, which could not wound our pride.

Other States have likewise, on extraordinary emergencies, hazarded to employ Slaves in their wars; but immediate, or conditional emancipation was, at the same time, held up, and most religiously bestowed on them, as the sacred retribution of gratitude. GOD forbid, we should act with less generosity and justice on similar occasions!

France, in the islands of Guadaloupe and Martinico, as well as Spain, in the island of Cuba, have, during the course of the last war, exhibited to us such laudable examples. The Slaves, whom they trusted with arms, in the defence of their territories, were not only allowed to dispose of their whole pay as they thought fit, but indiscriminately partook of every other advantage given to the freeborn soldiers of their respective States. Britain knows, and we may remember, that these freedmen, animated by such encouragements, fought with the greatest intrepidity. They were remarkably faithful, and none of them deserted.---Were they not certain, that, had they been guilty of that crime, or had they been made prisoners of war, the enemy would have sold them, in the same manner that they sold the Slaves who fell into their hands? But the owners were indemnified by the State to which they belonged, for the loss they sustained, on account of their Slaves, who were emancipated for having assisted in its defence.

Neither the Slaves who bear arms for us, nor their owners, have, as yet, obtained such advantages from any of the United States. Our non-emancipated soldiers are almost irresistibly tempted to desert to our foes, who never fail to employ them against us. There, at least, besides the uncontroled disposal of their whole pay, they have a chance for being gifted by the enemy, whom sound policy may inspire to be generous in this case, with that freedom, which our laws do not authorize them to claim as their reward from us, for whose liberty they daily expose their lives. It is true, that they are proportionally but few in the service; and yet, could we rest assured, that no great misfortune ever will arise from the want of benevolent resolves in their behalves, our domestic peace, and the jealousy of that honour which impels men to warlike atchievements, would demand the most serious attention of the Congress, respecting the political existence of inlisted Slaves, or the propriety of excluding them from being at any time employed, as soldiers or seamen, in our wars.

There is in the army and navy of the United States another class of oppressed men, whose singular usefulness, were they interested to remain with us, and whose power to do us numberless injuries, if provoked to fly to the enemy for an asylum, are of the greatest importance at this juncture. Their education, national prejudices and attachments, the moral principles of a considerable part of them, and the opprobrious state to which they are all very unjustly degraded, cannot have been considered in their different points of view, before they were invited to inlist; otherwise, the possibility of many evils which the resolve, relative to them, portends, in its original tenor, would have been discovered, and consequently prevented.

The oppressed persons here meant, are, few of them excepted, Europeans, and born in the dominions of Great-Britain. They are those unhappy beings, whom the covetousness and treachery of the British merchants, as well as the collusion of the British administration, have doomed, whether convicts or not, to temporary slavery amongst us, before we became free. Even now, these temporary Slaves are, to our dishonour! as remorselesly sold as the Africans, or their offspring; nay, the flagitiousness of the deed is aggravated by the mockery and hypocritical stile of the owners who advertise them for sale; who, ashamed of their own iniquitousness, vainly recur to subterfuges, that it may be extenuated in the minds of others--- It is THE TIME, not THE BODY, or the person, of the indented servant, of either sex, which is TO BE SOLD! The body or person of such servant is, however, subjected, not by law, but connivence, to the wanton barbarity or lewd attempts of the purchaser. It is, in fact, as absolutely subjected as the body or person of a Negro, man or woman, who is sold as a legal Slave.---Can it be much longer suffered, in this land of freedom, thus to sport with human nature?

Now that we are an independent people, the dissoluteness and oppression, which are inseparable from that impious trade, will have but a very short duration. They must cease of themselves at the expiration of the limited terms of servitude, the longest of which can scarcely exceed four years, from this time; and but few of our brethren will so long groan under the scandalous yoke. It is therefore unreasonable to believe, and it would be excessively cruel to insinuate, that any other consideration prevailed on our Delegates, to deprive themselves and their constituents of the god-like pleasure of giving unconditional deliverance from slavery to all the men, women and children of European descent, who had been betrayed into it, and sold to us, by their European brethren. But pardonable as the omission may be, neither humanity nor self-love will let us reflect upon it without regret.

Oh! may we soon blot out the reproach which that neglect has justly rendered us liable to, since we abolished the novercal government of Britain! May we soon impart, at least to those victims, devoted by her degenerate and unnatural sons to temporary slavery, the same blessings, to the enjoyment of which we are now restored! Let us endear ourselves to them by acts of justice :---let our selfishness and severity no longer strengthen the prejudices of their education, nor induce them to behold us as their oppressors and enemies.

They have already been courted to inlist in our service; but, unhappily for us, as well as for them, the indemnification allowed to the masters, was not a gift to the redeemed servants---It was no more than a loan to them.---They must discharge it out of their bounty money; and, if that be insufficient, out of their pay! An amazing number of these men eagerly seized the unexpected opportunity offered them, to rescue themselves from unlawful bondage; but the conditions on which they were to obtain their freedom, impressing no idea of gratitude on their minds, they determined to desert to the enemy, as soon as they could. In the mean while, most of them quickly disappeared from the corps in which they inlisted. They afterwards re-inlisted, and deserted, as often as they found officers who, over-anxious to fill up their companies with greater expedition, or led by sordid motives, were less inquisitive than they ought to have been.

The treasury of the United States has been, by these means, spoliated of an immense sum: The extravagant stipulations received, and so easily acquired by such unprincipled recruits, who have been mustered as Substitutes, for exempting Militia men from being draughted, have been squandered, together with the bounty money, in the most flagrant riots; and the lowest kind of profusion has been exhibited all over our territories. That profusion is, perhaps, one of the principal causes, which have concurred in raising the spirit of extortion with such stupendous rapidity, and to that progressive height, in every part of the United States, that it must now be speedily forced down, to a degree which may admit some toleration.----And indeed, should our absurd complaisance to extortioners, that is to traitors, continue but a few weeks longer, we might experience far greater woes than those we could reasonably fear from the combined malice and power of Great-Britain, unassisted by our own rapaciousness or conspiracy.

The service of the Militia men who have already procured, or may hereafter procure, substitutes of the cast we have described, will be lost to the United States, during the war, or three years; for, the wording of the recommendatory resolve of the Congress declaring that two Militia men shall be exempted from being draughted, if they procure one mustered substitute, the abuses which result from the resolve, are striking.----Every State which has made laws corresponding with the recommendation, will have reason to repent their compliance, two men being reputed in actual service, even after the desertion of their substitute. They are legally represented, and consequently exempted from being draughted, during the whole term

37. "Observations on the Slaves, and the Indented Servants inlisted in the Army, and in the Navy of the United States," signed Antibiastes, August 14, 1777. Library of Congress.

S

term stipulated in the inlistment of such deserted recruit.---Who can ascertain how many co-partnerships, consisting of the wealthy part of the indolent, or disaffected, may be legally entitled by a few mock-substitutes, to the exemption which the Congress meant to grant, for accelerating the completion of all the regiments on the new establishment, with effective soldiers?

But, the great reliance put on impunity, does infinitely greater injuries to our cause, than the pecuniary losses, fraudulent exemptions from personal service, or even the multiplied desertions, to all which we shall lie exposed, before several preventive resolves are issued, or during the operation of those which have been mentioned. The seducing prospect of the insuperable difficulties which obstruct legal conviction, presents itself to every dissolute man, employed on the recruiting service. The principles of a considerable part of the officers to whom that trust was committed, have been corrupted; and it is generally believed, that there are but few of them who have not, in some degree, caught the fatal infection;---few of them, who have declined entering into lucrative bargains with Militia men who wanted substitutes;---few of them have conscientiously availed themselves of all the means, which honour and duty bound them to use, for hindering deserters from carrying on their inlisting trade with impunity;---few of them have scrupled to pollute their hands with the supplies, which innumerable circumstances amply afforded them, for repairing, without the least danger of detection, the losses incidental to gaming, or for gratifying the most licentious appetites. Many, but too many of them, alas! have countenanced fraud, desertion and perjury.

Had the inlisted Slaves been paid for, at the joint expense of the United States;---had it been declared to them, that they were to be free at the end of the war, or a certain period of faithful service in our army or navy;---had the white servants been freed at the same joint expense;---had all these redeemed soldiers and seamen, white or black, been granted their full pay, the same bounty money and proportion of land, which other men, inlisted in the land or sea service, are allowed---great advantages would have been derived from such munificence. But those advantages would have been entirely negative; and, for this reason, the emissaries of our foes would have questioned their reality, before the melancholy experience of the effects, which opposite measures have produced, convinced the most superficial observer, that our conduct ought to be altered.

It may not be too late for administering the best remedy. Wisdom and patriotism will point it out to our Delegates, as well as the best mode of application. But let the limits, within which they will think fit to circumscribe their beneficence, be what they may, it seems that a general emancipation of the Slaves, inlisted in the army, or in the navy, ought immediately to take place; that the white or black freedmen ought to be fully re-imbursed of the sums deducted from their bounty or pay, to discharge what the masters of the indented servants shall have received for redemption money, or to pay the owners of the inlisted Slaves, for hire, or otherwise.

To give these resolves the fullest efficacy, they should be accompanied with a FREE pardon to all the non-commissioned officers, soldiers and seamen, then in actual service, who, before a certain day, were guilty of desertion, as well as to other deserters, who, not being in the service, will surrender themselves within a limited time. An act of indemnity for military crimes, which have been committed before a certain day, by any military man, who was under the rank of a field-officer, in the land or sea service, should be proclaimed at the same time; but fraud, embezzlement, cowardice, treason, and crimes which are capital at common law, should be excepted, together with such other crimes, and such persons, as the Congress might think proper to except from the benefit of this pardon. Without that prudent act of clemency, which, perhaps, better

than any other devise, will restore discipline in the army and navy, we shall have too many offenders to punish, or we must connive at the continuation of impunity, that is, in other words, at our own destruction.

If such like resolves be not soon adopted, and put into execution, we needlessly run great dangers, unless our redeemed soldiers and seamen, of whatever class or colour, be immediately discharged, and the Slaves for ever excluded from sharing in the honour of defending the Independence of the United States.

The fatal consequences attending the want of decisive resolutions on this momentous alternative, may be easily predicted by any person who reflects, that our implacable enemies are now opening the scene of their grand attack against us; an attack than which they have not yet made one more desperate against any nation. It may be objected that, should the Congress prefer the more generous part of the proposed resolution, the expense would be too considerable. It will certainly be great; but can it be imagined that impolitic œconomy ever can, with her contracted plans, supersede the claims of justice, or silence the loud warnings of alarmed safety, when confident republicans are to pronounce?

We, the members of the United States, have been---we still are, the accomplices of the Britons. We have received great emoluments from their profligacy, their insidiousness and savage cruelty, since they first undertook the slave trade. Blinded by the most superstitious reverence and partial affection, before their relentless oppression reduced us to choose between rapine or death, we were but too unwilling to suspect that their principles and actions wanted rectitude. The illusion gradually diminished; but, though much weakened, it did not cease to operate in their favour, until, deliberately declaring in their manifesto, that they had withdrawn their national assistance and protection from us, they, THEMSELVES, dissolved the inchantment, our oaths, and all reciprocal obligations!

Having often manifested our willingness to expiate the crimes, which our political connexion with Britain involved us into, we ought to reprobate every suggestion which tends to palliate their enormity. We ought publicly to confess them, with the heaven-taught humility and contrition of reformed penitents. Such instances of magnanimity will prove that we are rising superior to our former state. Let us therefore acknowledge that, had not our own cupidity and indolence prepared us for the seduction of the wily Britons, no--- not all their sophistry could have deluded us.---We never would have been tempted by them to purchase the Slaves they brought to us from the African shore! Reason, nature and religion would have made us recoil at the horrid act; and we must have execrated the seducers. But, we bought the devoted Africans! We bought them---to fix slavery upon them and their posterity!

Insatiate with such distant prey, the British monsters prowled in their own country, and brought to us for sale, such of their unhappy brethren whom they could seize upon. These too were our brethren---but, "deaf to the voice of consanguinity,"* we bought them; and numbers of them are still our Slaves!

Our complicity in those crimes was the joint guilt of the people who now compose the United States; let then the atonement be their joint act of piety. Let them produce fruits, that are worthy of their Independence, and convince Britain, that we really are that "VIRTUOUS PEOPLE" we have often declared ourselves to be. Before this can be clearly established by facts, her Parliament, never considering us as a formidable power, will remain persuaded, that our subjection to them is unavoidable, though it may be, for a long time, obstinately opposed by the generous, but insufficient efforts of a few enthusiastic patriots.

Philadelphia, August 14, 1777.

ANTIBIASTES.

* Declaration of Independence.

In his journal for September 20, 1777, Henry Melchior Muhlenberg, a Lutheran pastor, set down a conversation with two blacks, servants of an English family leaving Philadelphia: "They secretly wished that the British army might win, for then all Negro slaves will gain their freedom. It is said that this sentiment is almost universal among the Negroes in America." Certainly this sentiment was pervasive among blacks south of the Potomac. Writing to the president of Congress in February 1777, General Robert Howe recommended that seven to eight thousand regulars be retained in South Carolina at all times to control the "numerous black domestics who would undoubtedly flock in multitudes to the Banners of the enemy whenever an opportunity arrived." In 1778 the Georgia Assembly, afraid that "grave danger might arise from insurrections," ordered one-third of each county's troops to serve as a permanent local patrol.

In spite of the desperate ingenuity of the colonial governments—even New York had its "Commission for Detecting and Defeating Conspiracies"—the runaways bolted. Sometimes they were caught, as a South Carolina trial record makes clear. In early spring of 1776, two brothers asleep in the forecastle of their schooner tied to a wharf on the Potomac were surprised about midnight by four slaves owned by four nearby plantations. The slaves demanded that the boat be sailed to the Coan River and that "they should have the Guns to go on shore with . . . promising no hurt should be done. . . ." But "the negroes, not being able to Manage the Vessell," their white prisoners "stered to Maryland," where three of the slaves were captured. Charles and Kitt were sentenced to hang and Harry to receive thirty lashes on his bare back. Five springs later, in 1781, John Tayloe's slave Billy, accused of waging war against Virginia "in an armed vessel" of the British was found guilty of high treason. He was sentenced "to be hanged by the neck until dead and his head to be severed from his body and stuck up at some public cross road on a pole." Two of the six judges dissented: "A slave in our opinion Cannot Commit treason against the State not being Admitted to the Priviledges of a Citizen owes the State No Allegiance. . . ." Governor Thomas Jefferson apparently concurred, reprieving Billy until the legislature decreed that a slave could not be found guilty of treason.

More often, probably, the fugitives got through. In December 1777 a Baltimore newspaper described a spectacular escape from a Potomac plantation. Twenty-one blacks—fifteen men, two women, and four children—had broken into a barn in which the master had locked up his boat and had sailed away in it to the British. Three news items in Patriot papers of 1780 related the exploits of a black guerrilla leader, a veteran of Virginia's Ethiopian Regiment, operating in Monmouth County, New Jersey. During the first week of June, "Ty, with his party of about 20 blacks and whites, last Friday afternoon took and carried prisoners Capt. Barns Smock and Gilbert Vanmater," spiked the four pounder, and ran off with the artillery horses [figure 38]. A fortnight later, "Ty with 30 blacks, 36 Queen's Rangers, and 30 refugee tories, landed at Conascung . . . got

38. Extract of a letter from Monmouth County, June 12, 1780. *Pennsylvania Gazette and Weekly Advertiser,* June 21, 1780.

in between our scouts undiscovered" and "carried off" several whites and blacks as well as " a great deal of stock." There were casualties on both sides. In September, "72 men, composed of New-Levies, Refugees and Negroes . . . about an hour before day, attacked the house of Captain Joshua Huddy." The *"brave Negro Tye* [one of Lord Dunmore's crew]" was one of the wounded.

Thus, tens of thousands of slaves chose *their* way of striking for freedom. Most of them served the British—always short of men—as an indispensable labor force, in some cases armed with shovels and muskets. Many served as orderlies, mechanics, and artisans—and as cooks, carpenters, sawyers, teamsters, waggoners, turnwheelers, and blacksmiths. Some served as spies, guides, man-of-war men, and pilots. So rare are their names in the annals of the time, that two, at random, must suffice to hint at the host. In July 1776 Christopher Gadsden in reporting a victory in southern waters over an enemy squadron, appended a postscript: "As soon as the action began, the *Commodore* [a British ship] ordered to be put into a place of safety, negro Sampson, a black pilot." Six months later, north of New York, a Patriot colonel complained to his general that "a scouting party . . . brought in a stout negro fellow, the property of a Tory [*one Peck*], who is now with the enemy; and the negro has been employed as a spy to bring them accounts of our motion." Sampson and Peck were not at all unique.

Many, drilled in the manual of arms, saw action in the field. In April 1782, General Nathanael Greene informed Washington that the British had armed and put in uniform at least seven hundred blacks. The Ethiopian Regiment was not the only black unit. That same spring two members of a black cavalry troop, about a hundred strong, were killed in a skirmish at Dorchester, Virginia. Evacuating Boston, the royal army sailed to Halifax with a "Company of Negroes." Philadelphia had a "Company of Black Poneers." A Brunswick contingent under Baron von Riedesel, supporting Burogyne, took back to Germany its corps of black drummers. And just as blacks had fought with the British in the first skirmishes of the war, so they also fought in the last—and for the same reasons. In 1781 the General Assembly of British East Florida had offered to liberate any slave who showed courage in battle and to outfit him with a red coat and silver badge. Nine days after the signing of the Treaty of Peace in April 1783, a Tory colonel, Andrew Deveaux of South Carolina, with a task force of two hundred and twenty men, sailed out of St. Augustine in five privateers to recapture the Bahamas from Spain. The troops that debarked near Nassau and demanded the surrender of the Spanish fortress were both black and white.

When the British armies departed from the United States at the war's end, there went with them at least fourteen thousand blacks—six thousand from Charleston and four thousand each from Savannah and New York. Some were still the slaves of Tories; most were ex-slaves, whose possible path to freedom, in their eyes, had led to the losing camp of Dunmore, Clinton, and Cornwallis. They voyaged to Halifax, Jamaica, St. Lucia, Nassau, and England, grimly hopeful of the chance to begin a new life.

Some of the king's black troops did not leave in the British ships. William Bacon Stevens, in his *History of Georgia*, recorded in 1859 the known facts about a "corps" of some three hundred "runaway negroes, the leaders of which, having been trained to arms by the British during the siege of Savannah, still called themselves the 'King of England's Soldiers,' and ravaged both sides of the Savannah River, plundering and murdering, to the great alarm of the people; who also feared that the presence of this body of freebooters would lead to a general and bloody insurrection of the slaves in that vicinity." On May 6, 1786, a detachment of Georgia and South Carolina militia, guided by a few Catawba Indians, surprised the black village and assaulted the maroons in their improvised fortress which consisted of a rectangular breastwork of logs and cane about a hundred yards wide and half a mile long. Many of the "King of England's Soldiers" were killed or captured; some escaped into the tangled brakes.

The story of the black men, women, and children who sailed to Halifax with the British deserves to be better known as a part of the black history of the American Revolution. Here is a brief account of a single figure of some stature in that story.

Thomas Peters fought for his freedom in the service of the king, but that is only part of the saga of this black Moses—a cluster of fact and legend which relates him to the times of Martin Delany and Marcus Garvey.

Peters was an Egba of the Yoruba tribe, of royal birth, and "strong, far beyond the ordinary man" claim his descendants now living in Freetown, Sierra Leone. In the 1760s, he was kidnapped by the slave-ship *Henri Quatre* and ended up on an American plantation, perhaps in Louisiana. He was then in his twenties. Legend has it that his "master" kept him shackled. After his first attempt to escape, he wore a broad iron belt from which hung two massive linked chains which connected the ankle bands. He was whipped after each dash for liberty, and the third time he was branded.

On the eve of the Revolution, Peters was the slave of one William Campbell in Wilmington, North Carolina. When Lord Dunmore dangled the bait of freedom, he ran away into the British lines. Three years later, Sally, his wife-to-be, fled her master in Charleston, South Carolina. Peters fought with the British for the entire war and was twice wounded. No doubt his commitment to freedom, his courage, and his ability to lead brought him to the fore. His name appears as "Petters" with the rank of sergeant in "a Return of the Companies of Black Pioneers" for the thirteenth of September, 1783 [figure 39]. He later described himself as "a free Negro and late a Serjt. in the Regiment of Guides and Pioneers serving in North America under the Command of Genl. Sir Henry Clinton."

The war over, Peters and his veteran comrades asked the British to keep their promises. In May of 1784, the king's ships landed them in Nova Scotia. True, they were free, but where were the pledged farms? Peters hoped to work as a millwright. The reality was weasel words instead of farms, unclearable land for a few, slave-life apprenticeships to white Tories. In August, Peters and Murphy Still, another ex-sergeant in the Black Pioneers, petitioned the royal governor for an immediate grant of the promised acreage—to no avail. After six years of struggle, with his people behind him, he determined to go to London. As he later wrote, the trip was one of "much Trouble and Risk"; he was fifty years old, carrying a complaint against a hostile governor, an ex-slave voyaging alone.

In London, after initial hardship, it is possible that he received his first help from a brother African, Ottobah Cugoano, a Fanti who had been sold in the West Indies and brought to London as a servant. Four years earlier Cugoano had authored a celebrated book, his *Thoughts and Sentiments on the Evil and Wicked Traffic of Slavery and Commerce of the Human Species*. It was Cugoano who probably introduced Peters to the great English abolitionists, Granville Sharp, William Wilberforce, and Thomas Clarkson. Peters found his old commander-in-chief, Sir Henry Clinton, sympathetic to his cause. The upshot was that the abolitionists agreed to support the memorial that he had brought with him over the ocean, in which, "on Behalf of himself and others [of] the Black Pioneers and loyal Black Refugees" of Annapolis and New Brunswick, he demanded a "competent Settlement." He was "Attorney" for two groups: those "Black People . . . earnestly desirous of obtaining their due Allotment of Land and remaining in America"; and those who were "ready and willing to go wherever the Wisdom of Government may think proper to provide for them as free Subjects of the British Empire." The British secretary of state endorsed the petition and ordered the governor of Nova Scotia to comply.

Meanwhile another path had opened up for Peters—a path back to Africa. A few years earlier the English abolitionists, appalled by the hard lot of the black poor in England, had helped some four hundred blacks to begin a new life on the coast of Sierra Leone. A company had been formed to promote the idea. Why not offer the plan to the stranded, outraged black Nova Scotians—transportation to Sierra Leone and twenty acres for each settler? Peters said yes, returned to Canada, and rounded up his own group of eighty-four emigrants, including his wife and six children. In

39. Return of the Company of Black Pioneers commanded by Lt. Col. Allen Stewart, September 13, 1783. Photograph courtesy Colonial Williamsburg.

January of 1792, some twelve hundred settlers in fifteen ships sailed from Halifax for Freetown.

The rest belongs to the early history of the modern state of Sierra Leone. Although Thomas Peters died of fever only four months after returning to his native land, his name is imperishably linked to its history: kidnapped slave, branded fugitive, Tory soldier seeking his own freedom, early organizer of his own people for their return to the homeland, and finally, as his biographer has noted, a founding father of Sierra Leone.

PART III 👉

The

Black

Clergy

The genesis of the African-American church, north and south, under the tutelage of a handful of black apostles during the era of the Revolution, was not solely a religious milestone. "I entreat you to consider the obligations we lie under to help forward the cause of freedom," cried Richard Allen, who, in his old age, was to be the country's first black bishop, in his "Address to the People of Colour" in 1794. As Charles H. Wesley has observed, the rise of the black church during the birthing-time of the Nation, was an early assertion of "organized independence and self-expression" in the total life of Revolutionary black America.

FOUNDERS OF THE
AFRICAN BAPTIST CHURCH:
DAVID GEORGE, GEORGE LIELE,
ANDREW BRYAN

The determination of the southern slave to live his own religious life and to exploit the available forms of Christian association in order to construct a black solidarity beyond the slave quarters of a single plantation may be seen in the careers of three pioneer black Baptist preachers: David George, George Liele, and Andrew Bryan. At the close of the Revolution, the first two stayed in the King's camp: George continued his work in Canada and Africa, Liele in the West Indies, while Bryan built a church in Georgia.

David George: The first black Baptist church in America was gathered among the slaves at Silver Bluff in South Carolina between 1773 and 1775 by David George. The lineaments of its first pastor, George, born in Virginia in 1742, must be discerned in his eventful life. A runaway to South Carolina, he eluded the bloodhounds for two years, and then hid out with the Indians, first as a servant to Creek Chief Blue Salt, later to Natchez Chief King Jack, who in the early seventies sold him to a plantation on the Savannah River, twelve miles from Augusta. A Baptist slave, one Cyrus, awakened him to Christ, and he learned to read and write, helped by his master's children, with the Bible as primer and text. Not long after, a few slaves, baptized by a white minister, formed a church. "Then I began to exhort in church, and learned to sing hymns," George later recorded. "I was appointed to the office of an elder. . . . I proceeded in this way till the American War was coming on. . . . I continued preaching at Silver Bluff, till the church, constituted with eight, increased to thirty or more. . . ." When the British occupied Savannah in 1778 and his Patriot owner abandoned the plantation at Silver Bluff, George with his black flock—they had doubtless pondered Dunmore's offer of emancipation—took off for the British lines and freedom.

In Savannah during the next few years, George joined Liele and Bryan in preaching the word, but at the end of the war the three parted and went their separate ways—Liele to establish the Baptist Church in Jamaica, Bryan in Savannah. George never returned to Silver Bluff, where, after the Revolution, his old church revived under the guidance of the slave pastor, Jesse Peter. Instead, George and hundreds of his brothers sailed with the defeated British to Nova Scotia, where, for ten years, barely surviving lynch threat and arson ("they came one night and stood before the pulpit and swore how they would treat me if I preached again", he exhorted Baptist congregations, at first made up of black and white. In Shelburne, he was the first to open the doors of a Baptist church.

After a decade of selfless labor in the Canadian vineyard, George's story merges with that of Thomas Peters, the Tory corporal who, with his Black Pioneers, migrated in 1792 from Halifax to Freetown. David George also voyaged to Africa, where, with Peters, he became a founding father of Sierra Leone and planted the first Baptist church in West Africa.

George Liele: Of his origins, George Liele wrote: "I was born in Virginia, my father's name was Liele, and my mother's name Nancy; I cannot ascertain much of them, as I went to several parts of America when young, and at length resided in New Georgia; but was informed both by white and black people, that my father was the only black person who knew the Lord. . . ." In 1773 Liele moved with his master, a Baptist deacon by the name of Henry Sharp, to Burke County in Georgia, where a white minister brought him into the Baptist fold. He felt a call to preach. "Desiring to prove the sense I had of my obligations to God, I endeavoured to instruct the people of my own color in the word of God: the white brethren seeing my endeavours gave me a call at a quarterly meeting to preach before the congregation." Licensed as a probationer, for two years he carried the word to the slave quarters of plantations on the Savannah River from Silver Bluff, where he exhorted David George's newly gathered church, to the suburbs of Savannah.

Sometime before the Revolution, Deacon Sharp liberated the black preacher. In 1778, after Sharp had lost his life as a Tory officer, Liele joined the stream of black folk on their way to Savannah. There he met trouble when Sharp's heirs tried to re-enslave him, but the British officer he served backed him up. Wasting no time, he began immediately to gather a church and for three years, during the British occupation of Savannah, he inspired a growing congregation of black Baptists, slave and free. David George and Andrew Bryan listened to George Liele and learned.

When the British evacuated Savannah in 1782, Liele sailed with them to Jamaica, paying his passage as an indentured servant. Two years later, settled in Kingston with his family and fully free, he began again to preach, at first in a private home. Then, as he recalled, "I formed the church with four brethren from America." The preaching went well "with the poorer sort, especially the slaves," although whites "at first persecuted us both at meetings and baptisms." He fought back, drew up a "petition of our distresses," and wrung a promise of toleration from the Assembly. The church prospered. "I have baptized four hundred in Jamaica," he wrote in December 1791. "At Kingston I baptize in the sea, at Spanish Town in the river, and at convenient places in the country.

We have nigh *three hundred and fifty members;* a few white people among them. . . ."

There is little protest against slavery in Liele's letters to his white Baptist colleagues. He is candid if joyless about the concessions he had been forced to make for the sake of survival. To guarantee that he was no fomenter of revolt, he submitted to the authorities for their inspection every scrap of prayer used in his service. The "chiefest part of our society are poor, illiterate slaves, some living on sugar estates, some on mountains, pens, and other settlements . . . the free people in our society are but poor. . . . We receive none into the church without a few lines from their owners of their good behaviour towards them and religion. . . ." It is hard to decode the piety; the records are sparse. Is it significant that one of Liele's main interests was the promotion of "a *free school* for the instruction of children, both free and slave . . ."?

Looking back at forty, ten years after he had left Georgia with the British, George Liele, building a church on his own three acres at the east end of Kingston, seems to have been marking time.

I have a wife and four children. My wife was baptised by me in Savannah. . . . My occupation is a farmer. . . . I also keep a team of horses, and waggons for the carrying goods from one place to another, which I attend to myself, with the assistance of my sons. . . . I have a few books, some good old authors and sermons, and one large bible . . . a good many of our members can read, and are all desirous to learn. . . .

He kept in touch with other pioneer black Baptists which the stir of revolution had brought together. In his tally of their successes, is there a note of just pride in a collective enterprise, however limited by the powers that still rule, as they struggle to pierce the white fog of slavery to a clearer day?

The last accounts I had from Savannah were, that the Gospel had taken very great effect both there and in South Carolina. Brother Andrew Bryan, a black minister at Savannah, has two hundred members. . . . Also I received accounts from Nova Scotia of a black Baptist preacher, Brother David George, who was a member of the church at Savannah; he had the permission of the Governor to preach in three provinces. . . . Brother Amos is at Providence [Bahamas], he writes me that . . . he has about three hundred members. Brother Jessy Gaulsing, another black minister, preaches near Augusta, in South Carolina, at a place where I used to preach . . . has sixty members; and a great work is going on there.

Andrew Bryan: Andrew Bryan [figure 40] was born a slave at Goose Creek, South Carolina, about sixteen miles from Charleston, in 1737. In Savannah, during the war, he harkened to the words of George Liele, who baptized him and his wife Hannah in 1782. Nine months after Liele had departed for Jamaica, Bryan took up his work and began to preach to small groups—mostly blacks with a few whites—at Yamacraw, on the outskirts of Savannah. His master encouraged him, thought his influence on the slaves was "salutary," and allowed him to build a shack for wor-

40. Reverend Andrew Bryan, from a stained glass window in the First African Baptist Church, Savannah, Georgia.

41. The First African Baptist Church of Savannah established in 1788 by Andrew Bryan. Photograph ca. 1880.

ship, but hostile whites "artfully dispossessed" him. With the help of his brother Sampson, he tethered his flock in the swamps. On January 20, 1788, a white Baptist minister, Abraham Marshall of Kiokee, and the black minister, Jesse Peter of Silver Bluff certified the congregation as "the Ethiopian church of Jesus Christ" and ordained "beloved Brother Andrew to the work of the ministry . . . to preach the Gospel, and administer the ordinances, as God in his providence may call." Thus was formed the First Bryan Baptist Church, which lives today in Savannah [figure 41].

The organization of this church was an unhappy event for Georgia masters who feared servile insurrection. They quickly forbade their slaves to listen to Bryan's sermons. Even when a slave carried a pass, the whip of the patrol fell on his back; he was jailed and abused; meetings were heckled. In July of 1790, Marshall wrote from Savannah: "The whites grew more and more inveterate; taking numbers of them before magistrates [about fifty, including Sampson]—they were imprisoned and whipped . . . particularly *Andrew, who was cut and bled abundantly* . . . he held up his hand, and told his persecutors that he rejoiced not only to be whipped, but *would freely suffer death for the cause of Jesus Christ.*" After Jonathan Bryan, his owner, protested to the magistrates, Andrew was released and resumed preaching at Brampton, three miles from Savannah, in a barn on the plantation. By the end of 1791 he had brought hundreds into his church, although he had been forced to confront a critical problem: there were, in fact, three hundred and fifty slaves, already "converted," who could not be baptized because their masters did not think Christianity "salutary" for blacks.

Bryan was a stubborn saint. In 1792 he appointed four deacons, while brother Sampson, still a slave, helped as an assistant preacher. His church flourished: fifty of its members could read, three could write. When his master died, he bought himself free for fifty pounds, supported himself by his own labor, and built himself a home. In 1794, with the help of white Baptists, he raised enough money to erect a house of prayer.

A few days before Christmas in 1800, the Reverend Andrew Bryan wrote to a white Baptist colleague.

With much pleasure, I inform you, dear sir, that I enjoy good health, and am strong in body, tho' 63 years old, and am blessed with a pious wife, whose freedom I have obtained, and an only daughter and child, who is married to a free man, tho' she, and consequently, under our laws, her seven children, five sons and two daughters, are slaves. By a kind Providence I am well provided for, as to worldly comforts, (tho' I have had very little given to me as a minister) having a house and a lot in this city, besides the land on which several buildings stand, for which I receive a small rent, and a fifty-six acre tract of land, with all necessary buildings, four miles in the country. . . .

He owned "eight slaves"—members of his family—"for whose education and happiness, I am enabled thro' mercy to provide." His congregation now numbered about seven hundred blacks who

enjoy the rights of conscience to a valuable extent, worshiping in our families and preaching three times every Lord's-day, baptizing frequently from ten to thirty at a time in the Savannah, and administering the sacred supper, not only without molestation, but in the presence, and with the approbation and encouragement of many of the white people.

Soon Andrew Bryan was writing about his "large church," which was "getting too unwieldly for one body." Before long, there would be branches—the Second and Third Baptist churches in Savannah. The latter was guided by Henry Francis of Augusta, who had been purchased and liberated so that, as Bryan put it, he could come to Savannah "to exercise the handsome ministerial gifts he possesses amongst us, and teach our youth to read and write."

When Bryan died in 1812 at a ripe seventy-five, the white Savannah Baptist Association eulogized the "pastor of the First Colored Church in Savannah."

This son of Africa, after suffering inexpressible persecutions in the cause of his divine Master, was at length permitted to discharge the duties of the ministry among his colored friends in peace and quiet, hundreds of whom, through his instrumentality, were brought to a knowledge of the truth as "it is in Jesus."

☛ This brief account of the three founders can give only passing notice to other men of mark who were also present during the birthing time of the African Baptist Church in the new Nation. In Virginia—at Petersburg, Richmond, Charles City, Williamsburg, Gloucester, Isle of Wight—from 1776 to 1800, Baptist churches, some of them black and white, some all white, sprang up under the tutelage of black preachers. Of them, little more is known than their names: the Reverend Mr. Moses, Gowan Pamphlet, William Lemon, Uncle Jack, Thomas Armstead, and Josiah Bishop. Often even the name has been lost. Johann David Schoepf, traveling in Florida in 1784, noted in his journal as he stopped at St. Augustine: "Not far off an association of Negroes have a cabin, in which one of their own countrymen, who has set himself up to be their teacher, holds services. They are of the sect of the Anabaptists." Sometime before the turn of the century, Joseph Willis, a licensed black preacher born in South Carolina in 1762, headed for the western frontier. In November of 1804, at Vermilion, a hamlet about forty miles southwest of Baton Rouge, he preached the first Baptist (and Protestant) sermon west of the Mississippi.

FOUNDERS OF THE
AFRICAN METHODIST CHURCH:
RICHARD ALLEN, ABSALOM JONES,
PETER WILLIAMS

A catalytic moment in the early struggle for black religious independence in the United States occurred on a Sunday morning in Philadelphia during the fall of 1787. The delegates to the Constitutional Convention had already departed for their homes while George Mason was busy putting together the Bill of Rights. Years later, the venerable Richard Allen, Bishop of the African Methodist Episcopal Church, musing over his "trials and sufferings" in behalf of "Adam's lost race," recorded that moment.

A number of us usually attended St. George's Church in Fourth Street; and when the colored people began to get numerous in attending the church, they moved us from the seats we usually sat on, and placed us around the wall, and on Sabbath morning we went to church and the sexton stood at the door, and told us to go in the gallery. He told us to go, and we would see where to sit. We expected to take the seats over the ones we formerly occupied below, not knowing any better. We took those seats. Meeting had begun, and they were nearly done singing, and just as we got to the seats, the elder said, "Let us pray." We had not been long upon our knees before I heard considerable scuffling and low talking. I raised my head up and saw one of the trustees, H—— M——, having hold of the Rev. Absalom Jones, pulling him off of his knees, and saying, "You must get up—you must not kneel here." Mr. Jones replied, "Wait until prayer is over." Mr. H—— M—— said, "No, you must get up now, or I will call for aid and force you away." Mr. Jones said, "Wait until prayer is over, and I will get up and trouble you no more." With that he beckoned to one of the other trustees, Mr. L—— S—— to come to his assistance. He came, and went to William White to pull him up.
"By this time prayer was over," Allen concluded, "and we all went out of the church in a body, and they were no more plagued with us in the church."

Richard Allen: He was born a slave in Philadelphia ten years before the Boston Massacre. His master was the Quaker lawyer, Benjamin Chew, chief justice of Pennsylvania during the Revolution. Chew sold the Allen family—father, mother, and four children—into Delaware, near the town of Dover, to one Stokeley, who, as Allen recalled, was "an unconverted man," but "a good master" and a "father" to his slaves. In 1777 seventeen-year-old Richard was converted to Methodism along with his mother, sister, and elder brother. Shortly after, he joined the Methodist Society in his neighborhood and began to attend class meetings in the forest.

Our neighbors, seeing that our master indulged us with the privilege of attending meeting once in two weeks, said that Stokeley's negroes would soon ruin him; and so my brother and myself held a council together . . . so that it should not be said that religion made us worse servants; we would work night and day to get our crops forward. . . . At length, our master said he was convinced that religion made slaves better and not worse, and often boasted of his slaves for their honesty and industry.

When the Reverend Freeborn Garrettson, the Methodist circuit rider who had liberated his own slaves in 1775, preached from the text, "Thou art weighted in the balance, and art found wanting," Stokeley, conscience-stricken, "proposed to me and my brother buying our times" for sixty pounds hard cash or two thousand dollars in Continental paper. Somehow the Allen brothers raised their ransom.

I had it often impressed upon my mind that I would one day enjoy my freedom; for slavery is a bitter pill, notwithstanding we had a good master. But when we would think that our day's work was never done, we often thought that after our master's death we were liable to be sold to the highest bidder, as he was much in debt; and thus . . . I was often brought to weep between the porch and the altar.

Allen now went to work for himself, sawing cordwood and making bricks. "I was after this employed in driving of wagon in time of the Continental war, in drawing salt from Rehobar, Sussex county, in Delaware. I had my regular stops and preaching places on the road. . . . After peace was proclaimed, I then travelled extensively. . . ." From Delaware he made his way into West Jersey, preaching the Gospel at night and on Sundays, cutting wood for his bread on the weekdays. Like the Quaker abolitionist Jonathan Woolman, Allen wandered about the countryside. In east Jersey he was lamed by rheumatism; in Pennsylvania "I walked until my feet became so sore and blistered the first day, that I scarcely could bear them to the ground." At Radnor, twelve miles from Philadelphia, strangers took him in and bathed his feet. "I preached for them the next evening and "on Sabbath day to a large congregation of different persuasions." Staying on in Radnor for "several weeks," he inspired a small revival. "There were but few colored people in the neighborhood—the most of my congregation was white. Some said, 'this man must be a man of God; I never heard such preaching before'."

At the end of December in 1784, when sixty preachers gathered in Baltimore for the first organizing conference of American Methodism, it is probable that Allen was present, and in 1785 he accompanied the white itinerant as a "helper" on the Baltimore circuit. "My lot was cast in Baltimore," he remembered, "in a small meeting-house called Methodist Alley."

I had some happy meetings in Baltimore. . . . Rev. Bishop Asbury sent for me. . . . He told me he wished me to travel with him. He told me that in the slave countries, Carolina and other places, I must not intermix with the slaves, and I would frequently have to sleep in his carriage, and he would allow me my victuals and clothes. I told him I would not travel with him on these conditions.

Is there a hint of this precious alloy of firm spirit and plain dignity in the chalk and pastel portrait [color plate 4, following page 84] of twenty-five year old Richard Allen limned by an unknown artist at about this time? A later black Methodist bishop cherished this portrait and passed it on to his son, Henry Ossawa Tanner, the fine painter of scriptural themes who was Thomas Eakins' best pupil!

Rejecting Bishop Asbury's flawed offer, Allen continued to ride and preach on his own: "I received nothing from the Methodist connection. My usual method was when I would get bare of clothes, to stop travelling and go to work. . . . My hands administered to my necessities." It is possible to think of him at this time, wrote Charles H. Wesley, as "an unordained Methodist preacher . . . who could travel and preach without ministerial orders or authority from a conference." In the autumn of 1785, he returned to Radnor: "I killed seven beeves, and supplied the neighbors with meat; got myself pretty well clad through my own industry—thank God—and preached occasionally." The following year was a turning point. When, in February 1786, the Methodist elder in charge sent for him, he gave up his wanderings and journeyed to Philadelphia—where he would meet Absalom Jones.

Absalom Jones: He was born a slave in Sussex, Delaware (where Allen hauled salt), on November 6, 1746. As a child he learned to read, and with the pennies he managed to save he bought a speller and a Testament. When he was sixteen, his master took him to Philadelphia and put him to work in a shop where his job was "to store, pack up and carry out goods." A clerk taught him to write, and in 1766 he was permitted to study in night school. Four years later, he married one of his master's slaves and bought her freedom with money they earned working evenings for wages. (Since the child's status followed the mother's it was proper to liberate her first.) Working hard, they acquired a home. In 1784, while Allen was preaching in Pennsylvania and Maryland, Absalom Jones bought his own freedom. The couple continued in the employ of their old master and in time built two houses and rented them. When Richard Allen rode into Philadelphia to begin his historic work, Absalom Jones was already prominent among the black members of St. George's Methodist Episcopal Church.

For the next thirty-odd years, although they would seek the independence of the black church on different paths, Richard Allen and Absalom Jones would be co-workers and leaders in the striving of black people to achieve justice and equality.

☛When Allen arrived in Philadelphia, the Methodist elder in charge assigned him to preach at St. George's Church—at five in the morning. "I strove to preach as well as I could, but it was a great cross to bear. . . ." He had planned "to stop in Philadelphia a week or two," but his "labor was much blessed": "I soon saw a large field open in seeking and in-

83

structing my African brethren, who had been a long forgotten people and few of them attended public worship." He spread the Gospel all over the city, in the commons, and in the suburbs; "it was not uncommon for me to preach from four to five times a day." He "established prayer meetings" and "raised a society in 1786 of forty-two members," who subscribed largely towards finishing St. George's church, in building the gallery and laying new floors. . . ."

Yet Allen felt "cramped." "I saw the necessity of erecting a place of worship for the colored people," he wrote with a restraint that understated the historic nature of the decision. Indeed, no fanfare hailed the great idea. Ironically, when he proposed it to "the most respectable" blacks of the city, only three—all members of St. George's—agreed with him. One of them was Absalom Jones. The main opposition, however, came from the white Methodist clergy. The minister-in-charge in Philadelphia "was much opposed to an African church, and used very degrading and insulting language to us, to try and prevent us from going on." When they persisted in their desire for a separate place of worship, and continued to recruit blacks for Methodism, he grew frantic and soon barred their meetings: "We viewed the forlorn state of our colored brethren . . . destitute of a place of worship. They were considered a nuisance."

It was at this point, even as they remained a harrassed part of the Methodist Church that Allen and Jones made a critical decision: it was also necessary to organize the blacks of Philadelphia outside the church. The decision, of course, was primarily a maneuver in the battle for religious autonomy, but it really went further and broke new ground. The Free African Society in Philadelphia, which came into being during the spring of 1787, was "the first evidence which history affords," wrote Charles H. Wesley, "of an organization for economic and social cooperation among Negroes of the western world." Indeed, the opening sentence of its Articles of Association had the feeling of a great beginning: "We the free Africans and their descendants . . . do unanimously agree, for the benefit of each other. . . ." And the preamble rang out:

Whereas Absalom Jones and Richard Allen, two men of the African race, who, for their religious life and conversation have obtained a good report among men, these persons, from a love to the people of their complexion whom they beheld with sorrow . . . often communed together . . . in order to form some kind of religious society, but there being too few to be found under the like concern, and those who were, differed in their religious sentiments; with these circumstances they labored for some time, till it was proposed, after a serious communication of sentiments, that a society should be formed, without regard to religious tenets, provided, the persons lived an orderly and sober life, in order to support one another in sickness, and for the benefit of their widows and fatherless children.

It was six months later on that fateful Sabbath morning in November that Richard Allen, Absalom Jones, and William White were yanked from their knees by the white trustees of St. George's Church and "all went out of the church in a body, and they were no more plagued with us in the

Plate 1. Lt. Grosvenor and his Negro Servant Peter Salem. John Trumbull, 1786. Yale University Art Gallery.

Plate 2. James Armistead Lafayette. John B. Martin, ca. 1824. The Valentine Museum, Richmond, Virginia.

Plate 3. Agrippa Hull. Unidentified artist, 1848 (after daguerreotype, 1844). Historical Room, Stockbridge [Massachusetts] Library.

Plate 4. Richard Allen. Unidentified artist, 1784. Mrs. Dorothy Porter, Washington, D. C.

Plate 5. Absalom Jones. Raphaelle Peale, 1810. On indefinite loan to the National Portrait Gallery from The Wilmington Society of the Fine Arts, Delaware Art Museum.

Plate 6. Yarrow Mamout. Charles Willson Peale, 1819. The Historical Society of Pennsylvania.

Plate 7. Elizabeth Freeman. Susan Sedgwick, 1811. Massachusetts Historical Society.

Plate 8. Reverend Lemuel Haynes in the pulpit. Unidentified artist, ca. 1800-1820. Museum of Art, Rhode Island School of Design.

church." After that proud exit, recalled Allen, "We were filled with fresh vigor to get a house erected to worship God in." It was not easy. They hired a store room in which to pray by themselves, but "bore much persecution" from white Methodists. "We will disown you all," the elder threatened again and again. "We told him we were dragged off our knees in St. George's church, and treated worse than heathens; and we were determined to seek out for ourselves, the Lord being our helper."

☞ That radical vision—"to seek out for ourselves"— was already the organized aim of the Free African Society, a wider sodality of the black community created by Richard Allen and Absalom Jones. But as time went on, the society, whose members "differed in their religious sentiments," seemed slow to inaugurate a separate black church. Allen grew restive, absented himself from meetings, and in June of 1789 the society voted (Jones abstaining) to "discontinue" him as a member.

But Allen's view was really winning out. By the end of 1790, encouraged by Benjamin Franklin and Benjamin Rush, the society was ready to appoint a committee including Jones and a reinstated Allen to work on the problem. Writing to the abolitionist Granville Sharp in London, Rush told him of a plan to form "The African Church of Philadelphia," whose organizers had drawn up articles "so general as to embrace all and yet so orthodox in cardinal points as to offend none." Rush was right. The burgeoning black church belonged as yet to no sect. In August 1791, addressing "the Friends of Liberty and Religion," the "Representatives of the African Church in Philadelphia," terming themselves "the scattered and unconnected appendages of most of the religious societies of the city," sent out an appeal for funds. Allen was happy. "The first day the Rev. Absalom Jones and myself went out we collected three hundred and sixty dollars." Before long a "day was appointed" to break ground for the new church. "I arose early in the morning and addressed the throne of grace" and "as I was the first proposer of the African church, I put the first spade in the ground to dig a cellar for the same."

It was one thing to build a separate "African preaching-house," another to agree on what its doctrine should be. The question was debated at length in the Free African Society. "We then held an election, to know what religious denomination we should unite with." For Allen the vote was a disappointment—"there were two in favor of the Methodist, the Rev. Absalom Jones and myself, and a large majority in favor of the Church of England." Nor was his chagrin diminished when the "large majority" offered him the pastorate of a Protestant Episcopal church. He could not accept the call:

I was confident there was no religious sect or denomination would suit the capacity of the colored people as well as the Methodist; for the plain and simple gospel suits best for any people. . . . The Methodist were the first people that brought glad tidings to colored people.

When the majority made the same offer to Absalom Jones, he put aside doctrinal preference and accepted the pastorate.

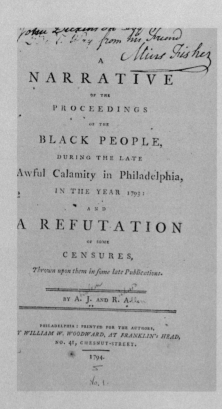

42. *A Narrative of the Proceedings of the Black People, During the late Awful Calamity in Philadelphia . . . 1793 . . . [yellow fever epidemic].* Library of Congress.

It was in this period of troubled groping for the correct religious way that an epidemic of yellow fever swept through the city during the summer of 1793 and ultimately killed five thousand Philadelphians, black and white, about a tenth of the population. Putting aside their doctrinal differences, the two black leaders got together (as they always would) to rally the city's blacks to fight the plague. Fifty physicians of Philadelphia, led by Dr. Rush, labored to stem death and panic. When, in early September, Rush published an appeal to the colored people of the city to assist in treating the sick and in burying the dead, Allen and Jones quickly responded: "We and a few others met and consulted how to act on so truly alarming and melancholy an occasion." After a conference with the mayor, they proceeded to their perilous tasks—Jones in charge of organizing the nursing of the sick, Allen of supervising the burial of the dead.

In their jointly authored classic, *A Narrative of the Proceedings of the Black People, During the Late Awful Calamity in Philadelphia*, 1794, [figure 42] a magnificent rebuttal of slanderous misrepresentations of the black role during the crisis, Allen and Jones with a kind of laconic eloquence described the heroic service of the black community: Soon after, the mortality increasing, the difficulty of getting a corpse taken away, was such, that few were willing to do it, when offered great rewards. The black people were looked to. We then offered our services in the public papers, by advertising that we would remove the dead and procure nurses. Our services were the production of real sensibility;—we sought not fee nor reward. . . . It was very uncommon at this time, to find anyone that would go near, much more, handle a sick or dead person. Of the group of prisoners in the town jail who "voluntarily offered themselves as nurses," two-thirds were "people of colour, who, on the application of the elders of the African church," had been liberated "to attend the sick at Bush-hill."

When the sickness became general, and several of the physicians died, and most of the survivors were exhausted by sickness or fatigue; that good man, Dr. Rush, called us more immediately to attend upon the sick. . . . This has been no small satisfaction to us; for, we think that when a physician was not attainable, we have been the instruments, in the hand of God, for saving the lives of some hundreds of our suffering fellow mortals. . . . We have bled upwards of eight hundred people. . . .

And there are unforgettable vignettes of the selfless "exercise of the finer feelings of humanity":

An elderly black woman nursed . . . with great diligence and attention; when recovered he asked what he must give for her services—she replied "a dinner master on a cold winter's day. . . ."

Caesar Cranchal, a black man, offered his services to attend the sick, and said, I will not take your money. I will not sell my life for money. It is said he died with the flux.

The white delusion that blacks were immune to the contagion—initially advanced but later retracted by Dr. Rush—exasperated Allen and Jones: Few have been the whites that paid attention to us while the black were

86

engaged in the other's service. We can assure the public we have taken four and five black people in a day to be buried. In several instances when they have been seized with the sickness while nursing, they have been turned out of the house . . . they have languished alone, and we know of one who even died in a stable . . . as many coloured people died in proportion as others. In 1792, there were 67 of our colour buried, and in 1793 it amounted to 305; thus the burials among us have increased fourfold, was not this in a great degree the effects of the services of the unjustly vilified black people?

Outraged by such ingratitude—"It is unpleasant for us to make these remarks, but justice to our colour demands it"—the authors of the *Narrative* seized the opportunity to castigate the racist ideology from which it flowed. Their "Address to those who keep Slaves, and approve the Practice," a short but powerful blast, is a green leaf from the early scripture of black liberation.

The judicious part of mankind will think it inreasonable, that a superior good conduct is looked for, from our race, by those who stigmatize us as men, whose baseness is incurable, and may therefore be held in a state of servitude, that a merciful man would not doom a beast to; yet you try what you can to prevent our rising. . . .

Allen and Jones would have none of this slaveholder logic: "We can tell you . . . that a black man, although reduced to the most abject state . . . can think, reflect, and feel injuries. . . ." Try "the experiment of taking a few black children, and cultivate their minds with the same care, and let them have the same prospect in view, as to living in the world, as you would wish for your own children, you would find upon the trial, they were not inferior in mental endowments. . . . We wish you to consider, that God himself was the first pleader of the cause of slaves. . . .   If you love your children, if you love your country, if you love the God of love, clear your hands from slaves, burden not your children or country with them."

The final note is portentous: "Will you, because you have reduced us to the unhappy condition our colour is in, plead our incapacity for freedom . . . as a sufficient cause for keeping us under the grievous yoke! . . . we appear contented . . . but the dreadful insurrections they [slaves] have made, when opportunity was offered, is enough to convince a reasonable man, that great uneasiness and not contentment, is the inhabitant of their hearts."

To far off Boston their fame would spread, and in the *Massachusetts Magazine*, in December 1793, an unknown admirer would publish a three-stanza "Eulogium in Honour of Absalom Jones and Richard Allen, Two of the Elders of the African Church, who Furnished Nurses to the Sick during the Late Pestilential Fever in Philadelphia":

> Brethren of man, and friend to human kind,
> Made of that blood which flow'd in Adam's vein!
> A muse who ever spurn'd at adulation's strains;
> Who rates not colour, but th' immortal mind,
> With transport guides the death redeeming plume;
> Nor leaves your names a victim to the tomb.

43. Pulpit constructed and used by the Reverend Richard Allen. Mother Bethel African Methodist Episcopal Church, Philadelphia.

☞ The plague at an end, Richard Allen and Absalom Jones turned their attention once more to the question of building the black church.

Rebuffed for the moment, Allen did not waiver in his conviction that the Methodist was the only right way for his people. Working as a master shoemaker with journeymen and apprentices in his employ, he put enough aside to buy a lot for his church. In early May of 1794 a goodly number of the city's blacks met with him "in order to consult together . . . to provide for ourselves a house to meet in for religious worship . . . separate from our white brethren."—"I bought an old frame," Allen recalled, "that had been formerly occupied as a blacksmith shop . . . and hauled it on the lot. . . . I employed carpenters to repair the old frame, and fit it for a place of worship. In July 1794, Bishop Asbury being in town I solicited him to open the church. . . . The house was called Bethel . . ." [figure 43].

☞ The house was called Bethel, but it would require more than a score of years to guarantee its independence, years of vigilance for Allen as he tried to cope with the hostility of Methodist "white preachers and trustees." His gift of wise leadership was soon recognized beyond the limits of his church. In 1795 he opened a day school for sixty pupils, and in 1804 he organized a "Society of Free People of Colour for Promoting the Instruction and School Education of Children of African Descent." While the country mourned the death of Washington, the *Philadelphia Gazette* printed Allen's Bethel sermon, in which he stressed the patriot who at the last had felt uneasy about the sin of slavery.

If he who broke the yoke of British burdens from the neck of the people of this land, and was called his country's deliverer, by what name shall we call him who secretly and almost unknown emancipated his bondmen and bondwomen, and became to them a father, and gave them an inheritance?

The Bethel Church prospered and Allen was ordained deacon and elder by Bishop Asbury. By 1810 there were almost five hundred worshippers in his congregation; five years later, there were more black than white Methodists in Philadelphia. Meanwhile Allen's message had spread.

Peter Williams: In New York City there was a black man named Peter Williams, who had been born in a cow shed—"in as humble a place as my Master," he would say with a smile. His owner was a tobacco merchant; the slave became an expert cigar maker. As a youth, converted to Methodism, he listened to the white preachers at sessions in the rigging loft. Early in 1778 the trustees of the John Street Methodist Episcopal Church purchased him for forty pounds sterling and made him sexton of the church. In the spring, as the British took over the city, he made off to New Brunswick in Jersey, lived with a Patriot family, and met his wife Molly, who later presented him with a son, Peter Junior (who would make his own mark in black religious history). Local record has it that he saved an outspoken clergyman from a British officer. In the fall of 1780, after the British evacuated New York, he and his wife returned to the John Street Church. They adopted an infant daughter. For the next sixteen years, he performed the duties of a sexton to the black and white congregation. Somehow, he pinched and scraped to buy his freedom. He was a favorite of the white Methodists, for he was a hardworking and gentle man. Observe the black sexton standing "at his post" in the door of the John Street Church, as sketched in Joseph B. Smith's watercolor of 1817 [figure 44].

Two years after Richard Allen opened the Bethel in Philadelphia something happened inside Peter Williams. There was no dramatic incident—nobody dragged him from his knees as he knelt in prayer—but one day, with a few of his black friends of the church, among them the future Bishop James Varick, he asked for a conference with Bishop Asbury. The blacks in the church had a "desire for the privilege of holding meetings of their own, where they might have an opportunity to exercise their spiritual gifts among themselves and thereby be more useful to one another." The bishop consented, and for the next three years they held separate meetings. Meanwhile Peter Williams, no longer sexton, was making good in his own tobacco business, acquiring a home, even some property. The legend is that he would not permit the racist name of a popular tobacco to be uttered in his shop. By 1799 the black Methodists of New York were ready to build their own house of worship,

89

44. The First Methodist Episcopal Church in America. Sexton Peter Williams stands in the doorway. Joseph Smith, watercolor, ca. 1817. Museum of the City of New York.

45. Peter Williams. Unidentified artist, ca. 1815. The New-York Historical Society.

and on July 30, 1800, Peter Williams laid the cornerstone of the new church, called Zion. In his portrait [figure 45], painted some time later by "a Frenchman from St. Domingo," he seems to exhibit a certain pride in the part he had played in planting the seed of the African Methodist Episcopal Zion Church of the future.

The Zion Church of Peter Williams was not the only offshoot of Richard Allen's Bethel. African Methodist Episcopal congregations would spring up in Baltimore and Wilmington, Delaware, as well as in Salem, New Jersey, and Attleboro, Pennsylvania, all of them suffering white Methodist harrassment even as they flourished. In April 1816, the leaders of these congregations met with Allen in Philadelphia to launch the first fully independent black church in the United States. Elected as its first bishop, he composed a hymn to celebrate the event:

> The God of Bethel heard her cries,
> He let his power be seen;
> He stopp'd the proud oppressor's power. . . .

In the portrait of middle-aged Richard Allen engraved around this time [figure 46], we can discern the black divine whom a later bishop of the same church, Daniel Payne, would describe as "a far-sighted churchman, modest without timidity, and brave without rashness. A lover of liberty, civil and religious. . . ."

90

Rev. Richard Allen

FOUNDER of the AFRICAN METHODIST EPISCOPAL CHURCH,
in the UNITED STATES of AMERICA, 1779.

Phila: Pub. by J. Dainty 1813.

46. Richard Allen. Stipple engraving, 1813. Library Company of Philadelphia.

91

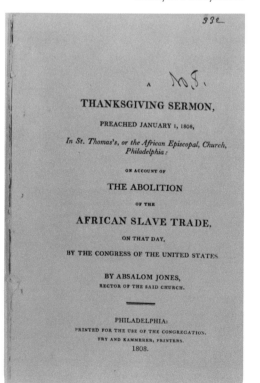

During that summer of 1794 when Allen opened Bethel, Absalom Jones dedicated the St. Thomas African Episcopal Church of Philadelphia [figure 47]. Ten years later the rector of St. Thomas's would be ordained the first black priest of the Episcopal denomination in the United States. Although the church was always his base, Jones's interests and energies during the next quarter century would be broadly enlisted in behalf of the welfare of his people. He would help organize a school for the black children of the city, found a society for the suppression of vice, create and direct an insurance company, and organize protest against the violation of black civil rights.

On December 30, 1799, the black community of Philadelphia, angered by kidnappings of free blacks on the coasts of Maryland and Delaware, made known their grievances to the president and Congress—"guardians of our rights, and patrons of equal and rational liberties" [figure 97]. Signed by Absalom Jones and seventy-five other "people of Colour, free men" of Philadelphia, the petition argued that the "solemn compact" embedded in the preamble to the federal constitution was being "violated" by the slave trade—"poor helpless victims, like droves of cattle, are seized, fettered, and hurried into . . . dark cellars and garrets" and "transported to Georgia." Root out the evil, Jones admonished. "Undo the heavy burdens" of this "grossly abused part of the human species, seven hundred thousand of whom . . . are now in unconditional bondage in these states. . . ." Was the Revolution real?—"if the Bill of Rights or the Declaration" is "of any validity, we beseech, that as we are men, we may be admitted to partake of the liberties and unalienable rights therein held forth." (Such anguish hardly touched the House, which saw in the petition a "tendency to create disquiet & jealousy.") Eight years later, in a sermon preached on January 1, 1808 [figure 48]—when the African slave trade came to its legal end— Jones proposed that the day "be set apart in every year, as a day of publick thanksgiving," so that the children might remember the crime that dragged their "fathers from their native country, and sold them as bondmen in the United States of Amerca." It was two years after this sermon during the winter of 1810 that Charles Willson Peale, the painter of the Patriot fathers, visiting his son's studio, was happy to find that Raphaelle had "painted a Portrait in oil of Absalom Jones a very excellent picture of the Revd. Gentleman" [color plate 5, following page 84].

49. Liverpoolware pitcher with a silhouette of Absalom Jones, ca. 1808. National Portrait Gallery.

Richard Allen and Absalom Jones, as they grew older, seemed to come even closer together, and with the Revolutionary veteran, James Forten, would form a kind of committee of leadership for the blacks of the city. When Jones and Forten decided to organize a Masonic Lodge for Pennsylvania, the local group of "white masons . . . refused to grant us a Dispensation, fearing that black men living in Virginia would get to be Masons, too." It was Prince Hall, founder of black Masonry during the Revolution, who journeyed from Boston in June of 1797 to install Jones as worshipful master and Allen as treasurer of the new lodge. In 1808, marking its tenth birthday, the members of the lodge marched to St. Thomas's, where Richard Allen, occupying the pulpit of his good friend Absalom Jones, preached a sermon to the black Masons. It is probable that the elegant Liverpoolware pitcher graced by Jones's silhouette [figure 49] and the mystic marks of Freemasonry was created to celebrate this anniversary.

Once again when Philadelphia was in the grip of crisis, Allen and Jones —long after they had collaborated to fight the yellow fever in 1793—were importuned to muster the aid of the black community. In 1814, as the British were threatening Philadelphia, the city's Committee of Defence called upon the two ministers to mobilize assistance. From the State House yard, 2,500 black citizens marched to Gray's Ferry and toiled on the defenses for two days. A battalion of black troops—with Revolutionary memories—was ready to march to the front when peace was declared.

The Reverend Absalom Jones passed away in the year 1818. His friend Richard Allen lived on and worked for a dozen busy years as the anti-slavery movement gathered force. In November 1827, in the columns of *Freedom's Journal*, the country's first black newspaper, the "aged and devoted Minister of the Gospel" castigated the colonizationists who would

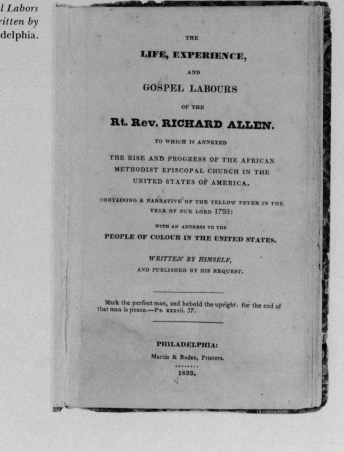

50. *The Life, Experiences and Gospel Labors of the Rt. Rev. Richard Allen, written by Himself.* Library Company of Philadelphia.

THE

LIFE, EXPERIENCE,

AND

GOSPEL LABOURS

OF THE

Rt. Rev. RICHARD ALLEN.

TO WHICH IS ANNEXED

THE RISE AND PROGRESS OF THE AFRICAN
METHODIST EPISCOPAL CHURCH IN THE
UNITED STATES OF AMERICA.

CONTAINING A NARRATIVE OF THE YELLOW FEVER IN THE
YEAR OF OUR LORD 1793:

WITH AN ADDRESS TO THE

PEOPLE OF COLOUR IN THE UNITED STATES.

WRITTEN BY HIMSELF,
AND PUBLISHED BY HIS REQUEST.

Mark the perfect man, and behold the upright: for the end of
that man is peace.—Ps. xxxvii. 37.

PHILADELPHIA:
Martin & Boden, Printers.
....
1833.

ship free blacks to Liberia because their presence in America made "the slaves uneasy." Wrote Allen: "This land which we have watered with our *tears* and *our blood* is now our *mother country.* . . ." Three years later, the pioneer "Convention of the People of Colour of the United States"— the first of many to follow—met in Bethel Church, presided over by Richard Allen, "Senior Bishop of the African Methodist Episcopal Churches." The convention recommended to the Nation that the Fourth of July be observed as a day of fasting and prayer [figure 50].

Side by side with Absalom Jones in the pantheon of early Afro-American history stands Richard Allen. Two years before his death, he was immortalized in David Walker's prophetic *Appeal*: "See him and his ministers in the states of New York, New Jersey, Pennsylvania, Delaware and Maryland, carrying the gladsome tidings of free and full salvation to the coloured people."

THREE BLACK MINISTERS:
JOHN MARRANT, JOHN CHAVIS,
LEMUEL HAYNES

David George, Andrew Bryan, George Liele, Richard Allen, Absalom Jones, Peter Williams—these six were the founders of the African-American church and shapers of the "organized independence and self-expression" of black people in America at the time of the Revolution. But there were hundreds of others, nameless and faceless for the most part, charismatic preachers of the slave quarters, potential Gabriel Prossers and Nat Turners, or loners, like wayfaring John Marrant, missionary to the Indians and chaplain of the African Masons. Some felt the impulse to mold the Christian story into a message for their black brethren, but, by accident of time and place, became stalwarts of the white church, where, by the sheer force of their talent, they achieved eminence, even fame, and paid a price for it, perhaps. Such were the Reverend John Chavis, a Presbyterian in the south, and the Reverend Lemuel Haynes, a Congregationalist in the north.

John Marrant: "I, John Marrant, born June 15, 1755, in New-York, in North-America, wish these gracious dealings of the Lord with me to be published, in hopes they may be useful to others"—so begins the autobiography of this black minister whose short life was so full of remarkable happenings. "My father died when I was little more than four years of age," he continues, "and before I was five my mother removed from New York to St. Augustine. . . . Here I was sent to school, and taught to read and spell. . . ." Eighteen months later the family moved to Georgia. His schooldays over at eleven, it was time now for John to be apprenticed to a trade. His mother packed him off to Charleston. One day, he wrote, "I passed by a school, and heard music and dancing. . . . I went home and informed my sister, that I had rather learn to play upon music than go to a trade." His mother objected, to no avail. After a year of study, the twelve-year-old boy could play the violin and French horn. He was "invited to all the balls and assemblies that were held in the town, and met with the general applause of the inhabitants."

One evening, two years later, the Reverend George Whitefield came to town. Planning some mischief—the scheme was to break up his meeting by a blast on the horn—young Marrant "was struck to the ground . . . speechless and senseless" by Whitefield's eloquence and could not deny the preacher's words: "Jesus Christ has got thee at last." He now began to "read the

95

Scriptures very much." When his family ridiculed his happy faith, he "took up a small pocket Bible and one of Dr. Watt's hymn books" and ran away from home, wandering in field and forest, starving himself into religious ecstasy.

In the woods, he met an Indian who befriended him. Hunting together for ten weeks, the red man taught the black youth some of his language, and after the season was over, the two headed for a village of the Cherokee Nation. Here there were trials in store for Marrant, who at moments seemed to hunger for Christian martyrdom. Jailed, strung up for torture, he turned to God: "I prayed in English a considerable time, and about the middle of my prayer, the Lord impressed a strong desire upon my mind to turn into their language, and pray in their tongue." A miracle occurred— the king of the Cherokees and his daughter were instantly converted. Cut down from the stake and bedecked in fine garments, Marrant lived well for nine weeks in the king's palace, where he "learnt to speak their tongue in the highest stile."

Unattached, unordained, a prophet in the wilderness, he now embarked upon his mission to the Indians, accompanied by a guard of fifty warriors, seeking out the Creeks, the Catawars, and the Howsaws. But the Indians he exhorted failed to respond to his Christian pleas: "When they recollect" that Christians "drove them from the American shores [they] have often united, and murdered all the white people in the back settlements. . . ." After six months of failure, he returned to the Cherokees, and against the will of his friend, the king, made up his mind to go back to Charleston. Back home, at first no one recognized him: "My dress was purely in the Indian stile; the skins of wild beasts composed my garments, my head was set out in the savage manner, with a long pendant down my back, a sash around my middle, without breeches, and a tomahawk by my side."

In Charleston he lived with his family "till the commencement of the American troubles." Then, chance placed him on the British side: "I was pressed on board the Scorpion sloop of war, as their musician. . . . I continued in his majesty's service six years and eleven months. . . . I was at the siege of Charles Town and passed through many dangers." In August of 1781 he was "in the engagement with the Dutch off the Dogger Bank, on board the *Princess Amelia, of 84 guns,*" a bloody affair in which he was wounded and ended up in the hospital at Plymouth. Discharged from the navy, he found his way to London where he worked for a "pious" cotton merchant for the next three years.

During this time in England, he saw his "call to the ministry fuller and clearer" and began to feel a concern for his black "countrymen." One day he received a letter from his brother in Nova Scotia, urging him to come over and preach, and he showed it to the evangelical, anti-slavery Countess of Huntingdon, who had been a friend and sponsor of Phillis Wheatley, the black poet of Boston. He was not idle: in London he continued to exercise his "gifts . . . in prayer and exhortation." When the countess counseled him to carry the word to Canada and invited him to join her independent group of Calvinist Methodists, he gladly consented and was ordained a minister of the sect in the spring of 1785. For the next few months, preaching "many sermons in Bath and Bristol . . . many precious souls experienced great blessings" from his labors. In August, before he sailed, he told the story of his life to the Reverend William Aldridge, who "arranged, corrected, and published" it. "John's narrative," commented *The Monthly Review* of London with a patronizing flourish, "is embellished with a good deal of *adventure,* enlivened by the *marvellous,* and a little touch of the *miraculous.* . . ." *The Narrative of the Life of John Marrant* would be reprinted nineteen times during the next forty years [figure 51].

So, like David George, John Marrant went to Nova Scotia to spread the gospel among his own people. At Birch Town, he assembled a Huntingdonian congregation of forty members and carried the Bible to the wigwams of the Canadian Indians. Marrant's *Journal,* printed in London in 1790, is a chronicle of his selfless toil in Nova Scotia—of endless journeyings to remote places, of passionate sermons to gatherings of black, white, and red. After four years of spiritual wrestling and physical hardship, Marrant apparently felt that he had done his work in Canada, and in the winter of 1789 he embarked for a new field of endeavor in New England.

In Boston, resuming his preaching without delay, he at first had a hard time of it, although the liberal Baptist minister, Dr. Samuel Stillman, came to his aid. "I was preaching at the west end of the town," the *Journal* relates, "to a large concourse of people, there were more than forty that had made an agreement to put an end to my evening preaching . . . they came prepared that evening with swords and clubs. . . ." He was not deterred (a Boston judge admonished the hoodlums), but opened a school and went off preaching to black and white groups as far as Bridgewater and Shoreham. Meanwhile, he had struck up a friendship with Prince Hall, "one of the most respectable characters in Boston," and in the spring the black civic leader invited him to fill the post of chaplain to the African Lodge of the Honorable Society of Free and Accepted Masons of Boston, the first black lodge in America, of which Hall, its founder, was Grand Master.

On June 24, 1789, the Reverend Chaplain John Marrant, in celebration of the festival of St. John the Baptist, delivered a memorable sermon to the black Masons of Boston [figure 52]—a discourse studded with passages of such uncommon beauty and power, one wonders how and when this self-taught wanderer ever mastered the eloquence that suffuses it. A jeremiad aimed against the "monsters" of white racism, it summons its hearers to a new sense of black worth and dignity.

Man is a wonderful creature, and not undeservedly said to be a little world, a world within himself, and containing whatever is found in the Creator.— In him is the spiritual and immaterial nature of God, the reasonableness of Angels, the sensitive power of brutes, the vegetative life of plants, and the virtue of all the elements he holds converse with in both worlds.—Thus man is crowned with glory and honour, he is the most remarkable workmanship of God. And is man such a noble creature and made to converse with his fellow men that are of his own order, to maintain mutual love and society, and to serve God in consort with each other?—then what can

97

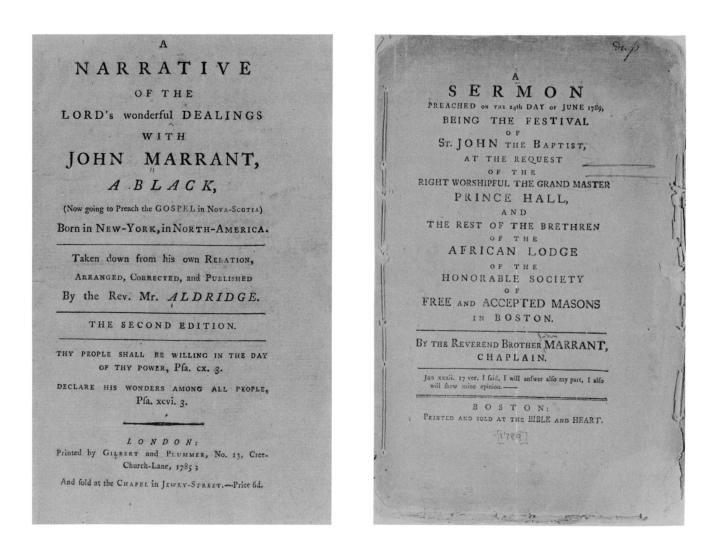

51. *A Narrative of the Lord's Wonderful Dealings with John Marrant.* Second edition, 1785. Library of Congress.

52. *A Sermon Preached on the 24th Day of June 1789....* Reverend John Marrant, 1789. American Antiquarian Society.

these God-provoking wretches think, who despise their fellow men, as tho' they were not of the same species with themselves, and would if in their power deprive them of the blessings and comforts of this life, which God in his bountiful goodness, hath freely given to all his creatures to improve and enjoy? Surely such monsters never came out of the hand of God. . . .

To his black audience, he counsels a just pride in their African forbears—"Tertullian, Cyprian, Origen, Augustine, Chrysotom . . . and many others." There are some, he tells them, who "despise those they would make, if they could, a species below them, and as not made of the same clay with themselves";

but if you study the holy book of God, you will there find that you stand on the level not only with them, but with the greatest kings on the earth, as

Men and as Masons. . . . Ancient history will produce some of the Africans who were truly good, wise, and learned men, and as eloquent as any other nation whatever, though at present many of them are in slavery, which is not a just cause of our being despised; for if we search history, we shall not find a nation on earth but has at some period or other of their existence been in slavery, from the Jews down to the English Nation, under many Emperors, Kings, and Princes. . . .

The Reverend John Marrant's sermon, preached to the black Masons of Boston when he was thirty-four years old, may be the high point of his checkered career. He had not much longer to live, missed his English friends, and yearned to return to London. For the next six months he prayed and exhorted in Massachusetts. On February 5, 1790, a company of black Bostonians, headed by Prince Hall, walked with him "down to the ship, with very heavy hearts." A year later his coffin was lowered into a grave of the Burial Ground on Church Street in Islington, a borough of London.

John Chavis: The case of John Chavis, the black Presbyterian preacher and school master, is one of brilliance and aspiration thwarted and choked, then perhaps betrayed, as white racism fastened itself firmly on the south after the Revolution.

Chavis was born free about 1763 in the West Indies or North Carolina and grew to manhood in Virginia. Almost nothing has been discovered to cast light on his early youth. When he was an old man, slighted by a few of his former pupils, he would declare proudly that he had been a "free born American and a revolutionary soldier." But where and when he fought we do not know, and for ten years after the war the record is silent. Then, in September of 1792, a brief entry on the rolls of the College of New Jersey (later Princeton University) reveals that "John Chavis a free Black man" of Virginia has been recommended for admission as a student by a Reverend John B. Smith. Tradition has it that Chavis's career was "the result of a wager that a Negro could not be educated," and that a few whites who perceived the extraordinary intellectual power of the man—he was now going on thirty—sent him to Princeton, which had permitted a few blacks and Indians to enter its classrooms. Chavis, it seems, became the pupil of old President John Witherspoon, who tutored him privately. For reasons unknown, he never graduated from Princeton, but continued his studies at an academy which after the Civil War was transformed into Washington and Lee University. There he completed a "regular course of Academical Studies."

Apparently he had been preparing himself in the usual subjects, classical and theological, for a career in the church, for at its regular meeting in the fall of 1799, the Presbytery of Lexington, Virginia, was asked to ponder the request of "John Chavis, a black man, personally known . . . of unquestionably good fame, & a communicant" to be ordained to the ministry. The reply was favorable and careful "considering that they, like their heavenly

Father, should be no respecter of persons, being satisfied with his narrative," the Presbytery "agreed, notwithstanding his colour, to take him under their care, for further trials in the usual form." In November 1800, at Timber-Ridge Meetinghouse, Chavis preached a sermon on the assigned text: "Believe on the Lord Jesus Christ & thou shalt be saved." Later the same year, the Presbytery saw fit "to license him to Preach the Gospel . . . hoping as he is a man of colour he may be peculiarly useful to those of his own complexion." Accordingly, in 1801, using cautious phrases that exude a sense of anxiety, the Presbytery directed that:

Mr. John Chavis, a black man of prudence and piety . . . be employed as a missionary among people of his own colour; and that for his better direction in the discharge of duties which are attended with many circumstances of delicacy and difficulty, some prudential instructions be issued to him by the assembly, governing himself by which, the knowledge of religion among that people may be made more and more to strengthen the order of society. . . .

It is quite clear that the Presbyters had no consuming desire to send abroad another Gabriel Prosser, who, during the summer of the previous year, with his brother Martin, a people's preacher, had organized an insurrection at religious gatherings and planned to take over Richmond for the slaves.

For the next thirty years, on and off, John Chavis rode his horse up and down country roads in Virginia, Maryland, and North Carolina as a Presbyterian missionary "under the Direction of the General Assembly," repeatedly instructed "to employ himself chiefly among the blacks and people of colour," and always performing to the satisfaction of his superiors, who praise him for executing his mission with "great diligence, fidelity and prudence." He was also an "acceptable preacher," now and then, to white congregations, one of whose members recollected that his sermons abounded "in strong common sense views and happy illustrations, without any effort at oratory or sensational appeals to the passions of his hearers."

In 1805 or thereabouts, settled in North Carolina as a minister of the Orange Presbytery and continuing his work as a riding missionary, Chavis decided to open a school where he could employ his correct English, good Latin, and fair Greek for the collegiate preparation of the sons of the white gentry. Recalling his own struggle for an education, it is probable that at the start he admitted to his classes the children of free blacks. That he could not for long resist the mounting intolerance of the times is evidenced by a notice he placed in the *Raleigh Register* during the summer of 1808: "John Chavis takes this method of informing the citizens of Raleigh" that he will "open an evening school for the purpose of instructing children of colour; as he intends, for the accomodation of some of his employers, to exclude all children of colour from his day school." And that he was still compelled to employ the strategy of "accomodation," doubtless behind a mask of irony, is evidenced again, twenty years later, in the same newspaper. "On Friday last," wrote Joseph Gales, its Whig editor, in an issue of April 1830, "we attended an examination of the free children of colour, attached to the school conducted by *John Chavis,* also colored, but a regularly educated Presbyterian minister. . . ."

To witness a well regulated school, composed of this class of persons—to see them setting an example both in behavior and scholarship, which their *white* superiors might take pride in imitating, was a cheering spectacle to a philanthropist. The exercises throughout, evinced a degree of attention and assiduous care on the part of the instructor, highly creditable, and of attainment on the part of his scholars almost incredible.

Gales was much pleased with Chavis's "sensible address," which closed the examination.

The object of the respectable teacher, was to impress on the scholars, the fact, that they occupied an inferior and subordinate station in society, and were possessed but of limited privileges; but that even *they* might become useful in their particular sphere by making a proper improvement of the advantages afforded them.

One shudders at the anguish Chavis must have suffered as he paid the price of protecting his black school from destruction. Years later—long after the school had ceased to exist—he would implore his white friend, Senator Willie P. Mangum, to refute the charge that "in going to Raleigh to Teach the children of the free people of colour" he had really intended to preach the abolitionist creed.

The uprising led by the self-taught black preacher, Nat Turner, in Southampton County, Virginia, during the summer of 1831 put an end to John Chavis's career as Presbyterian minister and classical schoolmaster. In North Carolina an "act for the better regulation of the conduct of Negroes" prescribed "thirty-nine lashes on his bare back" for any black under any pretense" who preached to his brothers. When Chavis complained of the "difficulties and embarassments" he suffered by this law, the Presbyters counseled him to comply "until God in his Providence" showed another way, and at the same time discouraged him from publishing—since he could no longer speak—an exegesis on the reconciliation of God and man by the sufferings of Christ.

In the official history of North Carolina, the Reverend John Chavis retains a certain fame as the greatly gifted teacher of the sons of the slavocracy—of future statesmen, among them a governor and a senator. He seemed to cherish a relationship of intimacy with some of the first families of the state. "In my boyhood life at my father's home," recalled a judge's son, "I often saw John Chavis . . . he was received by my father and treated with kindness and consideration, and respected as a man of education, good sense and most estimable character." A Granville County lawyer remembered: "I have heard him read and explain the Scriptures to my father's family repeatedly. His English was remarkably pure . . . his manner was impressive, his explanations clear and concise, and his views . . . entirely orthodox." With Willie Mangum, Chavis maintained a long friendship, as his letters to the senator, full of family news and sharp political counsel, demonstrate. But again, it would seem, at the high price of a grim accommodation. Writing to Mangum in April 1836, he declares his annoyance with the abolition petitions then stirring up the House and the country; but as he goes on, the tense rhetoric discloses the complex artifice of his uncomfortable position:

That Slavery is a national evil no one doubts, but what is to be done? It exists and what can be done with it? All that can be done, is to make the best of a bad bargain. For I am clearly of the opinion that immediate emancipation would be to entail the greatest earthly curse upon my brethren according to the flesh that could be conferred upon them especially in a country like ours.

"I suppose if they knew I said this," he concludes with tragic candor, "they would be ready to take my life, but as I wish them well I feel no disposition to see them any more miserable than they are."

When Chavis was seventy, the Presbytery resolved to support him as a "superannuated licentiate." In 1837, a year before his death, he managed to publish on his own his undelivered sermon on *The Extent of the Atonement.*

53. Lemuel Haynes. Frontispiece illustration from *Sketches of the Life and Character of the Reverend Lemuel Haynes* by Timothy Mather Cooley, 1837. Library of Congress.

Lemuel Haynes: A few years after that eminent divine, the Reverend Lemuel Haynes, A.M., the first black minister of the Congregational Church in America, had gone to his rest—an octogenarian whose years had stretched from the French and Indian War to the presidency of Andrew Jackson—Harper's published a full-scale memoir of his life and thought. His biographer, Timothy Mather Cooley, D.D., a white colleague in the church, began his account with a eulogy that linked his hero to history.

In various periods of time there have been Africans whose intellectual powers and attainments would be an ornament to any age or country. Among warriors few have held a higher rank than Hanno and Hannibal. The poetic works of Terence were admired in the Augustan age, and have survived the devastations of two thousand years. Cyprian, bishop of Carthage, whose memory is dear to all Christendom, and Augustine, bishop of Hippo, the successful defender of the church from Pelagius and his heresies, were sons of Africa.

It was in this distinguished company that the Reverend Lemuel Haynes belonged—a "sanctified genius" whose life story could "hardly fail to mitigate the unreasonable prejudices against the Africans in our land."

Lemuel Haynes [figure 53] was born in 1753 at West Hartford, Connecticut. His father (whom he never knew) was "of unmingled African extraction;" his mother "a white woman of respectable ancestry in New-England." Someone gave him a name. "When I was five months old," Haynes wrote, "I was carried to Granville, Massachusetts, and bound out as a servant to Deacon David Rose till I was Twenty-one. He was a man of singular piety. I was taught the principles of religion. His wife, my mistress, had peculiar attachment to me: she treated me as though I was her own child." (One painful day the lad had met his mother by accident in a nearby town. She had tried to elude him. "Vexed and mortified at such an instance of unnatural contempt," observed Dr. Cooley, "he accosted her in the language of severe but merited rebuke.") The deacon, one of Granville's pioneers, had to carve a farm out of the forest and for him Lemuel wielded the axe and guided the plow. There was a little time left over for education. "As I had the advantage of attending a common school equal with the other children," he remembered, "I was early taught to read, to which I was greatly attached, and could vie with almost any of my age." People said that "Lemuel Haynes got his education in the chimney-corner," where by the light of blazing pine knots, he devoured speller, psalter, and Bible. "At the age of fifty," a friend recalled, "he could repeat nearly the whole of Young's *Night Thoughts*, Milton's *Paradise Lost*, Watts's *Psalms and Hymns*, and large unbroken passages from different authors, and more of the sacred Scriptures than any man I ever knew." When Haynes was an old man, he often used to say, "If I were to live my life over again, I would devote myself to books."

Theology fascinated the Bible-struck youth. One evening, "greatly alarmed by the *Aurora Borealis*," as a "presage of the day of judgment," he experienced conversion. In the deacon's family, on Saturday night—a time of religious instruction—Lemuel usually read aloud a sermon by some worthy of the church. "One evening being called upon to read . . . he slipped into the book his own sermon . . . and read it to the family." The deacon was highly edified: "Lemuel, whose work is that which you have been reading? Is it Davies's sermon, or Watts's, or Whitefield's"? When the youth answered, "It's Lemuel's sermon," that moment was the start of a career. Since the parish at this time lacked a minister, Lemuel was frequently called upon to conduct the service and to read an approved sermon. Sometimes he read one of his own.

In 1774, at the age of twenty-one, his period of service to the deacon completed, Lemuel enlisted as a minuteman and spent a day a week training on the village green. Soon after the skirmish at Lexington, with Captain Lebbeus Ball's militia company he joined the army at the siege of Boston; and in 1776 marched in the expedition to Ticonderoga, where with Ethan Allen and the Green Mountain Boys he helped to take the fort from the British. Forty years later, in a sermon preached on George Washington's birthday, he would remind his listeners of his service in the Revolution: "Perhaps it is not ostentatious in the speaker to observe, that in early life he devoted all for the sake of freedom and independence, and endured frequent campaigns in their defence. . . ."

Back home from the front, white friends in Granville encouraged him to consider a life in the church. "I was solicited by some to obtain a collegiate education with a view to the gospel ministry. A door was opened for it at Dartmouth College, but I shrunk at the thought." At last he was persuaded to study "the learned languages" and in 1779 was invited by a clergyman in Canaan, Connecticut, to live with him and learn Latin. Now, he felt a "quenchless ardor" to master Greek as well, so that he might read

103

the New Testament in the original. A well-wishing pastor got him a position as a teacher in Wintonbury, and after school hours tutored him in Greek. In the fall of 1780 he thought he was ready, and several ministers of "high respectability," after examining him "in the languages and sciences, and with respect to his knowledge of the doctrines of the gospel, and practical and experimental religion, recommended him as qualified to preach the gospel." His first official sermon was on the text: "The Lord reigneth, let the earth rejoice," preached in a new house of worship to a white congregation in Middle Granville, which had unanimously invited him to supply its vacant pulpit. Three years later, he married a young white schoolteacher of the town, Elizabeth Babbit, whom he had helped to convert. "Looking to Heaven for guidance," remarked Dr. Cooley, "she was led with a consistent and justifiable delicacy, to make him the overture of her heart. . . . He consulted a number of ministers and . . . received their unanimous advice and sanction." (There were ten children, three sons: at the time of Elizabeth's death in 1836, two lived in New York, one a farmer, the other a physician; the third was a law student in Massachusetts.) In November 1785, Haynes was officially ordained by an Association of Ministers in Litchfield County, Connecticut, in response to the unanimous request of his Granville congregation, signed by Deacons Aaron Coe and Timothy Robinson, who had been his captain and colonel ten years before in the Revolutionary War.

Haynes' first call to fill a pulpit came from Torrington, Connecticut— the town in which five years later John Brown would first see the light— and after a preaching tour of Vermont during the summer of 1785, he settled down to his work. Although his sermons soon began to pack the meetinghouse, there were intolerant diehards in the congregation who were less than pleased with his dark skin. Dr. Cooley has preserved the memoir of one churchgoer who did not at first approve.

He was disaffected that the church should employ him, and neglected meeting for a time. At length curiosity conquered prejudice. . . . He took his seat in the crowded assembly, and, from designed disrespect, sat *with his hat on.* Mr. Haynes gave out his text, and began with his usual impassioned earnestness, as if unconscious of anything amiss in the congregation. "The preacher had not proceeded far in his sermon . . . before I thought him the *whitest* man I ever saw. My hat was instantly taken off and thrown under the seat, and I found myself listening with the most profound attention."

But others in his flock did not conquer their prejudice, and the "designed disrespect" of a clique forced him to leave Torrington after two years to seek another pulpit.

In March of 1788, he received his second call from a church in the west parish of Rutland, Vermont. Here, for the next thirty years, he would try to save souls, preserve doctrine untainted by liberal theology, and enlighten the backward on political questions. In Vermont, where freethinkers "extensively circulated Allen's 'Oracle of Reason,' and other infidel books," the thirty-five-year-old black minister would achieve a transatlantic reputation as a skillful and ruthless polemicist in theological dispute. Writing from Rutland in 1796, he would observe that he had never known "infidelity more prevalent. . . . Paine has advocates. I have attended to all his writings on theology, and can find little else but invective and the lowest kind of burlesque."

The years of the turn of the century, when the animated portrait in Cooley's memoir was probably painted, seem his most vigorous and productive. "Many, on seeing him in the pulpit," the biographer records, "have been reminded of the inspired expression, 'I am black, but comely' . . . the remarkable assemblage of graces which were thrown around his semi-African complexion, especially his eye, could not fail to prepossess the stranger in his favour." The papier-maché tray that shows Haynes exhorting from the pulpit of his white church might illustrate this passage [color plate 8, following page 84]. During these years, he defended the gospels according to Jonathan Edwards and George Washington in a barrage of eloquent discourse. In 1798 two of his sermons were printed for wider notice, one religious, the other political—although these blend at times—the first a manifesto on *The Important Concerns of Ministers*, the second an anti-Jeffersonian defense of the quasi-war with atheistical France. "I am preparing another political discourse for the press," he informs a friend in September of 1801. The title is imposing: *The Nature and Importance of True Republicanism: with a Few Suggestions Favorable to Independence. Delivered at Rutland, Vermont) the Fourth of July, 1801. It Being the 25th Anniversary of American Independence* [figure 54]. What is remarkable in this oration is not so much its passionate praise of the Revolution and "the rights of men," as its castigation of "monarchal government," where the "people are commonly ignorant . . . and know but little more than to bow to despots, and crouch to them for a piece of bread," for the truth of his argument will be illustrated by the sin of American slavery:

The propriety of this idea will appear strikingly evident by pointing you to the poor Africans, among us. What has reduced them to their present pitiful, abject state? Is it any distinction that the God of nature hath made in their formation? Nay—but being subjected to slavery, by the cruel hands of oppressors, they have been taught to view themselves as a rank of beings far below others, which has suppressed in a degree, every principle of manhood, and so they become despised, ignorant, and licentious. This shows the effects of despotism and should fill us with the utmost detestation against every attack on the rights of men. . . .

A few lines later, he asks a question: "On the whole, does it not appear that a land of liberty is favourable to peace, happiness, virtue, and religion, and should be held sacred by mankind?" The answer is a resounding yes—and that is all. Nowhere else during a half-century's utterance from pulpit or press does Lemuel Haynes make a public statement on the subject of race or slavery.

His fame flourished. He had close friends on the faculty of Middlebury College, whose trustees in 1804 conferred on him the honorary degree of Master of Arts—the first ever bestowed on a black in America. It is in the

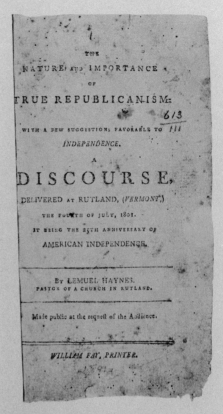

54. *The Nature and Importance of True Republicanism . . . A Discourse.* Lemuel Haynes, 1801. Library of Congress.

following year that his name becomes known beyond rural Vermont. The scene has a certain drama. Hosea Ballou, the distinguished champion of the doctrine of universal salvation, had been invited—unknown to Haynes, who had planned to visit a remote part of his parish on that day—to preach from his pulpit in the west parish of Rutland. When Ballou learned that Haynes would not be present for his sermon, he remarked that "the orthodox gentry generally *scud*" when he appeared to preach. Haynes decided to attend. He "had been repeatedly solicited to hear and dispute" with the Universalist, he tells us, "and had been charged with dishonesty and cowardice for refusing. He felt that some kind of testimony, in opposition to . . . error, ought to be made. . . ." Ballou lectured and Haynes—with little or no preparation—immediately replied. The result was the sermon called *Universal Salvation, a Very Ancient Doctrine* (of the Devil), which, during the next quarter century, as Dr. Cooley relates, was "printed and reprinted, both in America and Great Britain, till no one pretends to give any account of the number of editions." If the gentle Ballou felt that Haynes had identified him with the Serpent, he had every reason to think so, nor in the sharp exchange of letters of the following two years does Haynes abate a jot. His wrath was leveled against a Universalism which he saw as a doctrine that preached heaven for all and hell for none.

> Blest all who hunger and who thirst to find
> A chance to plunder and to cheat mankind;
> Such die in peace—for to them God has given,
> To be unjust on earth, and go to heaven.

So runs a parody of Ballou's creed which Haynes appended to his sermon. Would the sin of slavery be rewarded rather than punished? The sermon is silent on this question.

Meanwhile, life went on in its routine way. Haynes found himself in great demand as a speaker at ordinations, dedications, and funerals. He proved himself from time to time a magnetic revivalist. "His very colour," thought a brother cleric, "which marks the neglect and servitude of his race in this country, associated, as it was . . . with his high qualifications to entertain and instruct, became the means of increasing his celebrity and enlarging the sphere of his influence." In 1809 he was appointed field secretary of the Vermont Missionary Society. And all the while he labored on his farm, his early training standing him in good stead, in order to feed his large family.

The year 1814 was another memorable year for Haynes. As delegate of the General Convention of Ministers in Vermont, he attended the meeting of the General Association of Connecticut which gathered at Fairfield. On the way, there was an opportunity to visit New Haven and stop for a talk with the Reverend Doctor Timothy Dwight, president of Yale. Haynes' fame had in fact preceded him. In the Blue Church of New Haven, he preached to a full house. Professor Silliman was impressed with his "dignity and feeling," and President Dwight was moved to tears. At Fairfield, addressing one hundred ministers, the Reverend Humphrey, then pastor of the church in the town, and later president of Amherst College, recalled that Haynes used "no notes, but spoke with freedom and correctness." The sermon was so "rich in Scriptural thought . . . there was so much of truth and nature in it . . . hundreds were melted into tears." Did the black pastor perhaps feel lonely among his hundred white colleagues? "In meetings of councils and associations," wrote Dr. Cooley, without a smile, "where it was necessary to put two in one bed, one and another would say, *'I will sleep with Mr. Haynes!'*" And what would have been Haynes' reaction, one wonders, to the benevolent appraisal of a Vermont governor's wife, who was a member of his flock.

He ever held the station of man without blemish—never appearing to re-pine that God had not made him without a stain upon his skin: nor was he often called upon to remember it, unless more than ordinary tender-ness, manifested by others in their intercourse with him, should have reminded him of it.

New Haven and Fairfield were triumphs, but all was not going as smoothly back in Rutland. A partisan of the Federalists who did not mince his words in the pulpit, Haynes found himself in increasing conflict with most of his parishioners. Opposing the War of 1812, he nevertheless scorned the threat of New England secession, but his activity in the con-servative Washington Benevolent Society as well as his biting sarcasm in urging his political views at last brought matters to a crisis. Thus it was that during the spring of 1818 the pastoral relation between Lemuel Haynes and his Rutland church came to an end. The farewell letter of the black minister—he was now sixty-five—is far from pathetic.

It was thirty years ago . . . since I took the pastoral care of this church and people; the church then consisted of forty-two members; since which time, there have been about three hundred and twelve added to it . . . I have preached about five thousand five hundred discourses: four hundred of them have been funeral sermons. I have solemnized more than a hun-dred marriages. During this period we have had two remarkable seasons of the outpourings of the Spirit. . . .

"Never was a greater degree of stupidity discovered among us," he wrote to a friend, "I expected it. . . . It was mutual agreement. No impeachment of my moral or ministerial character was pretended. I fully acquiesce in the event. I have many calls to labor elsewhere."

The third call he now responded to was from Manchester, on the west side of the Green Mountains. It was here, in 1820, that he became involved in the celebrated case of the allegedly murdered Russell Colvin, a "wander-ing maniac" of the town. In 1813 Colvin had suddenly disappeared. Years passed and a charge of murder was pressed against his wife's two brothers, who were finally sentenced to hang. Haynes spent many hours with the doomed men, grew convinced of their innocence, but despaired of saving them. Seven years after the supposed crime and thirty-seven days before the time appointed for the execution, Russell Colvin, alive and well, wandered back to town. The event was the sensation of the day. Haynes' sermon on the facts and meanings of the case under the title, *Mystery Developed,* broadened into an interesting disquisition on religion and prisons and packaged with his "narrative of the whole transaction" and the trial records was a best seller for a decade.

Two years later, in 1822, when the excitement was over, he learned to his dismay that his flock in Manchester felt the need for a younger pastor. There was regret on both sides. In Vermont he had made good friends: Richard Skinner, congressman, judge, and anti-slavery governor; Joseph Burr, patron of the American Colonization Society; Stephen Bradley, who had introduced into the Senate the bill that abolished the African slave trade; and Chief Justice Royall Tyler, poet and playwright. Now, once again, Lemuel Haynes, at three score and ten, would resume his pilgrimage. This time it was over the border in New York, where, in the town of Granville, revered as Father Haynes, he would spend the last eleven years of his life. There would be preaching trips to New York City, Albany, and Troy, and back to his first church in Massachusetts. When, on September 28, 1833, at an even eighty, he breathed his last, he left in his own hand "an epitaph to be put upon my tombstone":

Here lies the dust of a poor hell-deserving sinner, who ventured into eternity trusting wholly on the merits of Christ for salvation. In the full belief of the great doctrines he preached while on earth, he invites his children, and all who read this, to trust their eternal interest on the same foundation.

When Samuel E. Cornish, editor of the New York *Colored American,* one of the earliest black newspapers in the country, received a copy of Dr. Cooley's biography of Lemuel Haynes for review, it is probable that he was not quite sure of what he ought to make of the "very interesting and useful memoir of Father Haynes . . . one of the Lord's worthies . . . published for the benefit of his children." He first gives a brief summary: "the Rev. Lemuel Haynes, best known as pastor of the congregational church in West Rutland, Vt., was the son of an African father and a white mother . . . he was disowned in childhood by his mother, but kindly taken up by a worthy farmer . . . by his own almost unassisted efforts, he made such attainments in science and learning, that he was called to the ministry, settled successively over two churches of white people—and through life enjoyed, in an uncommon degree, the respect of the whole community." But how could this miracle have come to pass in the United States? Sixty years after the Declaration of Independence, the black editor struggled for an answer: "He is the only man of *known* African descent, who has ever succeeded in overpowering the system of American *caste.* And this he did by wisdom and piety, aided also by the more favorable state of the times in which he lived."

PART IV ☞

The

Emergence

of

Gifts

and

Powers

On the Fourth of July, 1791, at a public meeting of the Maryland Society for the Abolition of Slavery, a physician by the name of George Buchanan delivered *An Oration Upon the Moral and Political Evil of Slavery.* The young doctor was a member of the American Philosophical Society, had studied medicine in Edinburgh and Paris, practiced in Baltimore, and would succumb to the yellow fever in Philadelphia while ministering to the victims of the plague—but his justest claim to fame is this remarkable *Oration,* a rare jeremiad of the white Revolutionary conscience uttered in a stronghold of slavery only a few years after the adoption of the Constitution of the United States.

Deceitful men! Who could have suggested that American patriotism would at this day countenance a conduct so inconsistent; that while America boasts of being a land of freedom, and an asylum of the oppressed of Europe, she should at the same time foster an abominable nursery of slaves to check the shoots of her growing liberty? Deaf to the clamors of criticism, she feels no remorse. . . .   Not even the sobs and groans of injured innocence which reek from every state can excite her pity, nor human misery bend her heart to sympathy. Cruel and oppressive she wantonly abuses the rights of man, and willingly sacrifices her liberty upon the altar of slavery. "What! will you not consider that the Africans are men"? Buchanan cries out "that they have human souls to be saved? that they are born free and independent? . . . the Africans, whom you despise, whom you more inhumanly treat than brutes, and whom you unlawfully subject to slavery, with the tyrannizing hands of Despots, are equally capable of improvements with yourselves."

Things pleasing rejoice them, and melancholy circumstances pall their appetites for amusements. They brook no insults, and are equally prone to forgiveness as to resentment; they have gratitude also, and will even expose their own lives, to wipe off the obligation of past favours; nor do they want the refinements of taste, so much the boast of those who call themselves Christians.

And now Buchanan becomes more specific. "Neither is their genius for literature to be despised; many instances are recorded" of "persons of eminence among them." He would cite a few: "Phillis Wheatley, who distinguished herself as a poetess—The physician of New Orleans—The Virginia calculator—Banneker, the Maryland Astronomer. . . ."

These were but a handful, who, in the time of transition from colony to Nation, here and there emerged, almost heroically, with a wide range of gifts and powers—poignant reminders of black creative genius that had not been free to flower, blighted for a century and a half by the pall of slavery. The impassioned orator had not had the time to speak of "many others whom it would be needless to mention." Here are a baker's dozen who somehow managed to breach the racist wall: first—a scientist, a colonizer, a frontiersman, a doctor, a mathematical prodigy; then—a medley of poets and writers, including the celebrated Phillis Wheatley, and a few artists, dimly discerned.

BENJAMIN BANNEKER

In the era of the Revolution, Benjamin Banneker of Maryland, astronomer, mathematician, and defender of black dignity against the aspersions of Thomas Jefferson, was a primary symbol of the self-evident truth that all men are created equal. Banneker achieved a transatlantic fame. In Paris, his name and work would be cited by the revolutionary abbé, Henri Gregoire. In London, Pitt, Fox, and Wilberforce would flourish his almanac in the House of Commons while the benches rang "with much Applause." Yet Jefferson never really forgave the sable scientist for speaking out. Who, in this historic encounter, finally emerged as the finer champion of the cause of humanity, may be clarified in the following notes.

A few pages must suffice to sketch in the first fifty years of Banneker's rich but simple life. In 1683 an English dairymaid named Molly Welsh, falsely accused of pilfering a bucket of milk, found herself part of a cargo of convicts, and was sold as an indentured servant to a tobacco farmer on the Patapsco River in tidewater Maryland. After working out her seven years, she rented some land on the nearby frontier, and farmed it alone for a number of years. Then, "from a ship anchored in the Bay," she purchased two African slaves. One, who had the name of Bannke or Bannaka, said he was the son of a chief, never gave up his African religion, and is described in tradition as "a man of bright intelligence, fine temper, with a very agreeable presence, dignified manners, and contemplative habits." A few years later, Molly liberated both her slaves, and—despite the laws against miscegenation—took Bannaka for her husband. One of their daughters, Mary, married a man from Guinea, the slave of a neighboring planter, who had baptized him Robert, and then set him free. Robert took the name of Banneky, or Banneker.

Their first child was Benjamin, born in 1731. Six years later, for 17,000 pounds of tobacco, Robert bought a farm of a hundred acres located ten miles from Baltimore, a village of thirty houses. The free Bannekers were an unusual family in Baltimore County, where fifteen years later, there were, roughly, only two hundred free blacks in a population of four thousand slaves and thirteen thousand whites. Benjamin's grandmother Molly taught him, via the Bible, to read and write, and sent him for a while to a one-room, interracial school presided over by a Quaker master. A black classmate recalled that young Benjamin was not fond of play—"all his delight was to dive into his books." He grew up as a farm boy, grumbled at his share of the chores, but even then displayed an interest in things mechanical and mathematical, long before he fell in love with the stars. The elaborate process of tobacco production fascinated the lad—he once tallied the number of steps in the operation, thirty-six from seed to cigar.

When he was twenty-two, Benjamin took it into his head to make with his own hands a clock that would strike the hours. His tools were primitive and up to this time he had never seen a book on the subject, perhaps not even a clock. "This first scientific achievement," writes Silvio A. Bedini in his recent biography of Banneker, "was associated with a theme that preoccupied him during the major part of his life. This was the theme of Time."

In all of his young life he had seen but two timepieces. One was a sundial; the other was a pocket watch. . . . Banneker conveyed his memories of the wheelwork of the watch into drawings, then he applied his natural mathematical skill into calculating the relative size and number of teeth of the wheels. First he drew a diagram of the wheels and gears, balance regulator, and spring barrel, then converted these into three dimensional parts . . . carving the wheels and pinions from selected pieces of hard-grained wood. . . . At last the movement was finished, and it was a successful striking clock . . . this miracle of untutored craftsmanship actually worked. . . . His fame spread rapidly throughout the valley. . . .

Completed in 1753, this clock, made almost entirely of wood, continued to strike the hours for more than half a century until its maker's death.

He was twenty-eight when his father died and willed him the farm, and for the next decade he lived alone with his mother. He was a good farmer, owned two horses and a few cows, sold honey from his beehives, cultivated a large garden for table and sale, and raised wheat and corn for his own use. Tobacco was his main market crop. He bought a book now and then when he could—a quarto Bible in 1763. He was the proud possessor of a flute, a violin, and some music books. He loved to devise mathematical puzzles, sometimes in verse. Now and then his neighbors came to marvel at his clock or to ask for help in arithmetic and letter writing. He favored the Quakers, but never formally became a Friend.

In 1772 two brothers named Ellicott came to the valley and in a few years built a complex of well-designed grist mills, which became the focus of a busy settlement with a post office and a general store. Banneker, now in his early forties, closely observed all the work—the details of construction, the semi-automated operation that converted wagons of grain into sacks of flour—and his farm helped to supply food for the laborers. The black farmer got to know the Ellicotts, and on his visits to the store there was palaver about politics and other matters. Banneker was restrained in his manner, but "when he could be prevailed upon to set this reserve aside," those within earshot discovered that he had "a great store of traditional lore which he had gathered from listening to others and particularly from the books he had read," and that he could tell "anecdotes which fitted the current subject under discussion." One of his favorite topics was "the history of the early settlement of the North American continent"—no doubt he pondered the role of the kidnapped Africans in that history. Occasionally, he would talk about his own life and his struggle for knowledge. He was a regular reader of the *Maryland Gazette* and the *Baltimore Advertiser,* two newspapers he could find in the Ellicott store.

Although Congress met briefly in Baltimore in 1776, the war touched the county only slightly—the Quakerish Banneker, in his late forties, physically not at all. By the spring of 1781, free blacks were subject to the draft and the idea of a regiment of slaves was discarded only because Maryland lawmakers felt that the blacks were needed for production and it was risky to put guns in their hands. The Ellicotts went to war and the mills suffered, especially from floods, but when they returned they rebuilt better than before.

Banneker's best friend among the Ellicotts was young George, almost thirty years his junior, an enthusiast of science and especially astronomy, who had imported from London a collection of texts, instruments, and globes. George Ellicott was "one of the best mathematicians, and also one of the finest amateur astronomers of the time," wrote his daughter Martha, "and was fond of imparting instruction to every youthful inquirer after knowledge who came to his house. As early as the year 1782, during the fine clear evenings of autumn, he was in the habit of giving gratuitous lessons on astronomy to any of the inhabitants of the village who wished to hear him. To many of these, his celestial globe was an object of great interest and curiosity." Banneker became intoxicated with astronomy. In the autumn of 1788, George lent him some texts, a sturdy table, and a few pieces of apparatus—"a pedestal telescope and a set of drafting instruments for making observations of the times of the stars in the meridian, of their southing, and of their rising and setting." Using his logarithmic tables, Banneker ambitiously attempted a projection of an eclipse of the sun and sent the results to George, who found a trifling error but was amazed at the feat, for he had given Banneker no instruction on the procedure to be used. When Banneker learned of his error, he was chagrined and went over his work. The fault, he found to his joy, was not his, but had stemmed from a disparity in two of his sources, the leading English authorities on astronomy, "the Learned Leadbetter" and the "wise Author Ferguson." Although he counted himself among the "young Tyroes in Astronomy," he confessed to George, his confidence had not been destroyed: "I Doubt not being able to Calculate a Common Almanack" [figure 55].

Was Banneker planning to become a black Poor Richard? A colonial institution as early as 1639, the almanac, that popular compendium of practical data—astronomical, meteorological, medical, agricultural, and almost everything else—seasoned with proverb, poem and jest, was, of course, no new thing in American life. "No one who would penetrate to the core of early American literature," commented Moses Coit Tyler, ". . . may by any means turn away, in lofty literary scorn, from the almanac—most despised, most prolific, most indispensable of books . . . the supreme and only literary necessity even in households where the Bible and newspaper were still undesired and unattainable luxuries." But the heart of the almanac was the ephemeris, calculated by the astronomer, as Bedini explains, "from a series of basic computations required to establish the positions of the sun, moon and planets each year, from which other calculations may be made:

Sir I received your Letter on the hand of Bell but found nothing Strange to me In the Letter Concerning the Number of Eclipses tho according to authers the Edge of the penumber only touches the Suns Limb in that Eclipse that I left out of the Number — Which happens April 14 day at 37 minutes past 7 O'Clock in the morning and is the first we shall have but since you wrote to me I Drew in the Equations of the Node which will Cause a Small Solar Defect but I did not intend to publish, I was not so very particular as I should have been, but was more intent upon the true method of projecting a Solar Eclips — It is an Easy matter for us when a Diagram is laid down before us to draw one in resemblance of it, but it is a hard matter for young Tyroes in Astronomy when only the Elements for the projection is laid down before him to draw his Diagram to any degree of Ceatainty ————

Says the Learned LEADBETTER the projection that I shall here describe, is that mentioned by Mr. Flamsted — When the Sun is in Cancer, Leo, Virgo, Libra, Scorpio, or Saggittary, the Axes of the Globe must lie to the right hand of the Axes of the Ecliptic, but when the Sun is in Capercorn, Aquarius, pisces, Aries, Taurus, or Gemini then to the left ————

Says that wise Author FERGUSON, when the Sun is in Capercorn, Aquarius, pisces, Aries, Taurus, and Gemini the Northen half of the Earths Axes lies to the right hand of the Axes of the Ecliptic, and to the left hand whilst the Sun is in the other Six Signs ————

Now Mr. Ellicott two such learned Gentlemen as the above mentioned, one in direct opposition to the other, Stagnates young beginners, but I hope the Stagnation will not be of long duration — for this I observe that Leadbetter Count the time on the path of Vertex 1. 2. 3. &c from the right to the left hand or from the Consequent to the Antecedent —— But Furguson on the path of the Vertex, Count the time 1. 2. 3 &c from the left to the right hand according to the order of Numbers, So that, that is regular Shale Componsate for irregularity — Now Sir if I can overcome this difficulty I Doubt not being able to Calculate a Common Almanack — So no more but remain yr faithfull friend

Mr George Ellicott
Octo. 13, 1789 ———   ——— B Banneker.

the solar and lunar eclipses, the times of rising and setting of the sun and moon, identification of remarkable days, weather forecasting on a daily basis, tide tables for the region, and similar date." Probably before he thought of publishing an almanac, encouraged by George Ellicott, Banneker had hit upon the idea of constructing an ephemeris, as he says later, "at the request of Several Gentlemen." George's young wife, Elizabeth, who had lent Banneker her own precious text on astronomy, called on him with a few of her friends early in 1790.

His door stood wide open, and so closely was his mind engaged that they entered without being seen. Immediately upon observing them he arose and with much courtesy invited them to be seated. The large oval table at which Banneker sat was strewn with works on astronomy and with scientific appurtenances. He alluded to his love of the study of astronomy and mathematics as quite unsuited to a man of his class, and regretted his slow advancement in them, owing to the laborious nature of his agricultural engagements, which obliged him to spend the greater portion of his time in the fields. . . .

At last, in the spring of that year, the calculations for the twelve months of 1791 were completed, and Banneker decided on his own to send off the ephemeris to the Baltimore printer, John Hayes. There was no prompt answer, and he chafed with impatience. When the printer finally replied that he had dispatched the ephemeris to Philadelphia for review by the well-known surveyor, Major Andrew Ellicott, Banneker could not wait. In May, he wrote to the Major.

I beg that you will not be too Severe upon me but favourable in giving your approbation . . . knowing well the difficulty that attends long Calculations and especially with young beginners in Astronomy . . . the Calculations was made more for the Sake of gratifying the Curiosity of the public, than for any view of profit, as I suppose it to be the first attempt of the kind that ever was made in America by a person of my Complection—

Whether Ellicott ever replied to Banneker is unknown, and Hayes did not publish Banneker's ephemeris that year. The black astronomer was, of course, deeply disappointed, but he was determined to persevere. Perhaps the next year would be a luckier one. He continued his calculations for 1792.

But now something else, an interlude of some importance in Banneker's life, interrupted his work for a few months.

From the Declaration of Independence to the inauguration of George Washington, eight cities had furnished sites for the meetings of Congress. It was time to establish a national capital. During the winter of 1791, the president appointed Major Andrew Ellicott to survey the district chosen for the new Federal City on the Potomac that would later be known as the District of Columbia. When the major asked George Ellicott to serve as his "scientific assistant," George strongly recommended the sixty-year-old

Banneker for the position. The major, who had seen Banneker's ephemeris, knew, of course, that he was qualified, and Thomas Jefferson, the secretary of state, approved the appointment. As the two were preparing to proceed on horseback to Georgetown, Elizabeth Ellicott busied herself with getting her husband's black friend ready for the journey: "Under the impression that Banneker would fall under the notice of the most eminent men of the country, whilst thus engaged," recalled her daughter Martha, she "paid a visit to his cottage [and] was careful to direct the appointments of his wardrobe, in order that he might appear in respectable guise, before the distinguished personages likely to be assembled there."

In early February they reached Alexandria and went on to Georgetown to begin their task. Banneker worked closely with Ellicott, kept notes on the progress of the survey, made the necessary calculations, and handled the astronomical instruments for establishing the base points. "It was the work, also, of Major Ellicott," wrote Martha, "under the orders of General Washington . . . to locate the sites of the Capitol, president's house, treasury, and other public buildings. In this, also, Banneker was his assistant." Banneker's deportment throughout the whole of this engagement, secured their respect, and there is good authority for believing, that his endowments led the commissioners to overlook the color of his skin to converse with him freely, and enjoy the clearness and originality of his remarks on various subjects. . . . He was invited to sit at table with the engineer corps, but, as his characteristic modesty induced him to decline this, a separate table was prepared for him in their dining room; his meals being served at the same time as theirs.

Banneker, in fact, spent most of his time in the observatory tent, where he also slept. It was only after Ellicott and his black "scientific assistant" were well under way in the survey that Jefferson notified Major Pierre Charles L'Enfant of his appointment to prepare drawings of the site and of specific government buildings.

In early March the *Georgetown Weekly Ledger* printed a notice, widely copied in the newspapers of Maryland and elsewhere.

Some time last month arrived in this town Mr. *Andrew Ellicott,* a gentleman of superior astronomical abilities. He was employed by the President of the United States of America, to lay off the tract of land, ten miles square, on the Potowmack, for the use of Congress;—is now engaged in this business, and hopes soon to accomplish the object of his mission. He is attended by *Benjamin Banneker,* an Ethiopian, whose abilities, as a surveyor, and an astronomer, clearly prove that Mr. Jefferson's concluding that race of men were void of mental endowments, was without foundation.

Whenever Banneker had time, he labored on his ephemeris for the coming year. At the end of April, when the major's two brothers arrived to assist him, Banneker was not sorry to start for home. He had learned something about practical astronomy from Major Ellicott, and he was eager to resume full-time work on his calculations. And there was the farm. Elizabeth remembered the day he got back.

On his return home, he called at the house of his friend George Ellicott to give an account of his engagements. He arrived on horseback, dressed in his usual costume, a full suit of drab cloth, surmounted by a large beaver hat.

He was in fine spirits, seeming to have been reanimated by the kindness of the distinguished men with whom he had mingled.

With his usual humility he estimated his own services at a low rate.

▃▃Benjamin Banneker published six almanacs, for the years 1792 to 1797, in twenty-eight editions, printed in Baltimore, Philadelphia, Petersburg, Richmond, Wilmington, and Trenton. The achievement was a notable one for at least two reasons: as a scientific feat by a self-taught philomath in his sixties; as a bold polemic aimed at those who denied equal intellect and humanity in black and white. "His notes remain as a monument to his love of astronomy and of his unflagging determination to master every aspect of the task he had set himself," Bedini observes. Was there something else that drove the black astronomer to the herculean effort embodied in his six years of ceaseless toil? ("A vast amount of work was required to calculate a single eclipse," adds Bedini, "which makes Banneker's accomplishment in this field all the more impressive. He had to make at least sixty-eight mathematical calculations to produce the ten elements required to construct a single eclipse diagram.") There is a clue, perhaps, in the letter he had sent to Major Andrew Ellicott during the spring of 1790 as he breathlessly awaited his verdict on the first ephemeris: "the Calculations was made more for the Sake of gratifying the Curiosity of the public, than for any view of profit, as I suppose it to be the first attempt of the kind that ever was made in America by a person of my Complection."

Inevitably the trail leads to Thomas Jefferson. It was in 1788, in Philadelphia, that the American edition of the *Notes on the State of Virginia* first saw the light. It is hardly possible that the Ellicotts did not own a copy of the book, more than probable that Banneker, either directly or through the press, was painfully aware of its slurs on the intellectual capacities of the blacks. "Comparing them by their faculties of memory, reason, and imagination, it appears to me," wrote Jefferson, "that in memory they are equal to the white; in reason much inferior, as I think one could scarcely be found capable of tracing and comprehending the investigations of Euclid; and that in imagination they are dull, tasteless, and anomalous . . . never yet could I find that a black had uttered a thought above the level of plain narration. . . ." In Georgetown, in the *Weekly Ledger,* Banneker had already seen himself cited as "an Ethiopian" who was the living rebuttal of Mr. Jefferson's opinion that blacks were "void of mental endowments." Now, back home in Maryland, his historic task was clear. *Banneker's Almanacs* would drive the point home.

When the ephemeris for 1792 was at last ready for the press, he quickly lined up a few printers in Georgetown and Baltimore, but his particular wish was to publish it in Philadelphia, where the stalwarts of the Society for the Abolition of Slavery—already aware of his work—saw eye to eye with his vision of an almanac that would combine scientific data with anti-racist argument. Everything went well, the ubiquitous Ellicotts assisting. George sent the ephemeris to his brother Elias in Baltimore, who in turn wrote to James Pemberton, the wealthy Quaker abolitionist and friend of John Woolman, Anthony Benezet, and Captain Paul Cuffe. "He is a man of strong Natural parts," wrote Elias, "and by his own Study hath made himself well Acquainted with the Mathematicks. About three Years ago he began to study Astronomy . . . became so far a proficient as to Calculate an Almanac. . . . He hath a Copy now ready for the Press for the Year 1792"—then added what all the Ellicotts knew was uppermost in Banneker's mind—"he is a Poor man & Would be Pleased With having something for the Copy but if the Printer is not Willing to give any thing He would rather let him have it for nothing than not to have it Published. He thinks as it is the first performance of the kind ever done by One of his Complection that it might be a means of Promoting the Cause of Humanity as many are of the Opinion that the Blacks are Void of Mental Endowments."

Pemberton lost no time. He immediately dispatched a copy of Banneker's ephemeris to David Rittenhouse, the Nation's foremost scientist, who had recently been appointed to succeed Benjamin Franklin as president of the American Philosophical Society. (Before that same society in 1775, in his famous oration on the wonders of astronomy, Rittenhouse had defended the equality of the blacks, who, "degraded from their native dignity, have been doomed to endless slavery by us in America, merely because *their* bodies may be disposed to reflect or absorb the rays of light, in a way different from *ours*.") A "very extraordinary performance," replied Rittenhouse, ". . . Every Instance of Genius amongst the Negroes is worthy of attention, because their oppressors seem to lay great stress on their supposed inferior mental abilities."

It was at this moment, during the summer of 1791, that Benjamin Banneker, feeling that the time was now ripe for spelling out his grand idea, wrote a letter to Secretary of State Thomas Jefferson, that deserves to be enshrined as a classic document of our literature—the black democratic challenge put to the chief ideologist of the American Revolution. No treatment of the black presence in that area would be complete without the whole of this manifesto, no future edition of *Notes on the State of Virginia* should ever omit it.

Maryland, Baltimore County,
Near Ellicott's Lower Mills August 19th. 1791.
Thomas Jefferson Secretary of State.
Sir, I am fully sensible of the greatness of that freedom which I take with you on the present occasion; a liberty which Seemed to me Scarcely allowable, when I reflected on that distinguished, and dignifyed station in which you Stand; and the almost general prejudice and prepossession which is so previlent in the world against those of my complexion.

I suppose it is a truth too well attested to you, to need of proof here, that we are a race of Beings who have long laboured under the abuse and censure of the world, that we have long been looked upon with an eye of contempt, and that we have long been considered rather as brutish than human, and Scarcely capable of mental endowments.

Sir, I hope I may Safely admit, in consequence of that report which hath reached me, that you are a man far less inflexible in Sentiments of this nature, than many others, that you are measurably friendly and well disposed towards us, and that you are willing and ready to Lend your aid and assistance to our relief from those many distresses and numerous calamities to which we are reduced.

Now, Sir, if this is founded in truth, I apprehend you will readily embrace every opportunity to eradicate that train of absurd and false ideas and oppinions which so generally prevail with respect to us, and that your Sentiments are concurrent with mine, which are that one universal Father hath given being to us all, and that he hath not only made us all of one flesh, but that he hath also without partiality afforded us all the Same Sensations, and endued us all with the same faculties, and that however variable we may be in Society or religion, however diversified in Situation or colour, we are all of the Same Family, and Stand in the Same relation to him.

Sir, if these are Sentiments of which you are fully persuaded, I hope you cannot but acknowledge, that it is the indispensible duty of those who maintain for themselves the rights of human nature, and who profess the obligations of Christianity, to extend their power and influence to the relief of every part of the human race, from whatever burthen or oppression they may unjustly labour under; and this I apprehend a full conviction of the truth and obligation of these principles should lead all to.

Sir, I have long been convinced, that if your love for yourSelves and for those inesteemable laws which preserve to you the rights of human nature, was founded on Sincerity, you could not but be Solicitous, that every Individual of whatsoever rank or distinction, might with you equally enjoy the blessings thereof, neither could you rest Satisfyed, short of the most active diffusion of your exertions, in order to their promotion from any State of degradation, to which the unjustifyable cruelty and barbarism of men may have reduced them.

Sir I freely and Chearfully acknowledge, that I am of the African race, and, in that colour which is natural to them of the deepest dye*, and it is under a Sense of the most profound gratitude to the Supreme Ruler of the universe, that I now confess to you, that I am not under that State of tyrannical thraldom, and inhuman captivity, to which too many of my brethren are doomed; but that I have abundantly tasted of the fruition of those blessings which proceed from that free and unequalled liberty with which you are favoured and which I hope you will willingly allow you have received from the immediate Hand of that Being from whom proceedeth every good and perfect gift.

Sir, Suffer me to recall to your mind that time in which the Arms and tyranny of the British Crown were exerted with every powerful effort, in

* My Father was brought here a Slave from Africa.

order to reduce you to a State of Servitude; look back I intreat you on the variety of dangers to which you were exposed, reflect on that time in which every human aid appeared unavailable, and in which even hope and fortitude wore the aspect of inability to the Conflict, and you cannot but be led to a Serious and grateful Sense of your miraculous and providential preservation; You cannot but acknowledge, that the present freedom and tranquillity which you enjoy you have mercifully received, and that it is the peculiar blessing of Heaven.

This, Sir, was a time in which you clearly saw into the injustice of a State of Slavery, and in which you had Just apprehensions of the horrors of its condition, it was now Sir, that your abhorrence thereof was so excited, that you publicly held forth this true and invaluable doctrine, which is worthy to be recorded and remembered in all Succeeding ages. "We hold these truths to be Self evident, that all men are created equal, and that they are endowed by their creator with certain inalienable rights, that amongst these are life, liberty, and the persuit of happiness."

Here, Sir, was a time in which your tender feelings for your selves engaged you thus to declare, you were then impressed with proper ideas of the great valuation of liberty, and the free possession of those blessings to which you were entitled by nature; but Sir how pitiable is it to reflect, that altho you were so fully convinced of the benevolence of the Father of mankind, and of his equal and impartial distribution of those rights and privileges which he had conferred upon them, that you should at the Same time counteract his mercies, in detaining by fraud and violence so numerous a part of my brethren under groaning captivity and cruel oppression, that you should at the Same time be found guilty of that most criminal act, which you professedly detested in others, with respect to yourselves.

Sir, I suppose that your knowledge of the situation of my brethren is too extensive to need a recital here; neither shall I presume to prescribe methods by which they may be relieved, otherwise than by recommending to you, and all others, to wean yourselves from those narrow prejudices which you have imbibed with respect to them, and as Job proposed to his friends "Put your Souls in their Souls' stead," thus shall your hearts be enlarged with kindness and benevolence towards them, and thus shall you need neither the direction of myself or others in what manner to proceed herein.

And now, Sir, altho my Sympathy and affection for my brethren hath caused by enlargement thus far, I ardently hope that your condour and generosity will plead with you in my behalf, when I make known to you, that it was not originally my design; but that having taken up my pen in order to direct to your as a present, a copy of an Almanack which I have calculated for the Succeeding year, I was unexpectedly and unavoidably led thereto.

This calculation, Sir, is the production of my arduous study, in this my advanced Stage of life; for having long had unbounded desires to become Acquainted with the Secrets of nature, I have had to gratify my curiosity herein thro my own assiduous application to Astronomical Study, in which

I need not to recount to you the many difficulties and disadvantages which I have had to encounter.

And altho I had almost declined to make my calculation for the ensuing year, in consequence of that time which I had allotted therefor being taking up at the Federal Territory by the request of Mr. Andrew Ellicott, yet finding myself under Several engagements to printers of this state to whom I had communicated my design, on my return to my place of residence, I industriously apply'd myself thereto, which I hope I have accomplished with correctness and accuracy, a copy of which I have taken the liberty to direct to you, and which I humbly request you will favourably receive, and altho you may have the opportunity of perusing it after its publication, yet I chose to send it to you in manuscript previous thereto, that thereby you might not only have an earlier inspection, but that you might also view it in my own hand writing.

And now Sir, I Shall conclude and Subscribe my Self with the most profound respect,

Your most Obedient humble Servant
Benjamin Banneker

Five days after Banneker had dispatched the above to Jefferson, George Ellicott wrote to James Pemberton: "Inclosed is a Coppy of a Letter which Benjamin Banaker wrote to Thos. Jefferson Secretary of State which he wrote himself and desired Me to send to thee it is his wish to have it put into the Allmanacke if its thought proper or in to the publick papers." (It is to be noted that Banneker was not being "used" by the Quaker abolitionists; the initiative was his own; the letter was to be printed, if possible, in the almanac—the printers were finally responsible for the insertion of editorial materials—or in the newspapers.) "Their is a small piece of poetry inclosed of Banaker's composing," Ellicott continued, "which he desires may be put under the Letter if its published." How eager Banneker was to ram home his humanitarian point may be sensed in these verses, that never got into print.

> Behold ye Christians! and in pity see
> Those Afric sons which Nature formed free;
> Behold them in a fruitful country blest,
> of Nature's bounties see them rich possest,
> Behold them herefrom town by cruel force,
> And doomed to slavery without remorse,
> This act, America, thy sons have known;
> This cruel act, relentless have they done.

Jefferson received Banneker's ephemeris and letter at Philadelphia, and replied on August 30.

SIR, I thank you sincerely for your letter of the 19th instant and for the Almanac it contained. No body wishes more than I do to see such proofs as you exhibit, that nature has given to our black brethren, talents equal to those of the other colors of men, and that the appearance of a want of them is owing merely to the degraded condition of their existence, both in Africa and America. I can add with truth, that no body wishes more ardently to see a good system commenced for raising the condition both of their body & mind to what it ought to be, as fast as the imbecility of their present existence, and other circumstances which cannot be neglected will admit.

I have taken the liberty of sending your Almanac to Monsieur de Condorcet, Secretary of the Academy of Sciences at Paris, and member of the Philanthropic society, because I considered it as a document to which your whole colour had a right for their justification against the doubts which have been entertained of them.

On the same day, Jefferson forwarded the ephemeris—but not Banneker's letter—to Condorcet, with a covering note.

I am happy to be able to inform you that we have now in the United States a negro, the son of a black man born in Africa, and a black woman born in the United States, who is a very respectable mathematician. I procured him to be employed under one of our chief directors in laying out the new federal city of the Potowmac, & in the intervals of his leisure, while on that work, he made an Almanac for the next year, which he sent me in his own handwriting, & which I inclose to you. I have seen very elegant solutions of Geometrical problems by him. Add to this that he is a very worthy & respectable member of society. He is a free man. I shall be delighted to see these instances of moral eminence so multiplied as to prove that the want of talents observed in them is merely the effect of their degraded condition, and not proceeding from any difference in the structure of the parts in which intellect depends.

Did Condorcet reply? We do not know. But seventeen years later, another distinguished Frenchman, the Abbé Henri Grégoire sent to Jefferson a copy of his recent book, *De la littérature des Negres,* which would shortly be translated and published in Brooklyn under the impressive title, *An Enquiry concerning the Intellectual and Moral Faculties and Literature of Negroes; Followed with an Account of the Life and Works of Fifteen Negroes and Mulattoes.* There were some writers, observed the revolutionary priest, who believed that nature has denied to black people "deep reflection, genius and reason. . . . We regret to find the same prejudice in a man, whose name is not pronounced amongst us, but with the most profound esteem or merited respect—we mean Jefferson in his 'Notes on Virginia.' "

To Grégoire, Jefferson responded, as Winthrop Jordan puts it, with "his usual protestations of inconclusiveness."

Be assured that no person living wishes more sincerely than I do, to see a complete refutation of the doubts I have myself entertained and expressed on the grade of understanding alloted to them by nature, and that to find that in this respect they are on a par with ourselves. My doubts were the result of personal observation on the limited sphere of my own State, where the opportunities for the development of their genius were not favorable, and those of exercising it still less so. I expressed them therefore with great hesitation . . . but whatever be their degree of talent it is no measure of their rights. . . .

But to his friend, Joel Barlow, Jefferson confessed that he had given Grégoire "a very soft answer." It is in this letter with its inaccuracies and innuendo, that his original opinion of Banneker and his achievement—and of the equality of the black intellect—comes clear.

Bishop Grégoire wrote to me on the doubts I had expressed five or six and twenty years ago, in the *Notes on Virginia,* as to the grade of understanding of the negroes. His credulity had made him gather up every story he could find of men of color (without distinguishing whether black, or of what degree of mixture), however slight the mention, or light the authority on which they are quoted. The whole do not amount in point of evidence, to what we know ourselves about Banneker. We know he had spherical trigonometry enough to make almanacs, but not without the suspicion of aid from Ellicott, who was his neighbor and friend, and never missed an opportunity of puffing him. I have a long letter from Banneker, which shows him to have had a mind of very common stature indeed. . . .

The black astronomer was three years in his grave when Jefferson wrote these nervous lines.

Although Banneker was eager to print his correspondence with Jefferson as a preface to his first almanac, a misunderstanding among the printers delayed its publication to the almanac for 1793. Almost at the same time, to ensure wider distribution by the Abolition Society, he published the letters as a separate pamphlet, which sold out rapidly and had to be reprinted in a second edition. In place of the letters, *Benjamin Banneker's Pennsylvania, Delaware, Maryland and Virginia Almanack and Ephemeris, for the Year of Our Lord, 1792 . . . and the Sixteenth Year of American Independence* opened with a preface by the printer-editors, who presented to the public *"an extraordinary Effort of Genius"*

calculated by a sable Descendant of Africa, who, by this Specimen of Ingenuity, evinces, to Demonstration, that mental Powers and Endowments are not the exclusive *Excellence of* white people, *but the Rays of Science may alike illumine the Minds of Men of* every Clime, *(however they may differ in the* Colour *of their Skin) particularly those whom Tyrant-Custom hath too long taught us to depreciate as a Race inferior in intellectual Capacity.*

There followed a short biography of Banneker—the earliest sketch of his life, reprinted again and again at home and abroad during the next few years—by the senator from Maryland, Dr. James McHenry of Baltimore, whom he had asked for help. (The senator, who had come over from Ireland in 1771, had studied medicine under Dr. Benjamin Rush, served as secretary to Washington and Lafayette during the war and then spent three years in the Continental Congress.) "I cannot but wish on this occasion," wrote McHenry, "to see the Public patronage keep pace with my black friend's merit."

I consider this Negro as a fresh proof that the powers of the mind are disconnected with the colour of the skin, or, in other words, a striking contradiction to Mr. *Hume's* doctrine, that "Negroes are naturally inferior to the whites and unsusceptible of attainments in arts and sciences." In every civilized country we shall find thousands of whites, liberally educated, and who have enjoyed greater opportunities of instruction than this Negro, his inferior in those intellectual acquirements and capacities that form the most characteristic feature in the human race.

The almanacs themselves, aside from the ephemerides of Banneker, were an innovation in the old genre, bringing together, as they did, the usual variety of useful science, general information—and humanitarian politics. There were extracts from *The Columbian Magazine* "On Negro Slavery, and the Slave Trade," which cited a comment on skin pigmentation by David Rittenhouse, passages from the debates in Parliament on the slave trade with an abstract of William Pitt's great speech, stanzas from "Wilkinson's Appeal to England in Behalf of the Abused Africans, Cowper's poem "On Liberty," and a typical filler to the effect that needles were "first made in London, by a Negro from Spain, in the reign of Q Mary." Phillis Wheatley's twelve lines from "On the Works of Providence" in the almanac for 1794 are introduced by the editors with the remark "that Africans and their Descendants are capable of attaining a Degree of Eminence in the Liberal Sciences BENJAMIN is not the only proof." Most notable, along with the letter to Jefferson in the almanac of 1793, was the first version of Benjamin Rush's "A Plan of a Peace-Office, for the United States," a landmark in the history of the search for alternatives to war, and an argument for peace with which Banneker no doubt fully concurred [figure 56].

The labours of the justly celebrated *Bannaker* will likewise furnish you with a very important lesson, courteous reader, which you will not find in any other Almanac, namely that the Maker of the Universe is no respecter of colours; that the colour of the skin is in no ways connected with strength of mind or intellectual powers. . . .   To the untutored Blacks, the following elegant lines of GRAY may be applied.

So ends the preface to the almanac for 1796:

> Full many a gem of purest ray serene,
> The dark unfathom'd caves of ocean bear:
> Full many a flower is borne to blush unseen.
> And waste its fragrance on the desert air.

with an added stanza:

> Nor you ye proud, impute to these the blame
> If Afric's sons to genius are unknown,
> For Banneker has prov'd they may acquire a name
> As bright, as lasting as your own.

☞ The portrait cut on wood that adorns the cover of the almanac of 1795 [figure 57] shows Banneker at sixty-four (he looks younger) in the plain Quaker garb he always wore. There would be two more almanacs, in 1796 and 1797, and then his work would be done. His health had begun to decline. A young friend of the Ellicotts' from Philadelphia, Susannah Mason, visiting the old man in the summer of 1796, "found the venerable star-gazer under a wide-spreading pear tree laden with delicious fruit. He

56. Excerpts from Benjamin Rush's "Plan of a Peace-Office for the United States" published in Banneker's *Almanack, and Ephemeris*, 1793. Library of Congress.

A PLAN OF A *PEACE-OFFICE*, FOR THE UNITED STATES.

AMONG the many defects which have been pointed out in the federal conſtitution by its antifederal enemies, it is much to be lamented that no perſon has taken notice of its total ſilence upon the ſubject of an office of the utmoſt importance to the welfare of the United States, that is, an *office* for promoting and preſerving perpetual *peace* in our country.

It is to be hoped that no objection will be made to the eſtabliſhment of ſuch an office, while we are engaged in a war with the Indians, for as the *War-Office* of the United States was eſtabliſhed in the *time of peace*, it is equally reaſonable that a *Peace-Office* ſhould be eſtabliſhed in the *time of war.*

The plan of this office is as follows:

I. Let a Secretary of Peace be appointed to preſide in this office, who ſhall be perfectly free from all the preſent abſurd and vulgar European prejudices upon the ſubject of government; let him be a genuine republican and a ſincere Chriſtian, for the principles of republicaniſm and Chriſtianity are no leſs friendly to univerſal and perpetual peace, than they are to univerſal and equal liberty.

V. To inſpire a veneration for human life, and an horror at the ſhedding of human blood, let all thoſe laws be repealed which authoriſe juries, judges, ſheriffs, or bangmen to aſſume the reſentments of individuals, and to commit murder in cold blood in any caſe whatever. Until this reformation in our code of penal juriſprudence take place, it will be in vain to attempt to introduce univerſal and perpetual peace in our country.

VI. To ſubdue that paſſion for war, which education, added to human depravity, have made univerſal, a familiarity with the inſtruments of death, as well as all military ſhews, ſhould be carefully avoided. For which reaſon, militia laws ſhould every where be repealed, and military dreſſes and military titles ſhould be laid aſide: reviews tend to leſſen the horrors of a battle by connecting them with the charms of order; militia laws generate idleneſs and vice, and thereby produce the wars they are ſaid to prevent; military dreſſes faſcinate the minds of young men, and lead them from ſerious and uſeful profeſſions; were there no *uniforms*, there would probably be no armies; laſtly, military titles feed vanity, and keep up ideas in the mind which leſſen a ſenfe of the folly and miſeries of war.

125

Benjamin Bannaker's
PENNSYLVANIA, DELAWARE, MARY-
LAND, AND VIRGINIA
ALMANAC,
FOR THE
YEAR of our LORD 1795;
Being the Third after Leap-Year.

BANNAKER.

—PRINTED FOR—
And Sold by JOHN FISHER, *Stationer.*
BALTIMORE.

57. Benjamin Banneker. Woodcut engraving on title page of Banneker's *Almanac,* 1795.
Maryland Historical Society.

came forward to meet us, and bade us welcome to his lowly dwelling. It was built of logs, one story in height, and was surrounded by an orchard. In one corner of the room was a clock of his own construction. . . . He took down from a shelf a little book, wherein he registered the names of those by whose visits he felt particularly honored. . . ." When Susannah, in a rhymed letter of admiration, praised him as a "man exalted high:"

> Conspicuous in the world's keen eye,
> On record now thy name's enrolled;
> And future ages will be told
> There lived a man named BANNEKER
> An African Astronomer!

he replied with thanks in a note penned "with trembling hands."

Banneker never married, lived alone on his farm, cooked his own meals. As his infirmities increased, he sold and rented his land, then gave all of it to the Ellicotts in exchange for a twelve-pound annuity guaranteed for the rest of his life. He puttered in his garden and orchard, watched the stars at night, went to sleep at dawn, studied his bees endlessly, made original observations on the seventeen-year locusts, hunted a bit, sat under his chestnut tree in the dooryard and played his violin and flute, drank a little too much at times, attended Quaker meetings now and then. The journal that he always kept was not abandoned. In it, he recorded his observations of nature, new mathematical puzzles in verse, his dreams, and the continuing calculations for new ephemerides that were never published. "The contents of Banneker's Manuscript Journal and his commonplace book," notes Bedini, "are unique records of an eighteenth-century almanac-maker . . . with a clear exposition of the method by which almanacs were calculated during this period of American scientific history."

About Banneker in his old age there was the aura of a sage. All who knew him at this time remembered his "very venerable and dignified appearance." One found it curious that "the statue of Franklin at the Library in Philadelphia" was "the perfect likeness of him." A young clerk who worked in the store at Ellicott's Mills in 1800 could never forget him. After hearing him converse, I was always anxious to wait upon him. After making his purchases, he usually went to the part of the store where George Ellicott was in the habit of sitting, to converse with him about the affairs of our Government and other matters. He was very precise in conversation and exhibited deep reflection . . . he seemed to be acquainted with every thing of importance that was passing in the country. . . .
"I remember Benjamin Banneker's personal appearance very well," wrote Thomas Ellicott: "he was quite a black man, of medium stature, of uncommonly soft and gentlemanly manners, and pleasant coloquial powers, and like *other* gentlemen of that day had not abstained from the use of intoxicating drink—though I think I never saw him improperly influenced by it."
As a young woman, George Ellicott's daughter, Martha, frequently saw Banneker at the Elkridge Quaker Meeting House: "His raiment was always scrupulously neat; that for summer wear, being of unbleached linen, was beautifully washed and ironed by his sisters . . . In cold weather he dressed

in light colored cloth, a fine drab broadcloth constituting his attire when he designed appearing in his best style."

His ample forehead, white hair, and reverent deportment, gave him a very venerable appearance, as he leaned on the long staff (which he always carried with him) in contemplation. . . . The countenance of Banneker had a most benign and thoughtful expression. . . . His figure was perfectly erect, showing no inclination to stoop as he advanced in years.

The end came in October of 1806 when he had almost reached his seventy-fifth year. Two days after his death, as his body was being lowered into the grave, his house, a few yards away, caught fire. The clock that he made with his own hands forty years before was consumed in the flames.

On October 28, 1806, the *Federal Gazette and Baltimore Daily Advertiser* printed a brief but pithy obituary.

On Sunday, the 9th instant, departed this life at his residence in Baltimore County, Mr. Benjamin Banneker, a black man, and immediate descendent of an African father. He was well known in his neighborhood for his quiet and peaceful demeanor, and, among scientific men, as an astronomer and mathematician.

In early life he was instructed in the most common rules of arithmetic, and thereafter, with the assistance of different authors, he was enabled to acquire a perfect knowledge of all the higher branches of learning. Mr. Banneker was the calculator of several almanacs, published in this as well as several of the neighboring States; and, although of late years none of his almanacs have been published, yet he never failed to calculate one every year, and left them among his papers.

Preferring solitude to mixing with society, he devoted the greater part of his time to reading and contemplation, and to no book was he more attached than the Scriptures.

At his death, he bequeathed all his astronomical and philosophical books and papers to a friend.

Mr. Banneker is a prominent instance to prove that a descendant of Africa is susceptible of as great mental improvement and deep knowledge of the mysteries of nature as that of any other nation.

Forty years later, the Reverend Daniel Alexander Payne, pastor (later bishop) of the African Methodist Church, who had lauded Banneker as a model for the young men of his Baltimore parish, organized a committee to raise a fund for erecting a monument to his memory. He tried to find the grave. At Ellicott's Lower Mills an old-timer led him to the site of the family burying ground.

Beneath two tulip-trees, so grown as to seem one, lay the mortal remains of the black astronomer of Maryland. A few yards to the north-west of the grave was the site of his house, not a vestige of which could then be seen. It was marked only by a shallow cavity, at the southeastern end of which stood a tall Lombardy poplar, said to be that which overshadowed the gable end of his house. . . ."

CAPTAIN PAUL CUFFE

On March 14, 1780, seven freemen, "Chiefly of the African Extract," living in the seacoast town of Dartmouth, Massachusetts, sent a protest to the legislature in Boston [figure 58]. Their grievance had a familiar ring—taxation without representation!

By Reason of Long Bondag and hard Slavery we have been deprived of Injoying the Profits of our Labouer or the advantage of Inheriting Estates from our Parents as our Neighbouers the white peopel do . . . & yet . . . we have been & now are Taxed both in our Polls and that small Pittance of Estate which through much hard Labour & Industry we have got together to Sustain our selves. . . .

Not only does such taxation "Reduce us to a State of Beggary," they claimed but

we are not allowed the Privilege of freemen of the State having no vote or Influence in the Election of those that Tax us . . . we are not alowed in voating in the town meating . . . nur to chuse an oficer . . . & we have not an equal chance with the white people neither by Sea nur by Land. . . .

and the final irony:

yet many of our Colour (as is well known) have cheerfully Entered the field of Battle in the defence of the Common cause and that (as we conceive) against a similar Exertion of Power (in Regard to taxation) too well known to need a recital in this place.

One of the seven who signed, and probably wrote, the petition was twenty-one year old Paul Cuffe, destined to make his mark in the world as master mariner, merchant, shipbuilder, philanthropist, and African colonizer. Like the ship's compass [figure 59] he left behind, Captain Paul Cuffe's life had many points and directions.

59. Compass used by Captain Paul Cuffe. New Bedford Whaling Museum.

☞ Paul's father, Cuffe Slocum, was born in Africa, purchased his own liberty from his Dartmouth master, married a Wampanoag girl, Ruth Moses, in 1746, acquired a hardscrabble farm on Martha's Vineyard, and raised a family of ten children. The seventh was Paul, born in 1759 on the island of Cuttyhunk, nine miles off New Bedford. When he was nineteen, two years after the Declaration of Independence, he and his brothers discarded the slave name of Slocum and adopted the first name of their father.

A boy of thirteen at the time of his father's death, he scarcely knew the letters of the alphabet, but with the aid of a tutor he learned to read and write. From the start, salt was in his blood. He studied navigation and mastered the rudiments of "latitude, lead, and lookout." At sixteen, when the acres his father had willed him proved worthless, like many other lads,

To The Honourable Council and House
of Representatives in General Court assembled for
the State of the Massachusetts Bay in New
England ———— March 14th A.D. 1780 ———
The Petition of Several poor Negroes & molattors
who are Inhabitants of the Town of Dartmouth Humbly
sheweth —— That we being Chiefly of the African
Extract and by Reason of Long Bondage and hard Slavery we
have been deprived of Enjoying the Profits of our Labour or
the Advantage of Inheriting Estates from our Parents as
our Neighbours the white people do having some of us not
Long Enjoyed our own freedom yet of Late Contrary to the
invariable Custom & Practice of the Country we have been
& now are Taxed both in our Polls and that small Pittance
of Estate which through much hard Labour & Industry we have
got together to Sustain our selves & families withal —— We
Apprehend it therefore to be hard Usage and will doubtless;
if Continued will) Reduce us to a State of Beggary whereby we
shall become a Burthen to others If not timely prevented by the Interposition
of your Justice & power or your petitioners father sheweth that we
apprehend ourselves to be Aggrieved, in that while we are not
allowed the privilage of freemen of the State having no vote or
Influence in the Election of those that Tax us yet many of our Colour
(as is well known) have cheerfully Entered the field of Battle in the
defence of the Common Cause (and that / as we Conceive) against
a similar Exertion of power (in Regard to taxition)
too well Known to need a Recital in this place ———
that these the

58. "Petition of Paul Cuffe and several poor Negroes & mulattoes who are Inhabitants of the
Town of Dartmouth," Massachusetts to the general court, March 14, 1780.
Massachusetts Archives.

130

Most honourable Court / we Humbley Besecch
they to take this into Considenration and Set us
(would) a Side from Paying tax or taxes or Cauge us to Be
Cleaired: for we ever have Been a people that
was fair from all these thing Ever since
the days of our four fathers and therefore we
take it as a head ship that we should Be So
delt By now in these difficulty times for their
is not to [crossed out] more then five or six that hath
a cow in this town and therefore in our
distress we Send unto the thee most Honourable
Court for Releaf under the peaceableness of thee
people and the mercy of God that we may Be
Releaved for we are not alowed in voating
in the town meating in nur to Chuse a nofisers
neither their was not one Ever heard in the
active Court of the Jenerel asembley in nur [fus?]
We poor dispiyed miserable Black people & we
have not an Eqrual Chance with white people
Neither By Sea nur By land therefore we
take it as a head ship that poor old negeros
should Be Rated which have Been in Bondage Some
thirty some forty and Some fifty years and now Just
got their Liberty Some By going into the servise
and Some By going to Sea and others By good
fortan and also poor distressed mungrels which
have no larning and no land and also no stock
neither where to put their head But Some
shelter them Selves into an old rotten hut
which the dogs would not Lay in

therefore wee pray that thoe may give no offence
at all by no means But that thoe most Honourable
Court will take it into Consideration as if it were
their own Case for we think it as to be a heard
ship that we should Be assessed and not be a
Loved as we may Say to Eat Bread therefore we
Humbley Beg and pray thee to plead our Case for
us o with thy people o god that thoe who have the
Rule in their hands may Be mercyfull unto the
poor and needy give unto thoe who ask of the
on he that would Borrow of thee turn thou not away
Empty o god Be mercyfull unto the poor and
give unto thoe who give ought unto the poor therefore
we Return unto thee again most honourable Court
that thou wouldest Consider us in theſe difficult times
for we Send in now come unto the not falſe words
neither with lieing Lips there fore wee think
that we may Be clear from Being Called tories tho
some of our Colour hath Rebelled and Done
Wickedly how ever we think that their is more
of our Collour gone into the wars acording to
the number of them into the Reſpecktive
towns then any other nation here and here away
therefore We Most Humbley Request therefore that
you would take our Unhappy Case into your Serious
Consideration and in your wisdom and Power Grant us
Relief from Taxation while under our present diſtreſſed
Circumſtances and your poor Petioners as in duty bound
Shall Ever pray &c   John Cuffe
Dated at Darmouth the 10th   Adventur Child
of February 5780

1367

Paul Cuffe
Samuel   his
         + gray
         marke
Pero   his houseland
       + mark
Isero his Ruſsell
       + mark
Pero   Cuggſhell

black and red, he shipped as a hand on a whaler bound for the Gulf of Mexico. (In the century to follow, men of color, including a few in his own family, would play a big part in the American whale fishery—as seamen, mates, harpooners, and occasionally captains; a black ironworker of New Bedford, Lewis Temple, would revolutionize the technique of the whale hunt with his invention of the toggle harpoon.) His second voyage was to the West Indies. On the third, in 1776, he was captured by the British and spent three months in a New York prison.

He then settled down on the coast at nearby Westport, worked a farm, and for the next two years resumed his study of navigation. The war still raged and it was hazardous to go to sea. He could not wait. With an older brother, he built an open boat to trade with towns on the Connecticut shore. When rough seas and Tory pirates time and again thwarted his enterprise, he returned to the plow.

It was around this time that Paul and his brother John, with five others of "African Extract," would berate the elected worthies of the state house for violating Revolutionary doctrine. We petitioned "for relief from Taxation in the days of our distress," John noted. "But we received non." The Cuffe brothers persisted, and late in the year took their case to the court of general sessions in Bristol County. For three years they had refused to pay taxes. When the collectors arrived to seize their property, there was none. In December of 1780 the brothers found themselves in the common jail in Taunton, and from there they fought their case. During the following spring, putting the issue squarely before town meeting, they demanded a vote as to "whether all free Negroes and molattoes shall have the same Privileges . . . as the white People have Respecting Places of profit choosing of officers and the Like together with all other Privileges in all cases . . . or that we have Reliefe granted us Joyntly from Taxation. . . ." The Cuffes finally had to pay—but by forcing the issue they hastened the day when taxation without representation, for anybody, was declared unconstitutional in the Bay State.

Fighting for his people's rights, Paul Cuffe was at the same time planning a career as mariner-merchant. His struggle to carry a cargo to Nantucket showed his mettle. First, he built a deckless boat "from keel to gun-wale." Tory pirates captured it. He built another, borrowed money for a cargo, foiled the pirates in the night, hit a rock, had to limp back and refit. When he finally made Nantucket, he could not sell his goods. On the second try there was a bit of profit, but on his way home the pirates stole all but the boat and, for good measure, beat him up. A third trip was so well rewarded that he procured a craft of eighteen tons and took on a hand to help.

In 1784 Alice Pequit, a woman of the Wampanoags, like his mother, chose Paul Cuffe for her husband. The war was over, the sea safer. He rented a small house on the Westport River and in his new boat sailed to Saint George for a haul of codfish—and thus founded a thriving fishing industry in his neighborhood for years to come. This was a turning point for the black captain. There would be partnerships with his Indian brother-in-law, Michael Wainer, a seasoned seaman. The vessels would get bigger, the voyages better. A new 25-ton ship, the *Sunfish,* made two trips to the Straits of Bell Isle and Newfoundland, the profits invested in a 42-ton schooner, the *Mary.* When, in 1793, with a crew of ten black whalemen, the *Mary* cruised the Atlantic (and encountered some trouble from a few white whaleships), Captain Cuffe himself hurled the harpoon that accounted for two of the leviathans. Back home, laden with oil and bone, the *Mary* proceeded to Philadelphia to exchange its goods for hardware to build a new and larger vessel. In 1795, Cuffe launched the *Ranger,* a 69-ton schooner, sold two smaller boats to buy a cargo, and sailed to Norfolk. This was probably his initial visit to the south, where at firsthand he could view slavery as a flourishing institution. At Vienna, on the Nanticoke River, where the *Ranger* dropped anchor to buy Indian corn, his *Memoir* relates that

the people were filled with astonishment and alarm. A vessel owned and commanded by a black man, and manned with a crew of the same complexion, was unprecedented and surprising. The white inhabitants were struck with apprehensions of the injurious effects . . . on the minds of their slaves, suspecting that he wished secretly to kindle the spirit of rebellion, and excite a destructive revolt among them.

(To be sure, four years earlier the slaves had risen in San Domingue, and five years later Gabriel would rise up in Virginia.) A lynch-minded gang tried to stop him "from entering his vessel or remaining among them." Somehow, by smile and guile, he disarmed the suspicious, sold his cargo, and carried three thousand bushels of corn back to Westport. When, after a second trip south, the market on corn thinned out, he set his sails for the north to fetch gypsum from Maine to Delaware, this opening up another new line of trade.

In between voyages, he was rooting himself in the Westport community as a benefactor of the town. Westport had no school—he proposed to his neighbors that they establish one, but, tired of the squabbles that arose, he built the schoolhouse with his own money on his own land and donated it "freely . . . to the use of the public." His parents had always gone to Quaker Meeting, and so had he. In 1808, he became a formal member of the Friends, sent one of his sons to a Quaker school in Philadelphia, and later paid out of his own pocket for half the cost of building a new meetinghouse in Westport. To the end of his life, his manner of body and soul would remind one of Woolman and Benezet.

Things continued to prosper for the black Yankee trader. He acquired an interest in a bark of 162 tons, the *Hero,* which rounded the Cape of Good Hope, and he would later build the 268-ton *Alpha,* which, with a black crew of seven, sailed south to Wilmington and Savannah, thence across the ocean to Helsingør and Göteborg, returning to Philadelphia with passengers and freight. His last and favorite vessel, the *Traveller,* would carry him to Africa. Nearing the half-century mark, Captain Paul Cuffe was a merchant-mariner of substance: he owned one ship, two brigs, and several smaller vessels—a small fleet—as well as considerable property in houses and land.

If the narrative thus far has the sound of an early American success story with Captain Paul Cuffe cast in the role of an Afro-Indian Benjamin Franklin, let it be said that all of it was but prelude to the serious saga of his remaining years. How could this son of a freed slave take his ease in a society that shackled his people? A few blacks, by talent, toil, and luck might survive prejudice and statute to become men of property in the new Nation. But what of the rest—the slaves and poor freemen? Anger and despair gnawed at his heart. Once, in New York, after he was well-known, a white Methodist preacher asked him, "Do you understand English"? He replied that some of the language was difficult for him: "That many persons who profess being enlightened with the true light, yet had not seen the evil of one brother professor making merchandise of and holding his brother in bondage."

The "true light" that he worked out for his own people, born of a profound disillusionment with the unfulfilled pledges of the Revolution, was an exodus of free blacks to Africa. If whites (as they said) refused to liberate their slaves only because they feared masses of inferior and dangerous black freemen in their midst, then let these freemen, present and future, of their own free choice, depart from America for a better life in their once native Africa. Thereby, in time, a number of worthy aims might be achieved: accelerated manumission and the doom of slavery in America; independent and free black societies in Africa; the economic development of Africa; the abolition of the slave trade; the "civilizing" of Africa by anti-slavery black Christians. The last was crucial to the devout Quaker. "The travail of my soul," he would often say, "is that Africa's inhabitants may be favored with reformation." Although he did not reject the idea of an additional colony of blacks somewhere in the United States, in Cuffe's evangelical vision, the logic of black exodus seemed clear enough. For him it did not mean, as some would later charge, the abandonment of the slaves by their free brothers, nor the weeding out of potential organizers of black liberation. On the contrary, the colonization of Africa, conducted by blacks of religion and talent, was the precondition, in the long run, for the ultimate emancipation of the slaves. To this idea, with all his resources of spirit and wealth, he would single-mindedly dedicate the last decade of his life.

For Cuffe, to think was to act—the most immediate task was to discover a fruitful place in Africa to begin the historic process. In Philadelphia, he discussed the matter with James Pemberton. "Since thy last being in this city," the Quaker merchant wrote him in June 1808, "the remembrance of thee has so frequently occupied my mind as to excite an inclination to write to thee, and particularly of thy sympathy expressed with the poor afflicted Inhabitants of Africa." From London, Pemberton had news of an association for "promoting the civilizations of the people" of Africa, whose members had "raised a considerable sum of money to engage persons of sobriety and other necessary qualifications" to go to Sierra Leone to offer instruction "in the art of Agriculture and other employments." Among the members of the African Institution were Thomas Clarkson, William Wilberforce, and Granville Sharpe. He had also heard that Zachariah Macau-

135

lay, the late governor of the colony, had said "that if Captⁿ Cuffey should incline to make a voyage to Sierra Leone," he would be welcomed with open arms. By September, Pemberton was more insistent. Clarkson and the rest were "anxious to receive all the assistance and encouragement they can from the friends of humanity" in America: "Now if thy concern for the good of the poor untutored people continues and finds the mind impressed with a sense that any portion of the work is alloted for thee to perform, I hope and trust thou wilt give it thy most serious consideration." Cuffe's response was quick. Although he felt "very feebel and all most worn out in hard service and uncapable of doing much for my brethren of the African Race," if God was pleased to choose him as an instrument "for that service," he was ready and willing.

Cuffe had been speaking with Quaker modesty. By the spring of 1809, his plans for going to Africa were well under way. Since Pemberton was no longer alive, he sought help from two other merchant Friends in Philadelphia, John James and Alexander Wilson:

I have for some years had it impressed on my mind to make a voyage to Sierra Leon in order to inspect the situation of the country, and feeling a real desire that the inhabitants of Africa might become an enlightened people. . . . And as I am of the African race I feel myself interested for them and if I am favored with a talent I think I am willing that they should be benefited thereby.

Could a letter be dispatched to London to find out "in case I engage in the whale fishery whether I could have encouragement such as bounty, or to carry the productions of the country duty free to England"? He was eager to make the trip by the next fall with "several families of good credit that may like to go." A year went by. Impatient, he laid his plans for the voyage before a committee of Westport Friends, whose enthusiastic letter of endorsement stated that the black captain was worth £5,000 and was "highly respected" by the Friends of Philadelphia. Unable to wait any longer, he rented his farm and asked his brother to look after his family. Paul would be gone for a year or two, wrote John to their sister, Freelove, in New York, on a "religious visit amongst the inhabitants of that Land, our own nation."

In the fall of 1810, Captain Cuffe sailed the *Traveller* out of Westport bound for Sierra Leone with a crew of nine black seamen. In Philadelphia, he conferred with Friends at the Arch Street meetinghouse, but when John James urged him to carry a cargo of corn to Cádiz, he replied that "it was not for profit or gain" that he "had undertaken this voyage." Departing from Philadelphia on New Year's Day of 1811, fifty-two days later he would record in his journal, with a sense of history, that "The dust of Africa lodged on our riggings."

For three months, Cuffe took notes on the possibilities of Sierra Leone as the land of promise for the blacks of America. There were conferences with the governor on the economic state of the colony, the control of the slave trade, and problems of settlement. He looked at things for himself—visited a school of thirty girls, went to Methodist meetings, distributed

Bibles, recorded without further comment that the "Mendingo men have the Scriptures in their tongue, viz the old testament, but deny the new testament. They own Mahomet a prophet." The longest entries in his journal reflect his eagerness to meet the local chieftains.

King Thomas came on board to see me. He was an old man, gray headed, appeared to be sober and grave. I treated him with civility, and made him a present of a bible, a history of Elizabeth Webb, a Quaker, and a book of essays on War: together with several other small pamphlets accompanied with a letter of advise from myself . . . for the use and encouragement of the nations of Africa. He and retinue were thirteen in number. I served him with victuals . . . but it appeared that there was *rum* wanting, *but none was given.*

A few days later there was a visit to the "Bullion Shore" to visit King George, who had earlier brought a gift of three chickens and who now "treated us very cordially."

In mid-May, invited by Wilberforce, Cuffe headed the *Traveller* for Liverpool, carrying with him a young African whom he had "taken as an apprentice . . . to instruct in navigation." The pages of his English journal are pervaded by a sense of excitement and discovery. During a busy month, he took in the sights of London, Liverpool, and Manchester. "We went over London Bridge to Lancaster's School, where were taught one thousand scholars by one master . . . the greatest gratification that I met with." In Manchester he spent a day in the factories, marveling at a woman who spun 150 threads at a time "under gaslight extracted from sea coal." In Liverpool, on a tour of the "blind school," it was "wonderful to see the . . . spinning, weaving, matting, carpeting, of many colors." There was a visit to Parliament, conferences with Wilberforce, Clarkson, William Dillwyn, who gave him Clarkson's book on the slave trade, and William Allen, whom he told that he planned "to build a house in Sierra Leone." His conversation with William Roscoe, the famous historian and author of *The Wrongs of Africa*—"He being a very warm friend for the abolishing the slave trade, many subjects took place between us"—focused on a question that would shortly become crucial as war between England and America threatened the African project.

He stated the necessity, and propriety of condemning all nations, that might be found in the trade. I likewise was favored to state to him the necessity there was of keeping open a communication between America, Africa and England in order to assist Africa in its civilization . . . the two powers to countenance it even if they were at variance, and to consider it as a neutral path.

A high point was his meeting with members of the African Institution, who praised him for "maintaining the good cause," following which he presented to its president, the Duke of Gloucester, who was a nephew of the king, "an African robe, a letter box, and a dagger to show that the Africans were capable of mental endowment." (Cuffe's "simplicity and strong natural good sense made a great impression upon all parties," noted William Allen in his diary. He found himself a celebrity of a sort, and in October could read in the *Liverpool Mercury* that his efforts were "gratifying to humanity." "Who that justly appreciates human character," asked the editor, "would not prefer Paul Cuffee, the offspring of an African slave, to the proudest statesman that ever dealt out destruction amongst mankind?"

In November the *Traveller* sailed back to Africa and, for another three months, Cuffe investigated Sierra Leone for its economic potential. Waterpower was abundant. He noted thriving crops—pineapples, Indian corn, and buckwheat. The Guinea grass grew so tall he could barely reach the top with the tip of his umbrella. He distributed seeds and silkworm eggs, and arranged for the indenture of four African apprentices to return with him to Westport.

Back home in the spring of 1812, Cuffe was reminded once more of what it meant to be a black man in America. The *Traveller,* arriving in American waters at the beginning of the war, had been condemned by a revenue cutter for bringing in a British cargo. Cuffe journeyed to Washington to speak personally with the secretary of war and President Madison. The day after the president had ordered the release of the *Traveller,* the Captain started home. In the Baltimore coach, he took a seat—and ran into trouble. In came a blustering powder-headed man with stern countenance. "Come away from that seat." I . . . sat still. . . . He then said, "You must go out of this for there is a lady coming in." I entered into no discourse with him, but took my seat; he took his beside me but showed much evil contempt. . . . When I arrived in Baltimore they utterly refused to take me in at the tavern or to get me a dinner unless I would go back among the servants. This I refused, not as I thought myself better than the servants, but from the nature of the case. I found my way to a tavern where I got my dinner. One imagines him, at these moments, standing tall in his dignity. On the trip to the capital, from Providence to Washington men of stature, black and white, had been eager to listen to his words. It was about this time that an obscure artist drew the Captain's portrait in silhouette and sketched beneath it his good ship *Traveller,* the ark of colonization [figure 60]. "In his person," wrote a black friend, "Capt. Cuffe was large and well proportioned. His countenance was serious, but mild. His speech and habit, plain and unostentatious. His deportment, dignified and prepossessing; blending gravity with modesty and sweetness, and firmness with gentleness and humility."

For the moment, he seemed a bit tired. Had he done his proper share of the work in preparing the exodus to the promised land? Was it time for others to carry the torch? He had intimated to William Allen a plan to settle in Sierra Leone. Now he decided against it, although this meant no slackening in his zeal. "Paul Cuffee doth not at present go to Africa," he informed Allen, "but shall send such characters as confidence may be placed in. At present it is thought that I may be as serviceable towards the promotion of the colony, as though I was to remove. However, as my wife is not willing to go, I do not feel at liberty to urge, but feel in duty bound to escort myself to the uttermost of my ability for the good cause of Africa." His plan, in fact, was to make a trip to Sierra Leone once a year, transport-

PAUL

CAPTAIN

CUFFEE

1812.

ENGRAVED FOR ABRM. L. PENNOCK, BY MASON & MAAS.

60. Captain Paul Cuffe. Wood engraving by Mason and Maas after drawing by
John Pole, 1812. Library of Congress.

ing settlers and cargo, and returning with African products. But there were difficulties. The voyage of the *Traveller* had lost money; the *Alpha* had just returned with a huge deficit; an uninsured bark on a whaling voyage around Cape Horn had disappeared.

The war, of course, was the great obstacle. He was ready to send over plows, wagons, and a sawmill. His four apprentices were schooled and eager to return. The idea of a whale fishery off the African coast seemed more feasible than ever. People were clamoring to be taken to Sierra Leone. He was frantic to get going again. In June of 1813 he sent a memorial to Congress requesting a license for the voyage, but the House refused to permit any commerce with a colony of the enemy.

His spirit would not down. One wintry day in 1815, as soon as the war was over, with thirty-eight black emigrants and a cargo of goods that pioneers could use, Captain Cuffe steered the *Traveller* for Africa [figure 61]. Only eight of the future settlers could pay for their passage. He made little of it, although the trip would cost him a small fortune; "all this was done," he wrote "without fee or reward—my hope is in a coming day." Ashore, in Sierre Leone, he was not idle. With the governor he inspected schools, compiled data on captured slave ships for the Abolition Society in Philadelphia, assailed the license houses that trafficked in slaves, urged that houses be built on the farms of the settlers. In the spring, the *Traveller* returned to Westport.

It was his final trip to Africa, and he seemed to know it. But there was work yet to be done in America. He kept in close touch with the organizers of the African Institution in New York and Philadelphia, wrote frequently to the colonists he had carried over, experienced moments of despair when he felt that the seed he had planted in Africa might perish. When the American Colonization Society, among whose first officers were Henry Clay and Andrew Jackson, began to be active early in 1817, its chief organizers went to Cuffe for information and advice. He gave freely of his knowledge of Africa. Perhaps he never suspected that the chief aim of the Society, for many of its founders, was a greater security for the institution of slavery in the United States. Perhaps, knowing this, he thought that he might co-operate with certain elements of the Society to further his own grand plan of colonization as the road to general emancipation. It is difficult to know. He had only a short time to live, and others would have to take up the problem.

☛ Is there anything in the record to show that Captain Paul Cuffe, towards the end of his life, ever doubted the validity of his back-to-Africa idea? After his second voyage to Sierra Leone, he had boasted that two thousand pleas for passage to Africa had reached him from the city of Boston. But Boston was not America. In Richmond in January of 1817 "a respectable portion of the free people of color" would resolve that they preferred to be "colonized in the most remote corner of the land of our nativity, to being exiled" in Africa. It is possible that Cuffe never heard of

In Senate of the U.S.
Jany 10 1814

Mr Gore from the committee appointed on the subject reports the following bill which was read & passed to the 2° Reading

attest Sam A. Otis Sy

An Act to authorize the President of the United States to permit the Departure of Paul Cuffee, from the United States, with a Vessel & Cargo for Sierra Leona, in Africa, and to return with a Cargo.

Be it enacted, by the Senate and House of Representatives, of the United States of America, in Congress assembled, that the President of the United States be, and He is hereby authorized, under such Regulations and Restrictions, as He may prescribe, to permit Paul Cuffee, & his Associates to depart from the United States, with a Vessel, not exceeding two hundred Tons Burthen, and Cargo, ~~~~~~~~ for Sierra Leona in Africa, and to return to said United States, with a Cargo, the Produce of Africa, any Law to the contrary notwithstanding.

141

61. Congressional act authorizing Paul Cuffe to take cargo to Sierra Leone, January 10, 1814. National Archives.

the Virginia protest, but during that same month the post brought a letter from Philadelphia which must have shaken his confidence. "I must mention to you," wrote his friend, James Forten, "that the whole continent seems to be agitated concerning Colonising the People of Colour." When, during the previous month, the American Colonization Society had published its program, "the People of Colour here was very much fritened at first. They were afrade that all the free people would be Compelled to go, particularly in the southern States." There had been "a large meeting of Males at the Rev. R. Allens Church the other evening. Three thousand at least atended, and there was not one sole that was in favour of going to Africa. They think that the slave holders want to get rid of them so as to make their property more secure."

Indeed, Forten himself had chaired the meetings, and with Richard Allen and Absalom Jones had signed his name to the document that boldly affirmed—"we never will separate ourselves voluntarily from the slave population of the country; they are our brethren by the ties of consanguinity, of suffering, and of wrong." Although Forten had transmitted this repudiation of deportation to his congressman from Philadelphia, he was deeply troubled, for the way for him was no longer "strate and clear." While his unalterable opinion was that blacks would "never become a people until they com out from amongst the white people . . . as the majority is decidedly against me I am determined to remain silent. . . ." (Before the year was out he would denounce colonization as a weapon of the slavocracy and would persuade William Lloyd Garrison to do likewise.)

How did Cuffe react to Forten's shattering news? There is perhaps a hint of doubt in his advice to his brethren to wait a year before they came to final judgment on the issue. A few months later, in the spring, his health began to fail. Yet how sacred for him was the cause of Africa may be gauged by a curious letter he wrote during those last sick days to a black confidence man, who had masqueraded as his son and had fleeced the unwary from New Bedford to Albany.

The great evil that thou hast embarked upon is not only against me as an individual. It is a national concern. It is a stain to the whole community of the African race. Wilt thou consider, thou imposter, the great number thou hast lifted thy hand against. . . . Let me tell thee that the manumission of 1,500,000 slaves depends on the faithfulness of the few who have obtained their freedom, yea, it is not only those who are in bondage, but the whole community of the African race. . . .

Seven months later Captain Paul Cuffe was buried with honors in the Quaker cemetery of Westport. From the pulpit of the Zion Church in New York, his co-worker, the Reverend Peter Williams, Jr., delivered a discourse in praise of a great and saintly lover of his people, whose "thoughts ran deep" [figure 62]. If, in his peroration, the preacher departed cautiously from the text of his eulogy to make a plea of forbearance, he was no doubt trying to answer a question that burned in the minds of his black audience.

Oh! what honor to the son of an African slave, the most respectable men in Great Britain and America, were not ashamed to seek to him for counsel

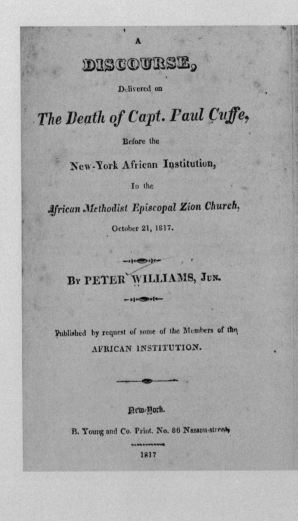

and advice. Moreover brethren, he was our friend. Let us not then hastily condemn a measure to which every fibre of his heart clung, and from which it could only be separated by the strong hand of death. . . .

The "measure" of which the preacher spoke was, of course, the colonization of Africa. "Let us suspend our judgments of it," he concluded, "until we see its further development. . . ." The injunction was prophetic. If it was the failure of the Revolutionary promise that stirred a segment of the black people to seek another way, there is a sense in which the standpoint first formulated by Captain Paul Cuffe—who saw himself as the champion of "the whole community of the African race"—has been a black thread running through American history to the present day.

143

JEAN BAPTISTE POINT DU SABLE

Benjamin Banneker and Paul Cuffe loom large and clear in the early annals of Afro-America. It is otherwise with Jean Baptiste Point du Sable. There is a mythic quality about this black pioneer who founded Chicago during the time of the Revolution. First of all, what was his real name—Sable, Saible, Sabre, Dessables? And what were his origins? Was he the son of a black maidservant and white master who had emigrated from Bourges to French Canada, or had he been born in Haiti, his parents a white planter and a free black woman?

Du Sable's name makes its first appearance in the historical record in the journal of the British commandant at Mackinaw, a New York Tory, one Colonel Arent Schuyler de Peyster, who, in an entry for July 4, 1779, describes him as "a handsome negro, (well educated and settled in Eschecagou) but much in the French interest." De Peyster tried to win him over to the royal cause. In August, Lieutenant Thomas Bennett of the King's Regiment wrote from St. Joseph's: "Baptiste Point au Sable I have taken into custody, he hopes to make his conduct to you spotless. . . ." Du Sable apparently had little interest in the issues of the war. He gave the lieutenant some information on the movements of hostile Indians. In September, Bennett reported to De Peyster that the Potowatomi were strongly disaffected. As for the black trader, he no longer distrusted him: "I had the Negro Baptiste point au Sable brought Prisoner from the River Du Chemin, Corporal Tascon who commanded the Party very prudently, prevented the Indians from burning his house, or doing him any injury, he secured his Packs &c which he takes with him from Michilimakinac, the Negro since his imprisonment has in every respect behaved with becoming a man in his situation, has many friends, who give him a good character." Du Sable was a big man in the area. In a "Speech to the Western Indians," which he later put into verse, De Peyster threatens a council of "Great Chiefs" that he has convened: they must become allies of the British

> Or, he will send them *tout au diable*,
>
> As he did Baptist *Point de Saible*.

Du Sable did not long remain a prisoner. During the summer of 1780, a delegation of Indians from a settlement of the British on the St. Clair River south of Port Huron demanded that the governor of the territory, Patrick Sinclair, oust their French overseer and appoint du Sable to replace him. Sinclair ordered his immediate release from the stockade and sent him in a sloop to take over the job.

The war over, du Sable hastened back to Chicago, where, years before, he had built a trading post and a house—the first in the city. The house was no rude hut. Perched on the north bank of the Chicago River, it measured forty feet long by twenty-two feet wide and was more than com-

144

63. Bill of sale of Jean Baptiste Point du Sable's Chicago property, May 1800.
Original unlocated; photograph courtesy *Ebony* Magazine

fortably furnished. There were four tables and seven chairs, a French wal-
nut cabinet with four glass doors, a bureau, a couch, a stove, a large feather-
bed; mirrors, lanterns, candlesticks, and, at one time, twenty-three pictures.
In addition to the house, there were two barns, a dairy, a mill, a bakehouse,
a poultry house, a workshop, as well as forty-four hens, thirty-eight hogs,
thirty head of cattle, two calves, and two mules. And tools: eight axes, eight
sickles, seven scythes, a variety of saws, a plow.

Du Sable and an Indian woman named Catherine had lived together
with their children for some time, and in 1788 a parish priest at Cahokia
officially made them man and wife. Their daughter, Suzanne, married a
Catholic. Their son, Jean Baptiste, Jr., left home and settled at Saint
Charles in Missouri.

Du Sable was general merchant, fur trader, farmer, and man of affairs in
the frontier community he had fashioned in the wilderness. He even owned
property elsewhere; in 1773 he had purchased thirty acres and a house in
Peoria, and eighteen years later received a grant of another four hundred
acres from the government. A visitor from Wisconsin who was in Chicago
about 1794 later recalled that he "was a large man; that he had a commission for some office, but for what particular object, or from what Government, I can not now recollect; he was a trader, pretty wealthy, and drank
freely."

Suddenly, in 1800, du Sable sold everything he owned in Chicago to a
white trader for twelve hundred dollars [figure 63]. Why? People invented

all sorts of reasons. One story was that before he had settled on the banks of the Chicago River, he had lived among the Peorias with a friend named Glamorgan, a brother San Domingan, who held vast Spanish land grants near Saint Louis; he now planned to return to Glamorgan and the Peorias to spend his last days. Another story, he had always aspired to become chief of the Potawatomis; now he joined them, but they denied him the headship.

The documents are more prosaic. From Chicago, he went to Saint Charles to live with his son. They owned property together in the city and county. His wife was dead. His son died in 1814. He went to live with his granddaughter, to whom he gave his house in Saint Charles on condition that she take care of him in his old age—she did not—and bury him in the Catholic cemetery of the town. Sixteen months later he had to apply for relief as a pauper, and after this he did not last long.

These are the bare facts with a bit of lore about the black frontiersman, Jean Baptiste Point du Sable. There is a tradition that the Potawatomis, who were there when he arrived, used to say: "The first white man to settle in Chicago was a Negro."

DR. JAMES DERHAM AND THOMAS FULLER

Back east in Philadelphia, a year after the ratification of the Constitution, the Abolition Society received a request from London to send over "accounts of mental improvement, in any of the blacks . . . in order the better . . . to contradict those who assert, that the intellectual faculties of the negroes are not capable of improvement equal to the rest of mankind." The redoubtable Dr. Benjamin Rush, friend of Richard Allen, Absalom Jones, and Benjamin Banneker, responded at once, supplying biographies of two extraordinary black men. One was a young New Orleans physician, Dr. James Derham, an ex-slave. "I expected to have suggested some new medicines to him;" remarked Dr. Rush after their first meeting, "but he suggested many more to me." The other was an aged "African slave, living in Virginia," one Thomas Fuller. "This man possesses a talent for arithmetical calculation"; thought Dr. Rush, "the history of which, I conceive, merits a place in the records of the human mind." The biographies of Derham and Fuller, subsequently published in the *American Museum* for January 1789, are the only existing sources for the lives of these gifted men, and they are here reprinted, since paraphrase would inevitably diminish the vigor of Rush's language.

There is now in this city [Philadelphia], a black man, of the name of James Derham, a practitioner of physic, belonging to the Spanish settlement of New Orleans, on the Mississippi. This man was born in a family in this city, in which he was taught to read and write, and instructed in the principles of christianity. When a boy, he was transferred by his master to the late dr. John Kearsly, jun. of this city, who employed him occasionally to compound medicines, and to perform some of the more humble acts of attention to his patients.

Upon the death of dr. Kearsley, he became (after passing through several hands) the property of dr. George West, surgeon to the sixteenth British regiment, under whom, during the late war in America, he performed many of the menial duties of our profession. At the close of the war, he was sold by dr. West to dr. Robert Dove, of New Orleans, who employed him as an assistant in his business: in which capacity he gained so much of his confidence and friendship, that he consented to liberate him, after two or three years, upon easy terms. From dr. Derham's numerous opportunities of improving in medicine, he became so well acquainted with the healing art, as to commence practitioner at New Orleans, under the patronage of his last master. He is now about twenty-six years of age, has a wife, but no children, and does business to the amount of three thousand dollars a year.

I have conversed with him upon most of the acute and epidemic diseases of the country where he lives, and was pleased to find him perfectly acquainted with the modern simple mode of practice in those diseases. . . . He is very modest and engaging in his manners. He speaks French fluently, and has some knowledge of the Spanish language. By some accident, although born in a religious family, belonging to the church of England, he was not baptised in his infancy; in consequence of which he applied, a few days ago, to bishop White, to be received by that ordinance into the episcopal church. The bishop found him qualified, both by knowledge and moral conduct, to be admitted to baptism, and this day performed the ceremony, in one of the churches in this city.

There is now living, about four miles from Alexandria, in the state of Virginia, a negro slave of seventy years old, of the name of Thomas Fuller, the property of mrs. Elizabeth Coxe. . . .   He is a native of Africa, and can neither read nor write. Two gentlemen, natives of Pennsylvania, viz. William Harthorne and Samuel Coates, men of probity and respectable characters, having heard, in travelling through the neighborhood in which this slave lived, of his extraordinary powers in arithmetic, sent for him, and had their curiosity sufficiently gratified by the answers which he gave to the following questions.

First. Upon being asked, how many seconds there are in a year and a half, he answered in about two minutes, 47,304,000.

Second. On being asked, how many seconds a man has lived, who is seventy years, seventeen days and twelve hours old, he answered in a minute and a half, 2,210,500,800.

One of the gentlemen, who employed himself with his pen in making these calculations, told him he was wrong, and that the sum was not so great as he had said—upon which the old man hastily replied, 'top, massa, you forget de leap year.' On adding the seconds of the leap years to the others, the amount of the whole in both their sums agreed exactly.

Third. The following question was then proposed to him: suppose a farmer has six sows, and each sow has six female pigs, the first year, and they all increase in the same proportion, to the end of eight years, how many sows will the farmer then have? In ten minutes, he answered, 34,588,-806. The difference of time between his answering this, and the two former questions, was occasioned by a trifling mistake he made from a misapprehension of the question.

In the presence of Thomas Wistar and Benjamin W. Morris, two respectable citizens of Philadelphia, he gave the amount of nine figures multiplied by nine. . . .

At the time he gave this account of himself, he said his memory began to fail him—he was grey-headed, and exhibited several other marks of the weakness of old age—he had worked hard upon a farm during the whole of his life, but had never been intemperate in the use of spiritous liquors. He spoke with great respect of his mistress, and mentioned in a particular manner his obligations to her for refusing to sell him, which she had been tempted to do by offers of large sums of money, from several curious persons.

One of the gentlemen (mr. Coates) having remarked in his presence, that it was pity he had not had an education equal to his genius; he said, "no massa—it is best I got no learning; for many learned men be great fools."

64. Obituary of Tom Fuller. *Columbia Centinel*, December 29, 1790. Library of Congress.

PHILLIS WHEATLEY

"I doubt not God is good, well-meaning, kind," muses Countee Cullen in the opening line of the great sonnet that ends with a couplet of doubt.

> Yet do I marvel at this curious thing:
> To make a poet black, and bid him sing.

It was so from the beginning in America. The first black poets who sang in print during the time of the Revolution, Phillis Wheatley and Jupiter Hammon, lucky to have humane masters, thanked God for snatching them from heathen Africa and never doubted that He would free the virtuous slave in heaven. Yet, here and there, the anguish that Cullen knew so well breaks through the facade of their comforting piety. Given the time and the place, it is no small miracle that in their finest passages these gifted slaves, even in a muffled way, could speak out as blacks in charged, poetic lines.

It has often been noted that Phillis Wheatley—"*Afric's* muse," as she called herself in her "Hymn to Humanity"—was the first black, the first slave, and the second woman to publish a book of poems in the United States. The editor of the recent edition of her complete works is of the opinion that

Her poems are certainly as good as or better than those of most of the poets usually included and afforded fair treatment in a discussion of American poetry before 1800.

Add to all this, that she was probably the first truly American poet in our literary history, for in some of the best passages of Boston's "Ethiopian poetess" her strong and graceful line plucked a uniquely American chord— what it meant to be black in white Revolutionary America. (Were the poems of Anne Bradstreet and Edward Taylor written in New or Old England? It is hard to tell.) And, of course, there is the unparalleled tale of her short, radiant life, of her early flowering genius.

Phillis first saw the light in Africa, Senegal perhaps. She liked to recall that her mother "poured out water before the sun at his rising" and in one of her major poems she would mourn with Niobe for her lost children. Seven years later, in the year 1761, she was put up for sale in a Boston slave market. Susannah, the wife of John Wheatley, a prosperous tailor, wanted a black girl to train as a domestic, although the Wheatleys already owned several household slaves. There, on the block, was this African child, "of a slender frame, and evidently suffering from a change of climate," naked except for a piece of dirty carpet. She was shedding her front teeth. Phillis quickly became a favorite. "She was not devoted to menial occupations, as was at first intended"; wrote her first biographer in 1834, "nor was she allowed to associate with the other domestics of the family, who were of her own color and condition, but was kept constantly about the person of her mistress." It is related that

her anxious mistress, fearful of the effects of cold and damp upon her already delicate health, ordered Prince (also an African and a slave) to take the chaise, and bring home her *protegee*. When the chaise returned, the good lady drew near the window, as it approached the house, and exclaimed—'Do but look at the saucy varlet—if he has'nt the impudence to sit upon the same seat with my Phillis!'

It is almost incredible that, as time went on, in the face of this tender assault on her African identity, the child could think of herself as a black among blacks.

The Wheatleys quickly discovered that they had purchased a prodigy. Susannah's daughter, Mary, found her an apt student of theology and literature. "Without any assistance from school education, and by only what she was taught in the family," wrote her master, "she, in sixteen months' time from her arrival, attained the English language . . . to such a degree as to read any, the most difficult parts of the Sacred Writings, to the great astonishment of all who heard her." She was eager to write—"her own curiosity led her to it"—and she tried the alphabet on the wall with chalk or charcoal. All "this she learned in so short a time, that in the year 1765 she wrote a letter" to the Reverend Samson Occom, the Indian minister, who, something of a poet himself, would later publish a hymnal for his people.

In 1767, when she was fourteen, she wrote her first poem, "To the University of Cambridge," thirty-two competent lines of blank verse which admonished unruly college boys to shun sin and follow Christ [figure 65]. The first stanza set a pattern for the next dozen years:

> While an intrinsic ardor bids me write
> The muse doth promise to assist my pen.
> 'Twas but e'en now I left my native shore
> The sable Land of error's darkest night.
> There, sacred Nine! for you no place was found.
> Parent of mercy, 'twas thy Powerful hand
> Brought me in safety from the dark abode.

The evidence is clear that the Wheatleys had done a good missionary job on the child—for her, Africa is a pagan inferno, and she is well out of it, thankful to be a slave in a good Christian household. Her final counsel to the students at Harvard is to avoid all "hateful vice":

> Suppress the sable monster in its growth,
> Ye blooming plants of human race, divine.
> An Ethiop tells you, tis your greatest foe,
> Its transient sweetness turns to endless pain,
> And brings eternal ruin on the Soul.

("An Ethiop tells you"—is it significant that six years later, when she revised the poem for the press, "The sable Land of error's darkest night" became

151

65. "To the University of Cambridge." Phillis Wheatley, 1767. American Antiquarian Society.

To the University of Cambridge   wrote in 1767

While an intrinsic ardor bids me write
The muse doth promise to assist my pen.
'Twas but e'er now I left my native Shore
The sable Land of errors darkest night
There, sacred Nine! for you no place was found.
Parent of mercy, 'twas thy Powerfull hand
Brought me in safty from the Dark abode.
To you, Bright youths! he points the height of Heav'n
To you, the knowledge of the depths profound.
Above, contemplate the ethereal space
And glorious Systems of revolving worlds.

Still more, ye Sons of Science! you've reciev'd
The pleasing Sound by messengers from heav'n,
The Saviours blood, for your Redemption flows.
See him, with hands stretch'd out upon the cross!
Divine compassion in his bosom glows.
He hears revilers with oblique regard
What Condescention in the Son of God!
When the whole human race, by Sin had fall'n;
He deign'd to Die, that they might rise again,
To live with him beyond the Starry Sky
Life without death, and Glory without End.—

Improve your privileges while they stay.
Caress, redeem each moment, which with haste
Bears on its rapid wing Eternal bliss.
Let hateful vice so baneful to the Soul,
Be still avoided with becoming care;
Suppress the sable monster in its growth,
Ye blooming plants of human race, divine
An Ethiop tells you, 'tis your greatest foe

Its transient sweetness turns to endless pain
And drags eternal ruin on the Soul.

" the land of errors, and *Egyptian* gloom," while "the sable monster" changed into "the deadly serpent"?)

The muse kept her promise to Phillis and during the next two years there were at least three more poems, the first a salute to King George, who was promised God's blessing if he cherished the liberty of the people—

> And may each clime with equal gladness see
> A monarch's smile can set his subjects free!

The second, an elegy on the death of her revered pastor, the Reverend Doctor Joseph Sewall of the Old South Church (whose father, the witch-trial judge, had written New England's first anti-slavery tract, *The Selling of Joseph*) was the first in a succession of occasional poems hailing or lamenting the births and deaths of Boston's elite. The third "On Being Brought from Africa to America," is worth reprinting here in full, for it is the first attempt of the young black poet to struggle for a position.

> 'Twas mercy brought me from my *Pagan* land,
> Taught my benighted soul to understand
> That there's a God, that there's a *Saviour* too:
> Once I redemption neither sought nor knew.
> Some view our sable race with scornful eye,
> "Their colour is a diabolic die."
> Remember, *Christians, Negroes,* black as *Cain,*
> May be refin'd, and join th' angelic train.

A black voice in the Christian white wilderness cries out in these lines. After all the obvious comments are duly made—she rejects her heritage, she accepts the myth of Cain, she expects her soul to be whitewashed in heaven —there is so much undiminished spirit in this little poem, it is the final proud image of the outraged girl asserting "our sable race" against their "scornful eye" that is rightfully stored in the mind.

No doubt, after she wrote out these early poems in her own pleasing hand, they circulated in manuscript beyond the family circle of the Wheatleys. Her name spread. When the Reverend George Whitefield breathed his last at Newburyport in September 1770, the *Massachusetts Spy* advertised for sale *An Elegiac Poem, On the Death of that celebrated Divine . . . By PHILLIS, a Servant girl of 17 years of Age, Belonging to Mr. J. WHEATLEY . . . but 9 Years in this Country from Africa* [figure 66]. To many blacks, Whitefield, although he did not preach abolition, was a crusading friend who spoke of a savior equally available to black and white. Thus, Phillis:

> Take him [Christ] my dear *Americans,* he said,
> Be your complaints on his kind bosom laid:
> Take him, ye *Africans,* he longs for you,
> *Impartial Saviour* is his title due:
> Wash'd in the fountain of redeeming blood,
> You shall be sons, and kings, and priests to God.

The broadside on Whitefield was Phillis's first published poem and launched her quickly into transatlantic fame. Reprinted almost immedi-

66. "An Elegiac Poem on the Death of . . .
George Whitefield." Phillis Wheatley, 1770.
Library Company of Philadelphia.

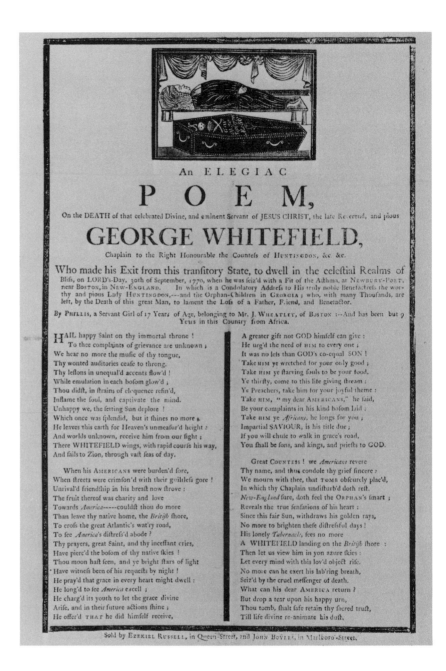

ately in Boston, Newport, New York, and Philadelphia, it found its way to
England the following year in Pemberton's *Heaven the Residence of Saints*.

She was becoming a person of eminence in the literary capital of the colonies, and she was pleased when she read in Dr. Benjamin Rush's *Address upon Slave-Keeping* that in Boston there was a "Negro Girl about 18 years of age, who has been but 9 years in the country, whose singular genius and accomplishments are such as not only do honor to her sex, but to human nature." People lent her books. Ministers, merchants, and scholars—"the most respectable Characters" of the town—visited and talked with her, read her poems. Eighteen of them later attested:

We whose Names are under-written, do assure the World, that the POEMS . . . were (as we verily believe) written by *Phillis,* a young Negro Girl, who was but a few Years since, brought an uncultivated Barbarian from *Africa,* and has ever since been, and now is, under the Disadvantage of serving as a Slave in a Family in this Town. She has been examined by some of the best Judges, and is thought qualified to write them [figure 67].

Among the judges were a royal governor, Thomas Hutchinson, as well as two governors of the Revolutionary future, James Bowdoin and John Hancock; the Reverend Charles Chauncey, pastor of the First Church, a Unitarian who rejected Whitefield's emotional style; Mathew Byles, poet and wit; and the Reverend Samuel Mather, son of Cotton. It was about this time that she became a baptized communicant and worshipped at the Old South Meeting House. "Whenever she was invited to the houses of individuals of wealth and distinction, (which frequently happened)," recalled a grandniece of Susannah Wheatley, "she always declined the seat offered her at their board, and, requesting that a side-table might be laid for her, dined modestly apart from the rest of the company." (Benjamin Banneker would do likewise in Georgetown. In either case, was it modesty or a complex pride that prompted the action?) A legend attached to the genesis of her first poem to be published in a magazine adds a detail to the scene. This "young *Negro woman* . . . a compleat sempstress, an accomplished mistress of her pen . . . a most surprising genius," a reader informs the editor of *The London Magazine* for March 1772, "being in company with some young ladies of family, when one of them said she did not remember, among all the poetical pieces she had seen, ever to have met with a poem upon RECOLLECTION, the *African* . . . took the hint," returned to her master's house, and invoking the muse—

> Mnme, begin; inspire, ye sacred Nine!
> Your vent'rous *Afric* in the deep design.

—the next day sent to the suggestor the elegant tour de force in Popean couplets called "Recollection."

That winter had been unkind to her and in the spring she was still "in a very poor state of health." The trouble was asthma and the Wheatleys packed her off to the country "for the benefit of its more wholesome air," although she returned to the city "to spend the Sabbath" with the family. Her illness did not keep her from her desk. To her friend, Obour Tanner, a young black woman living in Newport, Rhode Island, she wrote of her "great pleasure to hear of so many of my nation, seeking with eagerness the way of true felicity." She studied hard and went on with her reading in literature, sacred and profane. "She has a great Inclination to learn the Latin Tongue," John Wheatley noted, "and has made some Progress in it."

67. "To the Public." From *Poems on Various Subjects* by Phillis Wheatley, London, 1773. Library of Congress.

In her precocious advice to the students at Harvard, she had in fact revealed her own hunger for learning.

> Students, to you 'tis giv'n to scan the heights
> Above, to traverse the ethereal space,
> And mark the systems of revolving worlds. . . .
> Improve your privileges while they stay,
> Ye pupils, and each hour redeem. . . .

So, under Mary's tutelage and with the help of friends, she set herself the task of acquiring what amounted to a Harvard education, classical and neoclassical. She read voraciously—Christian scripture, ancient history and mythology, the classics (especially Virgil, Ovid, and Horace), Milton, Pope (she loved his translation of Homer and used his meter and rhyme in most of her verse), Gray, Addison, and Isaac Watts. She picked up as much as she could of geography and astronomy. All was grist for her poetic mill—sources of image, theme, and style in her varied work. And as she read, the couplets flowed. The story has come down that her "kind mistress indulged her with a light, and in the cold season with a fire, in her apartment during the night. The light was placed upon a table at her bed-side, with writing materials, that if anything occurred to her after she had retired, she might, without rising or taking cold, secure the swift-winged fancy, ere it fled."

Growing up in Boston during the decade that began with the martyrdom of Attucks, she followed political events with the zeal of an incipient patriot who "worshipped at Freedom's shrine." David was the hero and Goliath the villain of her longest poem. In August of 1772, the Earl of Dartmouth was appointed secretary of state for the colonies. As soon as the news arrived in Boston, the ailing black poet seized on the event—for Dartmouth had been Whitefield's friend and was close to the anti-slavery Countess of Huntingdon—as a good omen for the end of British tyranny in America.

> Hail, happy day, when, smiling like the morn,
> Fair *Freedom* rose *New-England* to adorn.

Thus she saluted Dartmouth in her opening lines, and went on:

> No more *America,* in mournful strain
> Of wrongs, and grievance unredress'd complain,
> No longer shall thou dread the iron chain,
> Which wanton *Tyranny* with lawless hand
> Had made, and with it meant t'enslave the land.

Her three key words here are *"America," "Tyranny,"* and "t' enslave," and they lead strategically to the next stanza—as splendid a statement of one facet of the black patriot position, three years before Bunker Hill, as can be found in the literature of the time.

> Should you, my lord, while you peruse my song,
> Wonder from whence my love of *Freedom* sprung,
> Whence flow these wishes for the common good,
> By feeling hearts alone best understood,
> I, young in life, by seeming cruel fate
> Was snatch'd from *Afric's* fancy'd happy seat:

What pangs excruciating must molest,
What sorrows labour in my parent's breast?
Steel'd was that soul and by no misery mov'd
That from a father seiz'd his babe belov'd:

Where, in these lines, is the notion of an earlier poem—"'Twas mercy brought me from my *Pagan* land"? And there is a new, independent note in the stanza's final couplet:

Such, such my case. And can I then but pray
Others may never feel tyrannic sway?

It was about this time, in the summer of 1772, that the idea of gathering her verse into a book first entered Phillis's mind. The manuscript was a sheaf of almost forty poems, some already in print, others known to a circle of friends and admirers. All that was needed was a poem to head the list— an ode of aspiration, in which she might implore the Muses to let her join the epic company, and at the same time an ode of identity, in which she might define herself and her world. "To Maecenas," the piece that would begin the book, is, of course, her grateful nod to the generous Wheatleys, but it is also a bold, initial statement of the blackness of the poet. After Homer and Virgil,

The happier *Terence** all the choir inspir'd,
His soul replenish'd, and his bosom fir'd;
But say, ye *Muses,* why this partial grace,
To one alone of *Afric's* sable race;
From age to age transmitting thus his name
With the first glory in the rolls of fame?

It was Phillis who placed the asterisk after the name of Terence to make sure the reader got the point—her footnote read: "*He was an African by birth."

In November, with a covering letter containing a few biographical notes, John Wheatley dispatched the manuscript to Archibald Bell, the London bookseller. News came from a London friend early in January. Bell had "waited upon the Countess of Huntingdon with the poems, who was greatly pleas'd with them, and pray'd him to read them; and often would break in upon him, and say, 'Is not this, or that, very fine? Do read another,' and question'd him much, whether she was *real*, without a deception?" Moreover, the Countess was "fond of having the book dedicated to her; but one thing she desir'd . . . to have Phillis' picture in the frontispiece. So that if you would get it done, it can be engraved here." The excitement in the Wheatley house must have been intense. A "deception"? There were eighteen Boston worthies who had signed a testimonial that she was indeed *"real."* The dedication to the anti-slavery Countess would be a distinct pleasure. The picture? Phillis had a friend who would do the job. One of those worthies, the Reverend John Moorhead, pastor of the Church of the Presbyterian Strangers, owned a slave who not only turned out verse himself, but also painted pictures. Scipio Moorhead's portrait of Phillis, quill in hand, demure, definite, and thoughtful, found the next ship out of Boston harbor, to be engraved in London as a frontispiece to the *Poems* [figure 68]. Susannah Wheatley said it was a fine likeness. What happened to Scipio's original, we do not know. (Could it have been one of the "fifty elegant Portrait Paintings [drawn from life]," titled "Phillis Wheatley, the celebrated African Poetess of Boston," noticed for sale in the *Columbian Gazeteer* ten years after her death?) What remains is Phillis's tribute "To S.M. A Young African Painter, On Seeing His Works" [figure 69]:

> To show the lab'ring bosom's deep intent,
> And thought in living characters to paint,
> When first thy pencil did those beauties give,
> And breathing figures learnt from thee to live,
> How did those prespects give my soul delight,
> A new creation rushing on my sight?
> Still, wond'rous youth! each noble path pursue,
> On deathless glories fix thine ardent view:
> Still may the painter's and the poet's fire
> To aid thy pencil, and thy verse conspire!

She waited eagerly for the book. But as her health continued to fail, the family doctor advised a voyage—the sea air might be good for her lungs. Why not send her to London, thought the Wheatleys, with their son, Nathaniel, who had already planned a business trip, where she might be on hand the day the volume came off the press? In May, she wrote her "Farewel to America" and in June was on the high seas.

London, for Phillis Wheatley, whose fame had preceded her, was, in a small way, a triumphal progress. The Countess of Huntingdon, who a decade later would sponsor the black preacher, John Marrant, introduced her to the reform-minded society of the day, where her conversational acuteness won her new friends. In July, Brook Watson, later a Lord Mayor of London, gave her a fine edition of *Paradise Lost,* which the Earl of Dartmouth matched with Smollet's new translation of *Don Quixote.* That same month Benjamin Franklin called, reporting to his cousin, Jonathan Williams, "Upon your recommendation I went to see the black poetess and offered her any services I could do her." (A few years later, she would dedicate to Franklin her second, never-to-be printed volume of poems and letters.) Her English friends pressed her to stay on in London for presentation at St. James to George III, but at the end of summer, Susannah Wheatley, ill in Boston, asked her to return.

Most important of all, as she was crossing the Atlantic her book of *Poems on Various Subjects, Religious and Moral* was being sought in London bookshops. By October she was back in Boston, writing to Obour Tanner that England had been a great experience: "The friends I found there among the nobility and gentry, their benevolent conduct toward me, the unexpected civility and complaisance with which I was treated by all, fills me with astonishment. I can scarcely realize it." Would Obour solicit subscriptions in Newport for her *Poems?* In January, the books arrived from London and were placed on sale on King Street, each volume, as the *Boston*

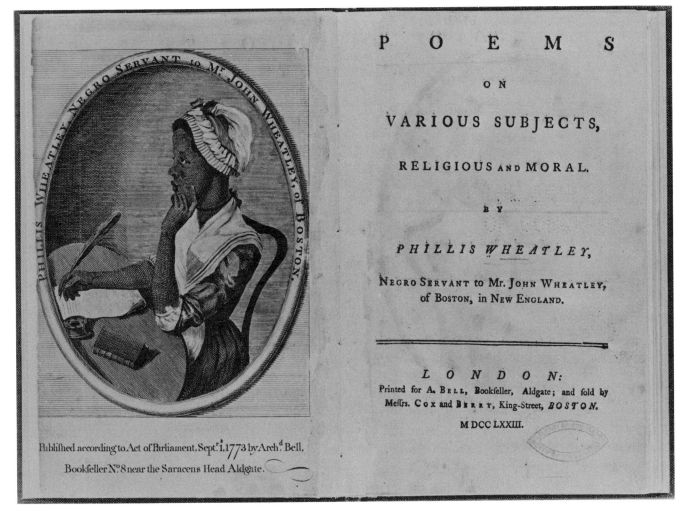

68 Phillis Wheatley. Frontispiece engraving after Scipio Moorhead and title page of
Poems on Various Subjects, Religious and Moral, London, 1773. Library of Congress.

Gazette put it, "Adorn'd with an Elegant Engraving of the Author." She
lost no time in posting seventeen copies to the Reverend Samuel Hopkins,
the disciple of Jonathan Edwards, who preached New Divinity and the
emancipation of the slaves in the First Church of Newport, at the same time
applauding his plan of helping "two negro men, who are desirous of returning to their native country to preach the Gospel." She hoped that the
prophecy of the psalmist was "now on the point of being accomplished,
namely, Ethiopia shall now stretch forth her hands unto God." More certain was the fact that a goodly number of readers, both white and black,
would stretch forth their hands towards the Ethiopian poetess of Boston.

159

69. "To S. M. [Scipio Moorhead], a young African
Painter . . ." from *Poems on Various Subjects* by
Phillis Wheatley, London, 1773. Library of Congress

To S. M. a young *African* Painter, on seeing
his Works.

TO show the lab'ring bosom's deep intent,
 And thought in living characters to paint,
When first thy pencil did those beauties give,
And, breathing figures learnt from thee to live,
How did those prospects give my soul delight,   5
A new creation rushing on my sight?
Still, wond'rous youth! each noble path pursue,
On deathless glories fix thine ardent view.
Still may the painter's and the poet's fire
To aid thy pencil, and thy verse conspire.   10
And may the charms of each seraphic theme
Conduct thy footsteps to immortal fame!
High to the blissful wonders of the skies
Elate thy soul, and raise thy wishful eyes.
Thrice happy, when exalted to survey   15
That splendid city, crown'd with endless day,
Whose twice six gates on radiant hinges ring:
Celestial *Salem* blooms in endless spring.

 Calm and serene thy moments glide along,
And may the muse inspire each future song!   20
Still, with the sweets of contemplation bless'd,
May peace with balmy wings your soul invest!

But when these shades of time are chas'd away,
And darkness ends in everlasting day,
On what seraphic pinions shall we move,   25
And view the landscapes in the realms above?
There shall thy tongue in heav'nly murmurs flow,
And there my muse with heav'nly transport glow:
No more to tell of *Damon's* tender sighs,
Or rising radiance of *Aurora's* eyes,   30
For nobler themes demand a nobler strain,
And purer language on th' ethereal plain.
Cease, gentle muse! the solemn gloom of night
Now seals the fair creation from my sight.

160

70. Letter from John Paul Jones to Hector McNeill concerning "the Celebrated Phillis" Wheatley. Not dated. The Pierpont Morgan Library.

Although the *London Magazine* denied her the "astonishing power of genius," it printed her "Hymn to the Morning" in "admiration of talents so vigorous and lively," and the *Poems* would be twice republished in England before the century was out. In America, during the next thirty years, at least seven editions would make her name and face familiar in Pennsylvania, New York, Connecticut, and New Hampshire.

In March of 1774, when Phillis was twenty-one, her beloved Susannah Wheatley died. She had been a mother and a friend rather than a mistress, as Phillis explained to Obour, and her departure signaled a new epoch in the poet's life. Whether she stayed on in the Wheatley home is not clear. What is certain is that her muse did not desert her after the publication of the book. A few months after her return from London, there is another broadside for sale in Boston, an elegy on the death of the artist Scipio's master, the Reverend John Moorhead. In May, she informs Obour that three hundred copies of the *Poems,* possibly the second London edition, have just come off the ship. In the *Royal American Magazine* of Boston for December there is a poem (and a reply) addressed "To Lieut R— of the Royal Navy" by *"Phillis, (a young* Affrican, *of surprising genius),"* with a Swiftian note by the editor that anticipates the answers that Jefferson would receive a decade later.

By this single instance may be seen, the importance of education. — Uncultivated nature is much the same in every part of the globe. It is probable

Europe *and* Affrica *would be alike* savage *or polite in the same circum-stances; though, it may be questioned, whether men who have no* artificial *wants, are capable of becoming so ferocious as those, who, by faring* sump-tuously every day, *are reduced to a habit of thinking it necessary to* their *happiness, to plunder the whole human race.*

There is some sentimental persiflage in the exchange between Phillis and the officer. "Paris, for Helen's bright resistless charms," she sings, "Made Illion bleed and set the world in arms," and in his "Answer" he replies to the "lovely virgin's praise" — "Behold with reverence, and with joy adore; The Lovely daughter of the Affric shore." One wonders whether Captain John Paul Jones's mysterious note [figure 70], written to a brother officer from the *Ranger* on an undated Friday, refers to an exchange of this sort.

I am on the point of sailing . . . pray be so good as put the Inclosed into the hands of the Celebrated Phillis the African Favorite of the Nine and of Apollo, should she Reply, I hope you will be the bearer.

More interesting, perhaps, than any romantic speculation about this liter-ary affair is Phillis's attempt, in her "Reply to the Answer," to recapture a memory of her African childhood in the poetic conventions of the day:

> And pleasing Gambia on my soul returns,
> With native grace in spring's luxuriant reign,
> Smiles the gay mead, and Eden blooms again,
> The various bower, the tuneful flowing stream,
> The soft retreats, the lovers golden dream,
> Her soil spontaneous, yields exhaustless stores;
> For phoebus revels on her verdant shores
> Whose flowery births, a fragrant train appear,
> And crown the youth throughout the smiling year. . . .

As the arguments of the Revolution reached the stage of arms, she found herself trapped in the crossfire of events, and after the Battle of Bunker Hill fled British-occupied Boston to join Obour Tanner in nearby Rhode Island. When Washington arrived in Cambridge to take command of the Ameri-can army, it was from Providence that she sent him a letter and a paean in verse. "Sir," wrote the poet and patriot, "I have taken the freedom to ad-dress your Excellency in the enclosed poem, and entreat your acceptance, though I am not insensible of its accuracies. Your being appointed by the Grand Continental Congress to be Generalissimo of the armies of North America, together with the fame of your virtues, excite sensations not easy to suppress." Her poem, too, was a weapon in "the great cause."

It is easy to understand why the Virginia general liked the poem. Unlike her pre-Revolutionary address to the Earl of Dartmouth, in which the poet-slave yoked British tyranny to black bondage, the ode to Washington is indicted by a raceless champion of Columbia—a name she invented for the new "land of freedom's heaven-defended race." For the aristocrat who owned slaves, or for the general who, at this point, barred blacks from the army, there was no discordant note in this hymn to independence.

162

Celestial Choir! enthron'd in realms of light,
    Columbia's scenes of glorious toils I write.
While freedom's cause her anxious breast alarms,
    She flashes dreadful in refulgent arms.

Nor was the general embarrassed by the offer of her final couplet:
    A crown, a mansion, and a throne that shine,
    With gold unfading, WASHINGTON! be thine."

"At first, with a view of doing justice to her great poetical genius," the general in early February confided to a friend, "I had a great mind to publish the poem; but not knowing whether it might not be considered rather as a mark of my own vanity, than as a compliment to her, I laid it aside. . . ." At the end of the month, he wrote to "Miss Phillis":

. . . a variety of important occurrences, continually interposing to distract the mind and withdraw the attention, I hope will apologize for the delay, and plead my excuse for the seeming but not real neglect. I thank you most sincerely for your polite notice of me, in the elegant lines you enclosed; and however undeserving I may be of such encomium and panegyric, the style and manner exhibit a striking proof of your poetical talents; in honor of which, and as a tribute justly due to you, I would have published the poem, had I not been apprehensive, that, while I only meant to give the world this new instance of your genius, I might have incurred the imputation of vanity. This, and nothing else, determined me not to give it place in the public prints.

If you should ever come to Cambridge, or near head-quarters, I shall be happy to see a person so favored by the Muses, and to whom nature has been so liberal and beneficient in her dispensations.

In fact, a month later both letter and poem found their way into the "Poetical Essays" section of *The Pennsylvania Magazine* [figure 71], whose editor, Thomas Paine, presented them to the public as *"written by the famous* Phillis Wheatley, *The African Poetess."* When later in the year she visited Washington at his headquarters, she was courteously received.

Two years later, in April 1778, Phillis Wheatley married John Peters, whose dim figure, it would seem, has been somewhat besmirched by her early white biographers. (The tone may be gauged by a passage in the first *Memoir* of 1834: "he wore a wig, carried a cane, and quite acted out *'the gentleman'* . . . he is said to have been both too proud and too indolent to apply himself to any occupation below his fancied dignity"). It is indeed difficult to reconstruct the six years of their wedded life. In 1805, when Grégoire was writing his book on the *Literature of Negroes,* he asked the French consul at Boston to gather some data on Phillis's last years. She "married a man of colour," the consul replied, notable for "the superiority of his understanding." Starting out as a grocer, he went on to become "a lawyer under the name of Doctor Peter, and plead before tribunals the cause of the blacks. The reputation he enjoyed procured him a fortune." What seems to emerge from the mélange of posthumous gossip and hearsay

X.

Let singular blessings America crown;
May the Congress be blest with immortal renown;
Each colony live in the true sisterly peace,
Whilst harmony, honour, and riches increase.
CHO. Oh! let freedom, &c.

The following LETTER *and* VERSES, *were written by the famous* Phillis Wheatley, *the African Poetess, and presented to his Excellency Gen.* Washington.

SIR,

I Have taken the freedom to address your Excellency in the enclosed poem, and entreat your acceptance, though I am not insensible of its inaccuracies. Your being appointed by the Grand Continental Congress to be Generalissimo of the armies of North America, together with the fame of your virtues, excite sensations not easy to suppress. Your generosity, therefore, I presume, will pardon the attempt. Wishing your Excellency all possible success in the great cause you are so generously engaged in. I am,

Your Excellency's most obedient humble servant,

Providence, Oct. 26, 1775.   PHILLIS WHEATLEY.
His Excellency Gen. Washington.

CElestial choir! enthron'd in realms of light,
   Columbia's scenes of glorious toils I write.
While freedom's cause her anxious breast alarms,
She flashes dreadful in refulgent arms.
See mother earth her offspring's fate bemoan,
And nations gaze at scenes before unknown!
See the bright beams of heaven's revolving light
Involved in sorrows and the veil of night!
   The goddess comes, she moves divinely fair,
Olive and laurel binds her golden hair:
Wherever shines this native of the skies,
Unnumber'd charms and recent graces rise.
   Muse! bow propitious while my pen relates
How pour her armies through a thousand gates:
As when Eolus heaven's fair face deforms,
Enwrapp'd in tempest and a night of storms;
Astonish'd ocean feels the wild uproar,
The refluent surges beat the sounding shore;
Or thick as leaves in Autumn's golden reign,
Such, and so many, moves the warrior's train.
In bright array they seek the work of war,
Where high unfurl'd the ensign waves in air.
Shall I to Washington their praise recite?
Enough thou know'st them in the fields of fight.
Thee, first in place and honours,—we demand
The grace and glory of thy martial band.
Fam'd for thy valour, for thy virtues more,
Hear every tongue thy guardian aid implore!
   One century scarce perform'd its destin'd round,
When Gallic powers Columbia's fury found;
And so may you, whoever dares disgrace
The land of freedom's heaven-defended race!
Fix'd are the eyes of nations on the scales,
For in their hopes Columbia's arm prevails.
Anon Britannia droops the pensive head,
While round increase the rising hills of dead.
Ah! cruel blindness to Columbia's state!
Lament thy thirst of boundless power too late.
   Proceed, great chief, with virtue on thy side,
Thy ev'ry action let the goddess guide.
A crown, a mansion, and a throne that shine,
With gold unfading, WASHINGTON! be thine.

71. Letter and poem written by Phillis Wheatley and presented to George Washington. Published in *The Pennsylvania Magazine*, April 1776. Historical Society of Pennsylvania.

is that John Peters, possibly a friend of Obour Tanner's, was a "respectable" citizen of Boston. In the 1830s, a granddaughter of Susannah Wheatley remembered that he "was not only a very remarkable looking man, but a man of talents and information, and that he wrote with fluency and propriety, and at one period read law." She "admitted, however, that he was disagreeable in his manners, and that on account of his improper conduct, Phillis became entirely estranged from the immediate family of her mistress. . . ." Nowhere does Phillis breathe a word of complaint against her husband. He seems to have been a black man of dignity, who valued himself, did not kowtow to patronizing whites, struggled to climb the educational and economic ladder, and failed.

One thing is clear. The marriage did not quench her poetic fire. On the front page of the *Evening Post and General Advertiser* for October 30, 1779, Phillis Wheatley, a *"female African,"* outlined her "Proposals" for publishing by subscription a new 300-page volume of "Poems & Letters on various subjects, dedicated to the Right Hon. Benjamin Franklin Esq: One of the Ambassadors of the United States at the Court of France," to be printed "as soon as a sufficient Number of Encouragers offer." The book was to contain thirty-odd poems—among the titles: "Thoughts on the Times," "Ocean," "Niagara," "Chloe to Calliope"—and thirteen letters, including one to Dr. Benjamin Rush and three to the Countess of Huntingdon. The way was still in progress and "Encouragers" did not flock to her standard. Life was bitter. At one point, John sat in jail for debt, while she scrubbed and washed in a cheap lodging house. There were three children —two died, a third lived on precariously. Always delicate, she found herself sick, poor, unable to find a printer willing to risk the new book. Yet she continued to write—a broadside elegy for the Brattle Street Church on the death of one of her old supporters, the "Learned Dr. Samuel Cooper," and a published four-page pamphlet in verse on *Liberty and Peace* [figure 72], which shows her frayed and tired. Her last piece in print, in the *Boston Magazine* of September 1784, is a consolation on the death of an infant son, which perhaps reflected the loss of her own last child. "This Poem," noted the editor, "was selected from a manuscript Volume of Poems, written by PHILLIS PETERS, formerly PHILLIS WHEATLEY—and is inserted as a specimen of her Work."

That winter she ceased to invoke the Muse. "Last Lord's day died, Mrs. PHILLIS PETERS, (formerly Phillis Wheatley), aged 31, known to the literary world by her celebrated miscellaneous Poems," so reads her obituary in the *Independent Chronicle* of December 9, 1784. In the same newspaper, a few months later appeared the following notice: "The person who borrowed a volume of manuscript poems etc of Phillis Peters . . . would very much oblige her husband, John Peters, by returning it immediately, as the whole of her works are intended to be published." When the first American edition of Phillis's book of 1773 was published in 1786, none of the thirty-odd new poems graced its pages. One of these days the manuscript may turn up. When it does, we will be able to read "the whole of her works."

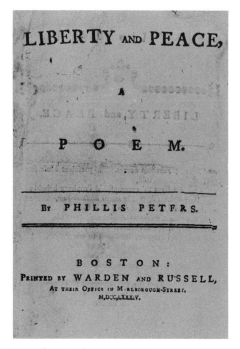

72. *Liberty and Peace, A Poem.* Phillis [Wheatley] Peters, 1784. The New-York Historical Society.

☞During the era of the Revolution, the "vent'rous Afric" was a critical image in the ongoing polemic between equalitarian and elitist. That she was black and a woman somewhat sharpened the issue. As with Benjamin Banneker, the reservations of Jefferson sparked the debate. (Recall how the black astronomer printed Phillis with the stars in his almanac.) "Misery is often the parent of the most affecting touches in poetry," begins the author of the *Notes on Virginia,* who, some years later, would say that "of all men living I am the last who should undertake to decide as to the merits of poetry."

Among the blacks is misery enough, God knows, but no poetry. Love is the peculiar oestrum of the poet. Their love is ardent, but it kindles the senses only, not the imagination. Religion indeed has produced a Phillis Wheatley; but it could not produce a poet. The compositions published under her name are below the dignity of criticism.

(The innuendo of fraudulent authorship would also be aimed at Banneker and Ignatius Sancho.)

Jefferson, of course, did not go unanswered. Gilbert Imlay, the Revolutionary captain whose name is linked to that of Mary Wollstonecraft, in his *Topographical Description of the Western Territory of North America* (1792) recorded that he was "ashamed, in reading Mr. Jefferson's book, to see, from one of the most enlightened and benevolent of my countrymen, the disgraceful prejudices he entertains against the unfortunate negroes," and singled out Wheatley in his rebuttal: "I will transcribe part of her poem on Imagination, and leave you to judge whether it is poetical or not. It will afford you an opportunity, if you have never met with it, of estimating her genius and Mr. Jefferson's judgment; and I think, without any disparagement to him, that, by comparison, Phillis appears much the superior. Indeed, I should be glad to be informed that a white upon this continent has written more beautiful lines." Grégoire, in Paris, reprinting three of her poems, was outraged: "If we were disposed to cavil, we might say, that to an assertion, it is sufficient to oppose a contrary assertion . . . but a more direct refutation may be made, by selecting some portions of her works, which will give us an idea of her talents. . . ." Dr. Samuel Stanhope Smith, member of the American Philosophical Society and president of the College of New Jersey, as late as 1810, discoursing on the *Causes of the Variety of Complexion and Figure on the Human Species,* echoing Imlay, was still demanding of "Mr. Jefferson, or any other man who is acquainted with American planters, how many of those masters could have written poems equal to those of Phillis Wheatley?"

There were others beside Jefferson, of course, whom Phillis Wheatley made uneasy. One Richard Nisbet, who, in the year of her *Poems,* published his tract, *Slavery Not Forbidden by Scripture,* was impatient with Dr. Benjamin Rush for citing "a single example of a negro girl writing a few silly poems, to prove that the blacks are not deficient to us in understanding," and two years later, Bernard Romans, in a natural history of Florida went out of his way to argue that "against the Phillis of Boston (who is the *Phaenix* of her race)," he could "bring at least twenty well known instances of the contrary effect of education on this sable generation."

But these were ineffectual voices drowned out by the wave of international acclaim. In 1774, Voltaire, who did not think highly of blacks, wrote to a friend: "Fontanelle was wrong to say there never would be Negro poets: there is right now a Negress who writes excellent verse in English," and five years later, his countryman, the Marquis de Barbé-Marbois, secretary of the French Legation in Boston, recorded in his diary that Phillis was a prodigy, "one of the strangest creatures in the country and perhaps in the whole world." In Göttingen, in 1806, the anthropologist, John Friedrich Blumenbach, defending the unity of mankind, cited blacks "who have distinguished themselves by their talents for poetry." He knew "English, Dutch, and Latin poems" by black poets, "above all, those of Phillis Wheatley of Boston, who is justly famous. . . ." Her volume of verse was a "collection which scarcely any one who has any taste for poetry could read without pleasure." And Thomas Clarkson, in his essay on slavery which shook the world, citing three of her poems, went on to remark, that "if the authoress was *designed for slavery* . . . the greater part of the inhabitants of Britain must lose their claim to freedom."

At home, she stirred tribute from other poets, black and white. In his second published poem, Jupiter Hammon, the black bard of Long Island, greeted her in a broadside *Address* [figure 75]. The month she died, a pseudonymous "Horatio" of State Street sent to the *Boston Magazine* an "Elegy on the Death of a late celebrated Poetess" [figure 74].

> As Orpheus play'd the list'ning herds among,
> They own'd the magic of his powerful song;
> Mankind no more their savage nature kept,
> And foes to music, wonder'd how they wept.
> So PHILLIS tun'd her sweet mellifluous lyre;
> (Harmonious numbers bid the soul aspire)
> While AFRIC's untaught race with transport heard,
> They lov'd the poet, and the muse rever'd.

During the summer of 1786, Dr. Joseph Ladd, a young New Englander practicing medicine in Charleston, South Carolina (where a few months later he would die in a duel), published a long poem on "The Prospects of America," in which the glory of the new Nation is illustrated by its greatest citizens, among them the poets, Freneau and Barlow—and "a negress . . . the authoress of some ingenious poems . . . entitled to a remembrance. . . .

> Here the fair volume shows the far-spread name
> Of Wondrous Wheatley, Afric's heir to fame,
> Well is it known what glowing genius shines,
> What force of numbers, in her polished lines:
> With magic power the grand descriptions roll
> Thick on the mind, and agitate the soul.

A decade later, in an issue of the *New York Magazine* for 1796, one "Matilda"—apparently a man—moved to verse "On Reading the Poems of Phil-

Dear Obour,

Tr: Fam. VII. 277.

1774
Mar. 21

I rec'd your obliging Letter, enclos'd in your rev'd Pastor's & handed me by his Son. I have lately met with a great trial in the death of my mistress, let us imagine the loss of a Parent, Sister or Brother the tenderness of all these were united in her. — I was a poor little outcast & a stranger when she took me in, not only into her house but I presently became a sharer in her most tender affections, I was treated by her more like her child than her servant, no opportunity was left unimprov'd, of giving me the best of advice, but in terms how tender! how engaging! this I hope ever to keep in remembrance. Her example by life was a greater monitor than all her precepts and Instruction, thus we may observe of how much greater force example is than Instruction. To alleviate our sorrows we had the satisfaction to see her depart in inexpressible raptures, earnest longings & impatient thirstings for the upper Courts of the Lord. Do, my dear friend, remember me & this family in your Closet that this afflicting dispensation may be sanctifyd to us. I am very sorry to hear that you are indispos'd, but hope this will find you in better health. I have been unwell the greater Part of the winter, but am much better as the spring approaches, Pray excuse my not writing to you so long before, for I have been so busy lately that I could not find leisure. I shall send the 5 Books you wrote for, the first convenient opportunity, if you want more, they shall be ready for you I am very affectionately your Friend

Phillis Wheatley

Boston March 21. 1774.

73. Letter from Phillis Wheatley to Obour Tanner telling of the death of her mistress Susannah Wheatley, March 21, 1774. Massachusetts Historical Society.

For the BOSTON MAGAZINE.

Elegy on the Death of a late celebrated Poetess.

IF conscious sense of genius yet re-
   mains,
Of lofty verse, and soft poetic strains;
Shall not the muse a grateful tribute
   rear.
And drop the silent, sympathetic
   tear.
If aught that glows within the friend-
   ly breast,
That weeps at tales of woe, or hearts
   opprest;
With me your sympathizing tribute
   pay,
And to her peaceful manes inscribe
   the lay.
   Ye! who her talents and her vir-
   tues knew,
With grief's spontaneous tears her
   urn bedew.
She too comply'd with nature's sa-
   cred tye,
She gently wip'd the sorrow-stream-
   ing eye,
As if by heaven inspir'd, did she re-
   late,
The souls grand entrance at the sacred gate! *
And shall the honour, which she oft
   apply'd,
To other's reliques, be to hers deny'd?
   O that the muse, dear spirit! own'd
   thy art,
To soften grief and captivate the
   heart,
Then should these lines in numbers
   soft array'd,
Preserve thy mem'ry from oblivion's
   shade;
But O! how vain the wish that
   friendship pays,
Since her own volumes are her greatest praise.

   As Orpheus play'd the list'ning
   herds among,
They own'd the magic of his powerful song;
Mankind no more their savage nature kept,
And foes to music, wonder'd how
   they wept.
So PHILLIS tun'd her sweet melli-
   fluous lyre;
(Harmonious numbers bid the soul
   aspire)
While AFRIC's untaught race with
   transport heard,
                              They

They lov'd the poet, and the muse
   rever'd.
What tho' her outward form did
   ne'er disclose
The lilly's white, or blushes of the
   rose;
Shall sensibility regard the skin,
If all be calm, serene, and pure with-
   in?
But ah! can beauty, or can genius
   save?
Genius and beauty moulder in the
   grave.
The modest graces, and the richest
   bloom,
The solemn toll soon ushers to the
   tomb.
Such the sad ruins of the human race,
That reptiles riot on the fairest face!
Hither let pride its sure criterion
   view;
In vain shall virtue plead, or honour
   sue;
Hither let luxury and av'rice find,
A cure for the distemper'd, canker'd
   mind.

   Tho' now the business of her life
   is o'er,
Tho' now she breaths and tunes her
   lyre no more;
Tho' now the body mixes with the
   clay;
The soul wings upward to immortal
   day;
Free'd from a world of wo, and scene
   of care,
A lyre of gold she tunes, a crown of
   glory wears.

   Seated with angels in that blissful
   place,
Where she now joins in her Creator's
   praise,
Where harmony with louder notes is
   swell'd,
Where her soft numbers only are
   excell'd.
                        HORATIO.

State Street, Dec. 1784.

* Page 488 of this vol.

74. "Elegy on the Death of a Late Celebrated Poetess" by Horatio. Published in The
Boston Magazine, December 1784. Bowdoin College Library.

lis Wheatley, the African Poetess," ended his tribute with a stanza that echoed her insight into the twofold meaning of liberty in the American Revolution:

> 'Til done! at length the long-withheld decree
> Goes forth, that Afric shall be blest and free;
> A PHILLIS rises, and the world no more
> Denies the sacred right to mental pow'r;
> While, Heav'n-inspirdd, she proves *her Country's* claim
> To Freedom, and *her own* to deathless Fame.

Long after her untimely death, another talented young black woman, sixteen-year old Charlotte L. Forten, daughter of the well-known Revolutionary veteran and abolitionist of Philadelphia, recorded in her journal on a Friday in July of 1854: "This evening read 'Poems of Phillis Wheatly,' an African slave, who lived in Boston at the time of the Revolution. She was a wonderfully gifted woman, and many of her poems are very beautiful. Her character and genius afford a striking proof of the falseness of the assertion made by some that hers is an inferior race. . . ." Only the other day, two centuries after Phillis's *Poems* first saw the light, another "vent'rous" young black poet, Nikki Giovanni, tracing her roots, was moved to say: "We have a line of strong poets. Wheatley, by her life style, was a strong woman intent on survival."

JUPITER HAMMON

The first published poem by a black American actually preceded Phillis Wheatley's book by a dozen years. It was printed in 1760 as a broadside in double-column with the title, *An Evening Thought. Salvation by Christ, with Penetential Cries: Composed by Jupiter Hammon, a Negro belonging to Mr. Lloyd, of Queen's-Village, on Long Island* . . . . "Believe me now my Christian friends," exhorted the poet-preacher over twenty years later in a stanza of the last poem he was to write:

> Believe your friend call'd Hammon:
> You cannot to your God attend,
> And serve the God of Mammon.

A few sparse notes, scraped together from some faded letters and printed lines, will have to serve as a life of this black Puritan of New York.

Jupiter Hammon was born a slave on October 17, 1711. His masters were the family of the Lloyds, manorial landlords and merchants of Long Island's north shore near Oyster Bay, and he served them his whole, long life. Possibly, as a child, he was allowed to attend the village school and later to read his master's books; in one of his discourses, he refers to the English divines, Burkitt and Beveridge, whose works were in Henry Lloyd's library. In May 1733, when he was twenty-two, he purchased from his master for seven shillings and six pence a Bible with Psalms. In his seventies, he claimed that he was still "able to do almost any kind of business"—which may indicate that he was a valued servant in house and market, a skilled farmhand and artisan, and able to save a bit by doing extra jobs for pay. When he was thirty, there occurred in nearby New York an event which must have made a deep impression on him: the discovery of an alleged conspiracy by the blacks of the city, with a few whites, to rise against their masters and the government. Thirteen slaves were burned at the stake, eighteen hanged (two in chains), and seventy banished to the West Indies.

When the Revolution came, the Patriot Lloyds fled Long Island as the British and Hessians took over, and Hammon went with them to Connecticut. All of his poems and discourses composed during the war were printed at Hartford. In 1782, when Prince William Henry, later King William IV, stopped over at the Lloyd Manor House, the black poet wrote a poem to celebrate the visit.

It is altogether possible that Jupiter Hammon was a preacher to the slaves in the communities of Long Island and Connecticut where he labored for the Lloyds. *An Evening Thought,* an antiphonal poem echoing the word "Salvation" in twenty-three of its eighty-eight lines, has all the ringing ecstatic hope for heavenly freedom with "tender love" that charges

171

An ADDRESS to Miss Phillis Wheatly, Ethiopian Poetess, in Boston, who came from Africa at eight years of age, and soon became acquainted with the gospel of Jesus Christ.

Miss Wheatly; pray give me leave to express as follows :

1.
O Come you pious youth ! adore
  The wisdom of thy God,
In bringing thee from distant shore,
  To learn his holy word.   *Ecclef. xii. 1.*

2.
Thou mightst been left behind,
  Amidst a dark abode ;
God's tender mercy still combin'd,
  Thou hast the holy word.   *Pfal. cxxxvi. 1, 2, 3.*

3.
Fair wisdom's ways are paths of peace,
  And they that walk therein,
Shall reap the joys that never cease,
  And Christ shall be their king.   *Pfal. i 1, 2, 3. Prov. iii. 7.*

4.
God's tender mercy brought thee here,
  Tost o'er the raging main ;
In Christian faith thou hast a share,
  Worth all the gold of Spain.   *Pfal. ciii. 1, 2, 3, 4.*

5.
While thousands tossed by the sea,
  And others settled down,
God's tender mercy set thee free,
  From dangers still unknown.   *Death.*

6.
That thou a pattern still might be,
  To youth of Boston town,
The blessed Jesus set thee free,
  From every sinful wound.   *2 Cor. v. 10.*

7.
The blessed Jesus, who came down,
  Unvail'd his sacred face,
To cleanse the soul of every wound,
  And give repenting grace.   *Rom. v. 21.*

8.
That we poor sinners may obtain
  The pardon of our sin ;
Dear blessed Jesus now constrain,
  And bring us flocking in.   *Pfal. xxxiv. 6, 7, 8.*

9.
Come you, Phillis, now aspire,
  And seek the living God,
So step by step thou mayst go higher,
  Till perfect in the word.   *Matth. vii. 7, 8.*

10.
While thousands mov'd to distant shore,
  And others left behind,
The blessed Jesus still adore,
  Implant this in thy mind.   *Pfal. lxxxix. 1.*

11.
Thou hast left the heathen shore,
  Thro' mercy of the Lord ;   *Pfal. xxxiv. 1, 2, 3.*

Among the heathen live no more,
  Come magnify thy God.

12.
I pray the living God may be,
  The shepherd of thy soul ;
His tender mercies still are free,
  His mysteries to u. fold.   *Pfal. lxxx 1, 2, 3.*

13.
Thou, Phillis, when thou hunger hast,
  Or pantest for thy God ;
Jesus Christ is thy relief,
  Thou hast the holy word.   *Pfal. xlii. 1, 2, 3.*

14.
The bounteous mercies of the Lord,
  Are hid beyond the sky,
And holy souls that love his word,
  Shall taste them when they die.   *Pfal. xvi. 10, 11.*

15.
These bounteous mercies are from God,
  The merits of his Son ;
The humble soul that loves his word,
  He chooses for his own.   *Pfal. xxxiv 15.*

16.
Come, dear Phillis, be advis'd,
  To drink Samaria's flood ;
There nothing is that shall suffice,
  But Christ's redeming blood.   *John iv. 13 14.*

17.
While thousands muse with earthly toys,
  And range about the street,
Dear Phillis, seek for heaven's joys,
  Where we do hope to meet.   *Matth. vi. 33.*

18.
When God shall send his summons down,
  And number saints together,
Blest angels chant, (triumphant sound)
  Come live with me for ever.   *Pfal. cxvi. 15.*

19.
The humble soul shall fly to God,
  And leave the things of time,
Start forth as 'twere at the first word,
  To taste things more divine.   *Mat. v. 3 8.*

20.
Behold ! the soul shall waft away,
  Whene'er we come to die,
And leave its cottage made of clay,
  In twinkling of an eye.   *Cor. xv. 51, 52, 53.*

21.
Now glory be to the Most High,
  United praises given,
By all on earth, incessantly,
  And all the host of heav'n.   *Pfal. cl. 6.*

Composed by JUPITER HAMMON, a Negro Man belonging to Mr. Joseph Lloyd, of Queen's Village, on Long-Island, now in Hartford.

*** The above lines are published by the Author, and a number of his friends, who desire to join with him in their best regards to Miss Wheatly.

75. "An Address to Miss Phillis Wheatley." Jupiter Hammon, August 4, 1778. The Connecticut Historical Society.

the earliest spirituals of the enslaved. The preacher calls and the flock responds—thus the "Penentential Cries."

> Dear Jesus unto Thee we cry,
>   Give us the Preparation;
> Turn not away thy tender Eye;
>   We seek thy true Salvation. . . .
> Lord hear our penentential Cry:
>   Salvation from above;
> It is the Lord that doth supply
>   With his Redeeming Love.

Jupiter Hammon wrote this hymn on Christmas Day of 1760, and for the next forty years, whenever he cried out in print to his black brothers and sisters, his theme, more or less, was always salvation. Yet there are hints towards the end of his career of a certain impatience, a feeling that freedom was possible—and desirable—in the Here as well as in the After.

It seems significant that his next poem of record, printed as a broadside eighteen years later when he was sixty-seven years old, is *An Address to Miss Phillis Wheatley* [figure 75] in twenty-one scripture-glossed quatrains, "published by the Author, and a number of his friends, who desire to join with him in their best regards" to "the Ethiopian Poetess." Five years after Phillis's *Poems* of 1773, Hammon echoes her sense of miracle in being rescued from pagan Africa.

> God's tender mercy brought thee here;
>   Tost o'er the raging main;
> In Christian faith thou hast a share,
>   Worth all the gold of Spain. . . .
> That thou a pattern still might be,
>   To youth of Boston town,
> The blessed Jesus set thee free,
>   From every sinful wound.

But did Hammon detect in her, at times, a note of frustration, even protest (which he took pains to conceal in his own poems)?

> Thou, Phillis, when thou hunger hast,
>   Or pantest for thy God;
> Jesus Christ is thy relief,
>   Thou hast the holy word.

The "holy word" of this stanza is tagged to Psalm XIII, in which "David complaineth of delay in help."

> How long wilt thou forget me O Lord? for ever? how long wilt thou hide thy face from me?
>
> How long shall I take counsel in my soul, *having* sorrow in my heart daily? how long shall mine enemy be exalted over me?
>
> Consider *and* hear me, O Lord my God: lighten my eyes, lest I sleep the *sleep* of death.

Hammon's next piece, of the following year, *An Essay on the Ten Virgins* has not yet turned up, although it was advertised in the *Connecticut Courant*, for December 14, 1779, "To be sold at the Printing-Office in Hart-

To be fold at the Printing-Office in Hartford,
An Eſſay on the Ten Virgins.
Compoſed by J U P I T E R H A M M O N, a Negro Man belonging to Mr. JOSEPH LLOYD, of Queen's Village on Long Iſland, now in Hartford.

ford" [figure 76]. There has survived, however, a work published three years later in the same town, Hammon's first sermon in print, *A Winter Piece: Being a Serious Exhortation, with a Call to the Unconverted: and a Short Contemplation on the Death of Jesus Christ.* "As I have been desired to write something more than Poetry," the black preacher began, "I shall endeavour to write from these words, Matthew xi, 28. Come unto me all ye that labour and are heavy laden." Although this sermon is very far from being a call to revolt, neither is it an exhortation to slaves to obey their masters. In places, it has the heat of a certain friction. Some whites have apparently objected to Hammon's preaching the word:

But it may be objected by those who have had the advantage of studying, every one is not calculated for teaching of others. To those I answer, Sirs, I do not attempt to teach those I know are able to teach me, but I shall endeavour by divine assistance to enlighten the minds of my brethren; for we are a poor despised nation, whom God in his wise providence has permitted to be brought from their native place to a christian land, and many thousands born in what are called christian families, and brought up to years of understanding. In answer to the objectors, Sirs, pray give me leave to enquire into the state of those children that are born in those christian families, have they been baptised, taught to read, and learnt their catechism? Surely this is a duty incumbent on masters or heads of families. Sirs, if you had a sick child, would you not send for a doctor?

Then he turns to his "Brethren for whom this discourse is designed"—some of whom, apparently, have looked at him askance as an upholder of slavery.

My dear Brethren, as it hath been reported that I had petitioned to the court of Hartford against freedom, I now solemnly declare that I never have said, nor done any thing, neither directly nor indirectly, to promote or to prevent freedom; but my answer hath always been I am a stranger here and I do not care to be concerned or to meddle with public affairs, and by this declaration I hope my friends will be satisfied, and all prejudice removed, Let us all strive to be united together in love, and to become new creatures.

His message was simply this: it was all in God's hands. If freedom, of body

174

or soul, was to be the fate of black or white, it must be bestowed as a gift from God.

Come my dear fellow servants and brothers, Africans by nation, we are all invited to come, Acts x, 34. Then Peter opened his mouth and said, of a truth I perceive that God is no respecter of persons, verse 35. But in every nation he that feareth him is accepted of him. My Brethren, many of us are seeking a temporal freedom, and I wish you may obtain it; remember that all power in heaven and on earth belongs to God; if we are slaves it is by the permission of God, if we are free it must be by the power of the most high God. Stand still and see the salvation of God, cannot that same power that divided the waters from the waters for the children of Israel to pass through, make way for your freedom.

The emphasis of Hammon's doctrine is that it applies equally to all.

My brethren, it is not we servants only that are unworthy, but all mankind by the fall of Adam, became guilty in the sight of God. . . . But how art we to forget that God spoke these words, saying, I am the Lord thy God, which brought thee out of the land of Egypt and out of the house of bondage. Exod. xx, 1. Thus we see how the children of Israel were delivered from the Egyptian service.

Both freedoms will come, must come, he concludes:

But the scripture hath told us, that we must not depend on the use of means alone. . . . Here we see if we are saved, it must be by the power of God's holy spirit. But my dear Brethren the time is hastening when we must appear.

But then, as if to mute the string of protest, he appends seventeen quatrains of his "Poem for Children with Thoughts on Death"—another series of pious homilies strung together in Hartford on New Year's Day of 1782.

Soon after *A Winter Piece* there followed another earnest discourse, *An Evening's Improvement. Shewing, the Necessity of beholding the Lamb of God . . . Printed for the Author, by the Assistance of his Friends.* "And now my brethren," Hammon begins, "seeing I have had an invitation to write something more to encourage my dear fellow servants and brethren Africans, in the knowledge of the Christian religion"—

let us behold the Lamb of God as having the power to make the blind to see, the dumb to speak, and the lame to walk, and even to raise the dead; But it may be objected and said by those that have had the advantage of studying, are we to expect miracles at this day? . . . Others may object and say, what can we expect from an unlearned Ethiopian? . . . Sirs, I know we are not to expect miracles at this day.

It is in this discourse that the "unlearned Ethiopian" has something to say about the war:

And now my dear brethren, I am to remind you of a most melancholy scene of Providence; it hath pleased the most high God, in his wise providence, to permit a cruel and unnatural war to be commenced. . . . Have we not great cause to think this is the just deserving of our sins. . . . Here we see that we ought to pray, that God may hasten the time when the people shall beat

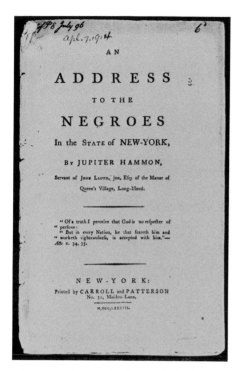

77. *An address to the Negroes in the State of New-York.* Jupiter Hammon, 1877. The New-York Historical Society.

their swords into ploughshares and their spears into pruning-hooks, and nations shall learn war no more.

In fact, the poem that concludes the sermon, "A Dialogue, Entitled, The Kind Master and Dutiful Servant"—a duet on Christian virtue rather than an injuction of holy obedience—is more than half devoted to the theme of *"the present* war." Hammon does not pray for the victory of either side; rather, he admonishes:

> Lay up the sword and drop the spear,
> And Nations seek for peace.

Looking back in 1786, Jupiter Hammon wrote:

When I was at Hartford in Connecticut, where I lived during the war, I published several pieces which were well received, not only by those of my own colour, but by a number of white people, who thought they might do good among their servants.

Hammon's last recorded work, *An Address to the Negroes in the State of New-York* [figure 77], was printed in his seventy-sixth year from a "manuscript, wrote in his own hand," with an unsolicited dedication to the members of the African Society in the City of New York. It has the feeling of a final utterance, a tone of legacy, to his "nation."

I think you will be more likely to listen to what is said, when you know it comes from a negro, one of your own nation and colour. . . . My age, I think, gives me some right to speak to you. . . . I have passed the common bounds set for man, and must soon go the way of all the earth.

One can understand from its opening pages why some "white people" thought Hammon's writings "might do good among their servants," for his first injunction is Paul's: "Servants be obedient to them that are your masters according to the flesh." He will not go into the question of "whether it is right, and lawful, in the sight of God, for them to make slaves of us or not"—but he is "certain that while we are slaves, it is our duty to obey our masters, in all their lawful commands, and mind them unless we are bid to do that which we know to be sin. . . ." One wonders about the reactions at this point of the members of the African Society, who noted Hammon's confession:

. . . I have great reason to be thankful that my lot has been so much better than most slaves have had. I suppose I have had more advantages and privileges than most of you, who are slaves, have ever known, and I believe more than many white people have enjoyed, for which I desire to bless God, and pray that he may bless those who have given them to me.

Were the unfree happy as they read Hammon's diatribes against swearing, stealing, and loitering? ("Some of you to excuse yourselves, may plead the example of others, and say that you hear a great many white people, who know more than such poor ignorant Negroes as you are, and some who are rich and great gentlemen, swear, and talk profanely; and some of you may say this of your masters, and say no more than is true.") Yet masters, sinful as they may be, must be served honestly by their servants. True, slavery is never condoned as a good—it is God's mystery, like an earthquake or a flood. The main force of Hammon's argument is to maintain the absolute equality of all men in what matters as infinitely important for him—the hereafter, which black and white can attain only by a life free of sin.

He will bring us all, rich and poor, white and black, to his judgment seat. If we are found among those who *feared his name,* and *trembled at his word,* we shall be called good and faithful servants. Our slavery will be at an end, and though ever so mean, low and despised in this world, we shall sit with God in his kingdom, as Kings and Priests, and rejoice for ever and ever.

Thus, the faultless logic of his advice—"to become religious, and to make religion the great business of your lives."

Hammon does not fault freedom: "Now I acknowledge that liberty is a great thing, and worth seeking for, if we can get it honestly" and "by our good conduct prevail on our masters to set us free. . . ." To "those Negroes who have liberty," his counsel is to be exemplary Christians, so that masters cannot use their sinfulness as a reason for refusing to free their slaves.

Yet, there are some lines in which Hammon seems to reject "Penetential Cries" and speak out as a man of the Revolution:

That liberty is a great thing we may know from our own feelings, and we may likewise judge so from the conduct of the white people in this war. How much money has been spent, and how many lives have been lost to defend their liberty! I must say that I have hoped that God would open their eyes, when they were so much engaged for liberty, to think of the state of the poor blacks, and to pity us. He has done it in some measure, and has raised us up many friends; for which we have reason to be thankful, and to hope in his mercy. What may be done further, he only knows. . . .

The lines leap out of the text—and ring like those of Banneker and Cuffe. But only for a moment.

This, my dear brethren, is by no means the greatest thing we have to be concerned about. Getting our liberty in this world is nothing to our having the liberty of the children of God. . . . What is forty, fifty, or sixty years, when compared to eternity?

And for further consolation:

There are but two places where all go after death, white and black, rich and poor; those places are Heaven and Hell.

Make no mistake: Hammon may have had the luck to be owned by a "good" master, but he will not therefore argue that the lot of the slave is a happy one. As a matter of fact, the misery of slavery is another argument for faith in eternity, "for God hath not chosen the rich of this world. Nor many rich, not many noble are called, but God hath chosen the weak things of this world. . . ."

Now, my brethren, it seems to me that there are no people that ought to attend to the hope of happiness in another world so much as we. Most of us are cut off from comfort and happiness here in this world, and can expect nothing from it. Now seeing this is the case, why should we not take care to be happy after death? Why should we spend our whole lives in sinning against God; and be miserable in this world, and in the world to come? If we do thus, we shall certainly be the greatest fools. We shall be slaves here, and slaves for ever.

Yet the final note, it must be admitted, is passive faith. Yes, "liberty is a great thing"—and this is what the Revolution might have meant for black people, too—but the whole question must be left in God's hands.

If you become Christians, you will have reason to bless God for ever, that you have been brought into a land where you have heard the gospel, though you have been slaves. If we should ever get to Heaven, we shall find nobody to reproach us for being black, or for being slaves. Let me beg of you, my dear African brethren, to think very little of your bondage in this life; for your thinking of it will do you no good. If God designs to set us free, he will do it in his own time and way. . . .

☞ The minutes of a meeting of the Acting Committee of the Pennsylvania Society for Promoting the Abolition of Slavery held on June 30, 1787, contained the following paragraph.

A Pamphlet wrote by Jupiter Hammon, servant to John Lloyd, jun. Esq. Queen's Village, Long-Island, and addressed to the African descendants in General, was laid before them. Impressed with a lively sense of the good effects that may result from a re-publication thereof, to those persons to whom it is particularly addressed, Ordered, that Daniel Humphreys be directed to print five hundred copies, for the purposes above mentioned.

Can it be that the Abolition Society, the sponsor of Banneker and Cuffe, thought that Hammon's message might serve as a weapon of the anti-slavery movement? Or was it simply that the virtuosity of mind displayed in the *Address* was still another disproof of Jefferson's doubt about the intellectual equality of the blacks? The final impression is perhaps one of sheer waste. For Jupiter Hammon was a genius of a sort and no time-serving hypocrite. He pursued his argument, for what it was worth, with skill and conviction. Who cannot respond to the tragic tension between the two utterances? "Liberty is a great thing," and, "if we should ever get to Heaven, we shall find nobody to reproach us for being black, or for being slaves." What finally remains is the sense of his titanic struggle for a position as a black and a slave in a white world that called itself Christian.

☞ Fortune was on Phillis Wheatley's side—when her portrait had to be done, she found nearby a black artist to do it. (Hers was the first portrait of a black with a name to be painted in America.) It was a sheer miracle that in those early days a few black Americans, transcending caste, began to paint pictures rather than fences.

We know, by brief report, a few facts about a handful of black artists and skilled craftsmen of the colonial and Revolutionary time. Isaiah Thomas, in his *History of Printing*, relates that in the Boston printing shop of Thomas Fleet, there was a black, an "ingenious man," who "cut on wooden blocks, all the pictures which decorated the ballads and small books of his

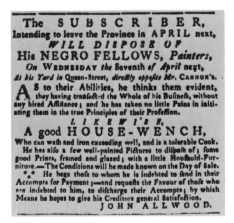

At Mr. *M'Lean's*, Watch-Maker near the Town-House, is a Negro Man whose extraordinary Genius has been assisted by one of the best Masters in *London*; he takes Faces at the lowest Rates. Specimens of his Performances may be seen at said Place.

78. Advertisement of a black portraitist. *Massachusetts Gazette,* January 7, 1773. Library of Congress.

master." A notice [figure 78] in the *Boston Newsletter* of January 7, 1773 reads as follows:

At Mr. *M'Lean's,* Watch-Maker near the Town-House, is a Negro Man whose extraordinary Genius has been assisted by one of the best Masters on *London;* he takes Faces at the lowest Rates. Specimens of his Performances may be seen at said Place.

In March of the same year in Charleston, South Carolina, an artist-artisan, John Allwood, on departing from the province, advertised [figure 79] in the *Gazette:*

... *DISPOSE OF* his NEGRO FELLOWS, *Painters.* ... As to their Abilities, he thinks them evident, they have transacted the Whole of his Business, without any hired Assistance; and he has taken no little Pains in initiating them in the true Principles of their Profession. ...   He has also a few well-painted Pictures to dispose of. ...

Thus far, we have neither their names nor their works.

A few dim names have survived in the record. In Newport, there was a black man of talent who hammered staves for his master. It was said—so reported a historian of Rhode Island in 1853—that Gilbert Stuart "derived his first impression of painting from witnessing Neptune Thurston, a slave, who was employed in his master's cooper-shop, sketch likenesses on the heads of casks, and remarked that if he had had an instructor he would make quite a celebrated artist." This, and nothing more. In the *Pennsylvania Packet* for May 1, 1784 [figure 80], one Benjamin Halsted of New York City offered a reward of eight dollars for the return of a valuable slave.

RAN-AWAY . . . a negro man, named JOHN FRANCES, *but commonly called* Jack: *he is about 40 years of age, five feet ten inches high, slender built, speaks good English, by trade a goldsmith; he generally affects to be very polite, and it's more than probable he may pass for a freeman. . . . All masters of vessels and others are forbid to harbour or carry him off at their peril.*

In Burlington, New Jersey, in the Friends' Burial-Ground, is the grave of the black clockmaker, Peter Hill, who probably knew John Woolman. In 1795, when he was twenty-seven years old, he won his freedom. A century

79. Advertisement by artist John Allwood to "Dispose of his Negro Fellows, Painters. . . ." South Carolina *Gazette,* March 8, 1773. Charleston Library Society.

Philadelphia, April 27.

Eight Dollars Reward.

RAN-AWAY from the subscriber, a negro man, named JOHN FRANCES, but commonly called JACK : he is about 40 years of age, five feet ten inches high, slender built, speaks good English, by trade a goldsmith; he generally affects to be very polite, and it's more than probable he may pass for a freeman. Said negro was carried to New York and left in charge of Mr. Ephraim Brasher, goldsmith, from whom he absconded, and returned to me after skulking about this city for a considerable time : had on when he went away, an old green coat, fustian waistcoat and breeches; a pair of half boots, but may probably change his dress. All masters of vessels and others are forbid to harbour or carry him off at their peril. Whoever takes up said negro and delivers him to John Le Telier, goldsmith in Market street, or to the subscriber in New York, shall have the above reward, and all reasonable charges paid. BENJAMIN HALSTED.

later, a few of his handsome clocks were still ticking away in houses of the neighborhood.

All these are but wraiths, shadows of a black creative presence in the time of the American Revolution, reminders that for every Wheatley, Banneker, or Cuffe a host of others, victims of racism, were forced to waste their gifts and powers.

180

PRINCE HALL: ORGANIZER

Prince Hall, Boston's most prominent black in the era of the Revolution, was not a poet or an artist, nor was he a preacher or a scientist. He was the founder of the world's first lodge of black Masons. But more than that, he was, in a sense, the first black organizer in American history. His gift was to show some of his people, in the new climate of independence, how they might get together in defense of their social, political, and economic rights. He devoted his whole life to grappling, in a refractory world, with a problem of the future, still unsolved.

He was not the only organizer, nor was his Masonic Lodge the only organization, outside the church, to unite the black people of his time. One of the earliest efforts to achieve a minimum of collective security was made at Newport, Rhode Island, during the fall of 1780, when Newport Gardner and a few friends established an African Union Society in that town. In hindsight, it would seem that a prime aim of the society was the sheer survival of the historic identity of the black community—its stated purpose was to keep a record of births, deaths, and marriages, to assist members in time of distress, to find apprenticeships for young men seeking a trade. There was sage advice for its members also: "We beseech you," counseled its founders, "to reflect that it is by your good conduct that you can refute the objections which have been made against you as rational and moral creatures. . . ." In Philadelphia, seven years later, Richard Allen and Absalom Jones, maneuvering to create a black church, felt the necessity, as "two men of the African race," to organize the Philadelphia African Society, "without regard to religious tenets . . . in order to support one another in sickness, and for the benefit of their widows and fatherless children." In that same year, Jupiter Hammon dedicated his last discourse to the New York African Society. In 1790, in South Carolina, a group of "free brown men," as they called themselves, in a "Preamble" to their "Rules and Regulations," taking into consideration

the unhappy situation of our fellow creatures, and the distresses of our widows and orphans, for the want of a fund to relieve them in the hour of their distresses, sickness and death; and holding it an essential of mankind to contribute all they can towards relieving the wants and miseries, and promoting the welfare and happiness of one another,

organized themselves into the Brown Fellowship Society of the city of Charleston. Indeed, in Hall's own city, in 1798, twenty years after he had pioneered the African Lodge, a group of non-Masonic blacks, feeling the need of another association "for the mutual benefit of each other"—to find jobs for the children, to support the widowed, attend the sick, and bury the dead—would constitute itself the African Society of Boston and print its *Laws* for all to see. Among its forty founders was Ceazer Fayer-

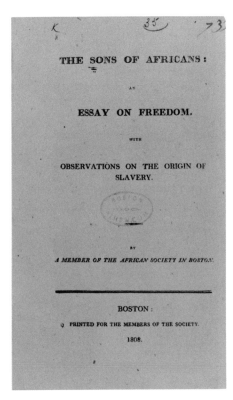

THE SONS OF AFRICANS:

AN

ESSAY ON FREEDOM.

WITH

OBSERVATIONS ON THE ORIGIN OF
SLAVERY.

BY

A MEMBER OF THE AFRICAN SOCIETY IN BOSTON.

BOSTON:

PRINTED FOR THE MEMBERS OF THE SOCIETY.
1808.

81. *The Sons of Africans: An Essay On Freedom.* 1808, Library Company of Philadelphia.

weather, who in 1777, like James Forten, had been a powder boy on a Revolutionary frigate. In 1808, one of its members would publish for the society an eloquent tract: *The Sons of Africans: An Essay on Freedom, with Observations on the Origin of Slavery* [figure 81].

The impulse towards unity surfaced earliest in Massachusetts between the martyrdom of Attucks and the Battle of Bunker Hill in the black petitions addressed to the general court. Although the name of Prince Hall is not signed to any of these petitions, it can be said, from one point of view, that the idea of African Lodge No. 1 was an outgrowth of the black solidarity fostered by these first bold attempts to force the Commonwealth to confront the anomaly of racism in the struggle for liberty. In fact, the first appearance of Prince Hall in the public record, two years after he had become a Free and Accepted Mason, was as a signer of a "petition of A Great Number of Blackes detained in a State of slavery in the Bowels of a free & Christian Country," demanding of the general court that slavery cease in Massachusetts.

☞ The pre-Revolutionary life of Prince Hall is still something of a mystery. For half a century historians have been repeating the passage of biography in Carter Woodson's *The Negro in Our History*.

Hall was born September 12, 1748, at Bridge Town, Barbados, British West Indies. His father, Thomas Prince Hall, was an Englishman, and his mother was a free woman of French descent. He was apprenticed as a leather worker . . . came to the United States in 1765 at the age of seventeen . . . applied himself industriously at common labor during the day and studied privately at night. Upon reaching the age of twenty-seven he had acquired the fundamentals of education. Saving his earnings, he had accumulated sufficient to buy a piece of property. He joined the Methodist Church, in which he passed as an eloquent preacher. His first church was located in Cambridge, Massachusetts. There he built up a prosperous congregation.

Recent studies of black Freemasonry have challenged parts of this version as based on lore and legend. (In the process, the familiar full-length portrait of Prince Hall, in wig and knee breeches, has been exposed as a clumsy forgery.) According to the new research, Hall was born around 1735, place unknown, and first crops up in the record during the late 1740s as the slave of one William Hall of Boston. He joined the Congregational Church on School Street, where the Reverend Andrew Croswell preached, in 1762, and the following year married Sarah Richie, a slave. In the spring of 1770, the year of the Boston Massacre, William Hall gave Prince his freedom, and that summer, a widower, he married Flora Gibbs of Gloucester.

Did Prince Hall fight in the American Revolution? Woodson believed that "he entered actively in the war and acquitted himself with credit." Others have stated that he fired a round at Bunker Hill. What is sure is that, whether or not he served the Revolution as a front-line soldier, he

Boston April ye 24th 1777

Col: Crafts. Reg:^t of Artilery

To Prince Hall b^r to 5 Drumheads
beleverd at Sundrey times To 8th may
£1-19-8

Rec^d ye above mention:d Drumheads for use of Said
Reg:^t James Ross Drum Major ——

Mr Com:^y General . Boston 8th may 1777.
This Certifies that the above Drum
heads are now In possession & use of the Reg^t of artil^y
£1. 19. 0 J Swan Maj Train

82. Bill of sale sent by Prince Hall to Colonel Crafts of the Boston Regiment of Artillery on April 24, 1777, for five leather drumheads. Massachusetts Archives.

did render it a service as a skilled craftsman, for there still exists a bill he sent to Colonel Crafts of the Boston Regiment of Artillery on April 24, 1777, for five leather drumheads [figure 82].

This ends the speculative part of Prince Hall's biography. The rest of his life, to his death at seventy-two in the year 1807, is fairly clear in its larger outlines.

☞ On March 6, 1775, six weeks before the skirmishes at Lexington and Concord, Prince Hall and fourteen other free blacks became members of an army lodge of Free and Accepted Masons attached to a British regiment stationed in Boston. When the British left the city, the black Masons who remained behind were given a qualified permit to meet as a lodge. They would have to wait until the end of the war for a permanent charter. Given their need to get together, why did Prince Hall and his friends choose to join the Masons? Recall the five petitions of Boston's blacks to the general court in 1773 and 1774. (When James Swan reprinted his argument against slavery in 1773, contending that "no country can be called free where there is one slave," he revealed that he had done so "at the earnest desire of the Negroes in Boston.") Recall that these petitions had been fruitless, and that Abigail Adams had written John of a "conspiracy of the negroes," who had drawn up a "petition to the [British] governor, telling him that they would fight for him provided he would arm them, and engage to liberate them if he conquered." Was this Prince Hall's mood as he listened to the white British officers inviting him to become a member of the army lodge? Or was it simply this, that "true Masonry," as he often repeated, had "something in it Divine and Noble and Diffuses Universal love to all Mankind?" One thing seems certain: searching for a form of solidarity that might structure the efforts of the petitioners, when the offer came, his organizing mind saw it as a possibility of a sort. Seize the day!

Two years later, on January 13, 1777, eight blacks of Boston and nearby signed a petition to the general court "humbly" demanding the abolition of slavery. The first four signers, heading the list—Lancaster Hill, Peter Bess, Brister Slenser, and Prince Hall—were Masons. What they signed was, in fact, an almost exact copy of the petition rejected by Governor Gage on May 25, 1774— with a few additional sentences that updated it to the second year of the Revolution. Abolish slavery and restore "the Natural Right of all men," Hall and his fellow petitioners beseeched the legislature, so that the "Inhabitance of these Stats" might no longer be chargeable with the inconstancey of acting themselves the part which thay condem and oppose in others. . . ." Although Hall and his friends were not alone in making the demand—a few white allies drew up a bill to abolish the nefarious practice—in the end the legislature passed the buck by referring the matter to the Congress of the Confederation. The abolition of slavery in Massachusetts, by judicial construction, would have to wait until the close of the war.

For the next five years the town records list Hall as taxpayer and voter, but there is no news of the lodge—no doubt many of its members were away, serving in the ranks on land and sea. But the lodge had survived. When, in December 1782, the black Masons celebrated their traditional Feast of St. John, a Boston newspaper, reporting the event, facetiously referred to the "St. Blacks' Lodge of Free and Accepted Masons." The reply was restrained, but angry:

with due submission to the public, our title is not St. Black's Lodge; neither do we aspire after high titles. But our only desire is that the Great Architect of the Universe would diffuse in our hearts the true spirit of Masonry, which is love to God and universal love to all mankind. These I humbly conceive to be the two grand pillars of Masonry. Instead of a splendid entertainment, we had an agreeable one in brotherly love. The letter was signed—"Prince Hall, Master of the African Lodge No. 1, Dedicated to St. John."

The African Lodge, however, was still without a charter. Two years later, in March of 1784, Hall wrote to London: "this Lodge hath been founded almost eight years and we have had only a Permit to Walk on St. John's Day and to Bury our Dead in a manner and form . . . we hope you will not deny us nor treat us Beneath the rest of our fellowmen, although

Poor yet Sincere Brethren of the Craft." London was eager to grant the charter, but red tape delayed its delivery for three years. Finally, Captain James Scott, a brother-in-law of John Hancock, carried it over the ocean in the spring of 1787. African Lodge No. 1, renumbered 459, was now formally organized with Prince Hall as Master.

The years 1786 and 1787 were a time of trouble in Massachusetts. The sound of the auctioneer's hammer was loud in the land. A new revolution had broken out on the mortgaged farms of the western half of the state. In the county conventions and in the guerilla bands, veterans of the war, who had returned to debt-ridden fields, demanded of the legislature a moratorium on sales and evictions, emergency grants of paper money, the curbing of the courts, and abolition of the lawyers. It was only after a pitched battle at Springfield Arsenal in January of 1787, when the army of Governor Bowdoin routed the insurgent troops under Captain Daniel Shays, that the men of property and standing in the state were able to quiet their fears about agrarians and levelers taking over the State House in Boston.

What stand would Prince Hall and the African Lodge take on the Shays Rebellion? The white Masons supported the government against the rebels. In an appraisal of their own interests, could the black city folk of Boston find much in common with the tax-laden farmers of the west? Among the few blacks who lived west of the valley of Connecticut, were there even a handful who burned farms? Although slavery had already been abolished in Massachusetts, white hostility still abounded, and the battle for full citizenship had yet to be won. No doubt there was sympathy for the dispossessed of the countryside in the hearts of urban and maritime blacks. But there was also the problem of the survival of the black community in Boston. When, in the fall of 1786, a call went out for volunteers to march to the West, the black organizer made up his mind: "We, by the Providence of God, are members of a fraternity that not only enjoins upon us to be peaceable subjects to the civil powers where we reside," Prince Hall wrote to Governor Bowdoin at the end of November,

but it also forbids our having any concern in any plot of conspiracies against the state where we dwell; and as it is the unhappy lot of this state at the present date, and as the meanest of its members must feel that want of a lawful and good government, and as we have been protected for many years under this once happy Constitution, so we hope, by the blessing of God, we may long enjoy that blessing; therefore, we, though unworthy members of this Commonwealth, are willing to help and support, as far as our weak and feeble abilities may become necessary in this time of trouble and confusion, as you in your wisdom shall direct us. That we may, under just and lawful authority, live peaceable lives in all godliness and honesty, is the hearty wish of your humble servants, the members of the African Lodge. . . .

Nine years later, the historian-minister, Jeremy Belknap, after a conversation with Prince Hall, wrote to Judge Beverly Tucker in Virginia: "In time of the insurrection, 1786, they offered their service to Governor

Bowdoin, to go against the insurgents, to the number of 700; but the council did not advise sending them, and indeed there was no necessity for their services." Seven hundred black troops seem a very large number—perhaps, Prince Hall was speaking not only for the lodge, but for the whole black community of coastal Massachusetts. Why did Governor Bowdoin and his council turn down Hall's offer? In November, there was a great need for government troops—the crisis at Springfield Arsenal was a month in the future. Were the upper classes of the state still fearful of black conspiracy, a bit nervous about the idea of putting arms on the shoulders of seven hundred blacks? On the other hand, rereading Hall's letter, the tone seems somewhat anxious, as if he were trying too hard to say: "We blacks are against conspiracy, will help you suppress it, please don't suspect us."

Prince Hall's reaction to Bowdoin's rejection of his services may be illuminated by a subsequent communication he signed and sent a month later to the State House—a petition to the general court by seventy-three "African Blacks," whose mood and message strike a note very different from that of November's offer to join the fight against Shays. This petition of January 4, 1787, is a remarkable document [figure 83]. During the spring of 1773, four Boston slaves organized a movement to persuade the general court to legislate for the "*Africans.* . . one day in a week to work for themselves," in order to earn enough to buy freedom and "leave the province. . . as soon as we can, from our joynt labours, procure money to transport ourselves to some part of the Coast of Africa, where we propose a settlement." Now, fourteen years later, a committee of twelve of the African Lodge, headed by its Grand Master, Prince Hall, spelled out the idea of a return to the motherland in passionate detail, five years before the Tory black veterans sailed from Canada to Africa, twenty-three years before Captain Paul Cuffe's first voyage to Sierra Leone. The first major statement on the subject in Afro-American history— yet never printed from the original manuscript—it deserves to be better known.

We, or our ancestors have been taken from all our dear connections, and brought from Africa and put into a state of slavery in this country; from which unhappy situation we have been lately in some measure delivered by the new constitution which has been adopted by this state, or by a free act of our former masters. But we yet find ourselves, in many respects, in very disagreeable and disadvantageous circumstances; most of which must attend us so long as we and our children live in America.

This, and other considerations, which we need not hear particularly mention, induce us earnestly to desire to return to Africa, our native country which warm climate is much more natural and agreable to us; and for which the God of nature has formed us; and where we shall live among our equals and be more comfortable and happy, than we can be in our present situation; and at the same time, may have a prospect of usefulness to our brethren there.

This leads us humbly to propose the following plan to the consideration

83. Signers of the petition of January 4, 1787, to the general court of Massachusetts [including Prince Hall]. Massachusetts Archives.

of this honourable Court. The soil of our native country is good and produces the necessaries of life in great abundance. There are large tracts of uncultivated lands which if proper application were made for them it is presumed, might be obtained, and would be freely given for those to settle upon, who shall be disposed to return to them. When this shall be effected by a number of Blacks sent there for this purpose, who shall be thought most capable of making such an application, and transacting this business; then they who are disposed to go and settle there shall form themselves into a civil society, united by a political constitution, in which they shall agree. And those who are disposed, and shall be thought qualified, shall unite, and be formed into a religious society, or christian church; and have one or more blacks ordained as their pastors or Bishops: And being thus formed, shall remove to Africa and settle on said lands.

These must be furnished with necessary provisions for the voyage; and with farming utensils necessary to cultivate the land; and with the materials which cannot at present be obtained there and which will be needed to build houses and mills.

The execution of this plan will, we hope, be the means of enlightening and civilizing those nations who are now sunk in ignorance and barbarity: and may give opportunity to those who shall be disposed, and engaged to promote the salvation of their heathen brethren, to spread the knowledge of Christianity among them and perswade them to embrace it. And schools may be formed to instruct their youth and children, and christian knowledge be spread through many nations who now are in gross darkness; and christian churches be formed and the only true God and Saviour be worshiped and honored through that vast extent of country, where are now the habitations of cruelty under the reign of the prince of darkness.

This may also lay a happy foundation for a friendly and lasting connection between that country and the United States of America, by a mutual intercourse and profitable commerce, which may much more than overbalance all the expence which is now necessary in order to carry this plan into effect.

This leads us to observe, that we are poor and utterly unable to prosecute this scheme or to return to Africa without assistance. Money is wanted to enable those who shall be appointed, to go to Africa, and procure lands to settle upon; and to obtain passage for us and our families; and to furnish us with the necessary provisions, and the utensils and articles that have been mentioned.

We therefore humbly and earnestly apply to this honourable Court, hoping and praying that in your wisdom and goodness, you concert and prosecute the best method to relieve and assist us either by granting a brief for a collection in all the congregations in this State, or in any other way, which shall to your wisdom appear most expedient.

The House received the petition and buried it in committee.

Africa might seem the only solution in times of deepest despair. Meanwhile, there were battles to be fought on the home front. Nine months later, in October 1787, Prince Hall was ready with another "petition of a great number of blacks, freemen of this Commonwealth," this time an assault on the system of racist discrimination in education. Taxed as citizens, and

willing to pay our equal part of these burdens, we are of the humble opinion that we have the right to enjoy the privileges of free men. But that we do not will appear in many instances, and we beg leave to mention one out of many, and that is of the education of our children which now receive no benefit from the free schools in the town of Boston, which we think is a great grievance, as by woful experience we now feel the want of a common education. We, therefore, must fear for our rising offspring to see them in ignorance in a land of gospel light . . . and for not other reason can be given this they are black. . . .

Denial of free schools for black freemen was indeed "a great grievance," but during the following winter the institution of slavery flourishing in the rest of the country struck a harder blow at their very existence. In early February 1788, three black Bostonians, named Wendham, Cato, and Luck (the last, a Mason), were decoyed by Captain Solomon Babson aboard his sloop *Ruby* with the promise of work. While they were toiling in the hold, the ship set sail for Salem, where according to the *American Hearld*, "he inveigled a number more of unfortunate blacks on board." Prince Hall lost no time in rallying the Masons to protest the outrage. On February 27, once more a "greet Number of Blacks" addressed a petition to the general court. "It is a truly original and curious performance," confided the Reverend Belknap to a friend, "written by the Grand Master of the Black Lodge," and signed by twenty-two of its members, "justly Allarmed at the enhuman and cruel Treetment that Three of our Brethren free citizens of the Town of Boston."

What then are our lives and Lebeties worth if they may be taken a way in such a cruel & unjust manner . . . we are not uncensebel that the good Laws of this State forbedes all such base axones: Notwithstanding we can aseur your Honners that maney of our free blacks . . . have Entred on bord of vessels as seamen *and* have been sold for Slaves . . . maney of us who are good seamen are oblidge to stay at home thru fear. . . .

The grievance went beyond the incident to the source of the outrage— the slave trade itself.

Your Petitioners have for sumtime past Beheld whith greef ships cleared out from this Herber for Africa and there they ether steal or case others to steal our Brothers & sisters fill there ships holes full of unhappy men & women crouded together, then set out to find the Best markets seal them there like sheep for the slarter and then Returne near like Honest men; after haven sported with the Lives and Lebeties fello men and at the same time call themselves Christians: Blush o Hevens at this.

The previous year the Quakers of Boston had already urged the legislature to put an end to the slave trade. The petition of the black Masons now spurred the Boston clergy to do likewise. The threefold pressure in the general court was effective: on March 26 the court passed an act "to pre-

84. *A Charge Delivered to the Brethren of the African Lodge on the 25th of June, 1792.* Prince Hall, 1792. Library of Congress.

vent the slave trade, and for granting relief to the families of such unhappy persons as may be kidnapped or decoyed away from this Commonwealth."

Meanwhile, Governor Hancock and the French consul in Boston had sent letters to the governors of all the islands of the West Indies advising them of the crime. The outcome was unexpectedly a happy one. "I have one piece of good news to tell you," wrote Belknap, in high spirits.

The Negroes who were kidnapped fron hence last winter are returned. They were carried to St. Bartholomew's and offered for sale. One of them was a sensible fellow, and a Free mason. The merchant to whom they were offered was of this fraternity; they were soon acquainted; the negro told his story, they were carried before the governor, with the ship master and the supercargo. . . .

When, at the end of July, the three kidnapped men returned to Boston, the African Lodge arranged the festivities. "The morning after their arrival here," Belknap continued,

they made me a visit, being introduced by Prince Hall, who is one of the head men among the blacks in this town. The interview was affecting— There, said Prince, this is the gentleman who was so much your friend, and petitioned the Court for us—alluding to the share which I had in the petition against the slave trade. They joined in thanking me. . . .

A battle had been organized and won, and it was a glad morning for Hall. But there was a flaw in the victory. While the gentlemen of the court were willing to stifle the slave trade with Africa, they were not yet ready to treat people of color as full citizens. Thus, a day after the court had closed the ports of the state to slave ships from Africa, the same court, ostensibly to reduce the cost of pauperism to its citizens, ruled that blacks who fled slavery were no longer welcome in the home of the free. Indeed, any "African or Negro" resident in the Commonwealth who could not produce "a certificate from the Secretary of the State" in which he had formerly lived as a "citizen," would be thrown into jail and whipped if, after legal warning, he did not get out. When, during the following year, Prince Hall's friend, John Marrant, the new chaplain of the African Lodge, delivered his sermon at the annual Festival of St. John, his excoriation of the sins of white chauvinism was doubtless directed against this inhuman law. (In 1800, when news arrived in Boston that Gabriel Prosser had tried to organize an insurrection of the slaves in Virginia, a "Notice to Blacks" appeared in the newspapers of Massachusetts listing the names and places of two hundred and forty "African or Negroes . . . Indians and Mulattoes," warning them "to depart out of this commonwealth." One-fourth of the banished blacks were members of the African Society of Boston. *The Gazette of the United States* reprinted the names with this remark: "The following notice has been published in the Boston papers: It seems probable, from the nature of the notice, that some suspicions of the design of the negroes are entertained, and we regret to say there is too much cause.")

Three years later, Prince Hall himself, "at the hall of Brother William Smith of Charlestown," gave the discourse in celebration of the Festival

190

of St. John, duly published as *A Charge Delivered to the Brethren of the African Lodge on the 25th of June, 1792* [figure 84]. Careful, as usual, to proclaim that black Masons had had "no hand in any plots or conspiracies or rebellion," he was impatient that black taxpayers were still denied free schools for their children. Four years later, he would memorialize the selectmen of Boston on that subject, and finally establish a school for black children in his house. Still irked by the decree of expulsion blasted by Marrant, and further irritated by the hostility of white Masons to the African Lodge, he traced the early history of Freemasonary from the defense of Jerusalem by the Order of St. John to the establishment of Christianity south of the Mediterranean by "our Fathers," the African saints—and focused his points in a "Query."

Whether at that day, when there was an African church, and perhaps the largest Christian church on earth, whether, if they were all whites, they would refuse to accept them as their fellow Christians and brother Masons; or whether there were any so weak, or rather foolish, as to say, because they were blacks, they would make their lodge or army to common or too cheap? Sure this was not our conduct in the late war; for then they marched shoulder to shoulder, brother soldier and brother soldier, to the field of battle. . . .

The answer is clear: "he that despises a black man for the sake of his colour, reproacheth his Maker. . . ."

The abrasive attitudes of white Masons continued to rankle. Belknap, investigating the situation in 1795, asked "a white gentleman of the craft, of good information and candour," for his opinion. "The African Lodge, though possessing a charter from England," he replied, "meet by themselves; and white masons not more skilled in geometry, will not acknowledge them. . . . The truth is, they are *ashamed* of being on *equality* with blacks." When Belknap queried Prince Hall, his answer was circumspect, but closed on a taut, ironic note:

Harmony in general prevails between us as citizens, for the good law of the land does oblige every one to live peaceably with all his fellow citizens, let them be black or white, We stand on a level, therefore no preeminence can be claimed on either side. As to our associating, there is here a great number of worthy good men and good citizens, that are not ashamed to take an African by the hand; but yet there are to be seen the weeds of pride, envy, tyranny, and scorn, in this garden of peace, liberty and equality.

Two years later, in June of 1797, at Menotomy (West Cambridge), addressing the African Lodge again at the Feast of St. John [figure 85], the "Right Worshipful Prince Hall," after recalling these brethren who had departed "to the Grand Lodge above," and flaying the merchants who traded in human flesh, described certain "weeds of pride, envy, tryanny, and scorn, in this garden of peace, liberty and equality."

Patience I say, for were we not possess'd of a great measure of it you could not bear up under the daily insults you meet with in the streets of Boston: much more on public days of recreation, how are you shamefully abus'd, and that at such a degree that you may truly be said to carry your lives

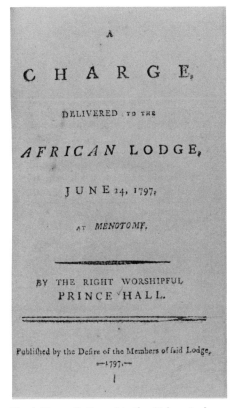

85. *A Charge Delivered to the African Lodge, June 24, 1797, at Menotomy.* Prince Hall, 1797. Library of Congress.

191

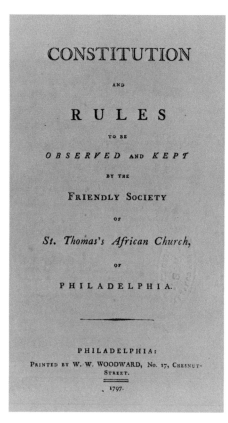

86. *Constitution and Rules to be Observed and Kept by the Friendly Society of St. Thomas's African Church of Philadelphia.* 1797. Library Company of Philadelphia.

in your hands, and the arrows of death are flying about your heads; helpless old women have their clothes torn off their backs, even to the exposing of their nakedness; and by whom are these disgraceful and abusive actions committed, not by the men born and bred in Boston, for they are better bred; but by a mob or horde of shameless, low-lived, envious, spiteful persons, some of them not long since, servants in gentlemen's kitchens, scouring knives, tending horses, and driving chaise . . . many in town who hath seen their behaviour to you, and that without provocation—twenty or thirty cowards fall upon one man—have wonder'd at the patience of the Blacks: 'tis not for want of courage in you, for they know that they dare not face you man for man, but in a mob, which we despise. . . .

Yet, all was not gloom. In Haiti, black leaders had arisen to change the course of imperialist history.

My brethren, let us not be cast down under these and many other abuses we at present labour under: for the darkest is before the break of day. My brethren, let us remember what a dark day it was with our African brethren six years ago, in the French West-Indies. Nothing but the snap of the whip was heard from morning to evening; hanging, broken on the wheel, burning, and all manner of tortures inflicted on those unhappy people for nothing else but to gratify their masters pride, wantonness, and cruelty: but blessed by God, the scene is changed; they now confess that God hath no respect of persons, and therefore receive them as their friends, and treat them as brothers. Thus doth Ethiopia begin to stretch forth her hand, from a sink of slavery to freedom and equality.

If genuine liberty had begun "to dawn in some of the West-Indian islands, "then, sure enough, God would act for justice in New England too, and "let Boston and the World know, that He hath no respect of persons; and that that bulwark of envy, pride, scorn and contempt, which is so visible to be seen in some . . . shall fall, to rise no more." This, in fact, was the message of the great organizer and law-giver, Moses, who had been "instructed by his father-in-law, Jethro, an Ethiopean" in "the first and grandest lecture that Moses ever received from the mouth of man. . . ." It was in this mood during that same month, that Prince Hall headed for Philadelphia to charter its first African Lodge and to install the Reverend Absalom Jones—who had just launched the benevolent Friendly Society of his St. Thomas's African Church [figure 86] as its Worshipful Master.

The charge delivered to the lodge at Menotomy was Prince Hall's last published utterance. He still had ahead of him a decade of useful work. In June of 1807, testifying in a legal process, he stated that he was "a leatherdresser and labourer aged about seventy years," but the Reverend William Bentley, Hall's good friend, in his diary entry for September 20 of the same year, referred to him as "the leading African of Boston & author of several masonic addresses." A fortnight later, he was dead. Six Boston newspapers printed the obituary of "Mr. Prince Hall, aged 72, Master of the African Lodge." His funeral was a Masonic one. The following year his brethren of the lodge honored the great black organizer and servant of his people by changing its name to "The Prince Hall Grand Lodge."

OLAUDAH EQUIANO:
THE IMAGE OF AFRICA

Even as white America fought for its own nationhood, it carried on a war against the nations of Africa, shipping across the ocean cargoes of captives, each a member of a nation and culture in the black motherland. The paradox troubled not a few Patriots, but by 1776 the apologists of slavery had easily resolved it as they fashioned a grand strategy for the suppression of white guilt and black revolt. Let the "Dark Continent" be construed as actual Hell, the abode of the devil and total depravity—a nonplace inhabited by nonpeople—and let this be believed as gospel truth. Ergo, was it not right to destroy the memory of the motherland—of its tongues, its arts, its wisdoms—in the minds of the enslaved, to erase all sense of an honorable and historic identity, to obliterate the very image of Africa, so that the kidnapped, robbed of their heritage, might be divided, ruled, and denationalized by the new Nation? How else explain the fact that during the first two centuries of slavery in America, only a few black voices, furnishing images of a real Africa and real Africans, were permitted in print to demolish the myth of a nonpast?

Most eloquent of these voices was that of a black man who, in his boyhood, was the subject of an African king and lived the rest of his days as slave and freeman in Europe and America. When, in 1789, he gave to the world *The Interesting Narrative of the Life of Olaudah Equiano, or Gustavus Vassa,* he was careful to complete his title with the words, *the African, Written by Himself.* The added phrase gives the timber of his voice, for the writer, neither Afro-American nor Anglo-African, was indeed an African, speaking for the black family of the pan-African world. Not long after Phillis Wheatley's death, he too became a transatlantic celebrity, when the twelve chapters of his *Narrative,* printed first in London and then, in 1791, in New York—with his bold ebony face looking out of the frontispiece— ran through eight editions in five years [figure 88]. One of "the rarest historical documents," Charles H. Nichols has rightly called it in his compendious study of the slave narrative. A classic of its genre, probing a wide range of deeply human themes and recounting the evolution of a bewildered, exiled slave into a statesman of his people, it surely ranks with the autobiographies of Benjamin Franklin and Frederick Douglass. Concrete and vigorous in the style of Defoe, there is a Swiftian quality in the tale of this black Gulliver who explores white worlds and opens wide his eyes in wonder and horror.

Olaudah Equiano, whose book, as he put it, was "the history of neither a saint, a hero, nor a tyrant," is a complex figure still awaiting a full-length portrait. What can be offered here is the merest sketch of his rich life with a few scattered passages, in his own good words, from *The Interesting Narrative.*

193

GUSTAVUS VASSA,

OR

Olaudah Equiano

A NATIVE AFRICAN FROM THE COAST OF GUINEA

*who, after being freed from American Slavery, made voyages
to Europe, the West Indies, &c. and accompanied an Expedition
to explore a North West passage. He was a worthy, pious, and
enlightened Negro, and published his own Narrative dedicated
to the British Parliament.*

87. Olaudah Equiano [Gustavus Vassa]. Unidentified artist. Engraving, not dated. The New-York Historical Society.

194

☛ Equiano first saw the light of day in the nation of Benin, in the interior of eastern Nigeria, where the language was Ibo. "This Kingdom," he begins, "is divided into many provinces or districts: in one of the most remote and fertile of which, I was born, in the year 1745, situated in a charming fruitful vale, named Essaka.... I had never heard of white men or Europeans, nor of the sea; and our subjection to the king of Benin was little more than nominal." His father, in whose household there were "many slaves," was an *enbrenche* or chief, and Essaka was ruled by its chiefs, who "decided disputes and punished crimes." In most cases, the trials were short and "the law of retaliation" prevailed.

Adultery, however, was sometimes punished with slavery or death; a punishment which I believe is inflicted on it throughout most of the nations of Africa: so sacred among them is the honour of the marriage bed.... The men, however, do not preserve the same constancy to their wives, which they expect from them; for they indulge in a plurality....

The "mode of marriage" was a happy ritual; at the end of the ceremony, there was a festival "celebrated with bonfires and loud acclamations of Joy, accompanied with music and dancing." Indeed, says Equiano,

We are almost a nation of dancers, musicians and poets. Thus every great event such as a triumphant return from battle or other cause of public rejoicing is celebrated in public dances.... The assembly is separated into four divisions, which dance either apart or in succession, and each with a character peculiar to itself. The first division contains the married men, who in their dances frequently exhibit feats of arms and the representation of a battle. To these succeed the married women, who dance in the second division. The young men occupy the third: and the maidens the fourth. Each represents some interesting scene of real life, such as a great achievement, domestic employment, a pathetic story, or some rural sport.... This gives our dances a spirit and variety which I have scarcely seen elsewhere. We have many musical instruments, particularly drums of different kinds, a piece of music which resembles a guitar, and another much like a stickado. These last are chiefly used by betrothed virgins, who play on them on all grand festivals.

The land was a happy and equal one—and its people beautiful.

Every one contributes something to the common stock; and as we are unacquainted with idleness, we have no beggars.... Those benefits are felt by us in the general healthiness of the people, and in their vigour and activity; I might have added too in their comeliness. Deformity is indeed unknown amongst us, I mean that of shape ... in regard to complexion, ideas of beauty are wholly relative. I remember while in Africa to have seen three negro children who were tawny, and another quite white, who were universally regarded by myself, and the natives in general, as far as related to their complexions, as deformed. Our women too were in my eye, at least uncommonly graceful, alert, and modest to a degree of bashfulness....

It was this kind of society that shaped the mind of Olaudah Equiano, the youngest and favorite son of his family.

I was trained up from my earliest years in the art of war: my daily exercise

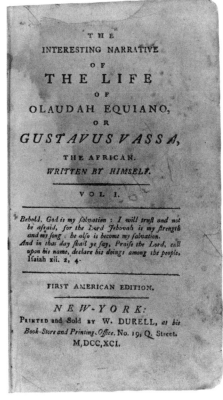

88. *The Interesting Narrative of the Life of Olaudah Equiano or Gustavus Vassa, the African. Written by Himself.* First American edition, 1791. Howard University Library.

was shooting and throwing javelins; and my mother adorned me with emblems, after the manner of our greatest warriors.

But the idyl too early came to an abrupt close: "In this way I grew up till I was turned the age of eleven when an end was put to my happiness. . . ."

Kidnapped by native raiders, carried southward in a sack, sold and resold (and observing, in the process, a variety of black societies), pampered as a slave in an African household, the young boy was eventually marched to the deck of a slave ship riding at anchor, waiting for cargo.

I was immediately handled and tossed up to see if I were sound by some of the crew. . . . When I looked round the ship too and saw a large furnace or copper boiling and a multitude of black people of every description chained together, every one of their countenances expressing dejection and sorrow, I no longer doubted of my fate. . . . In a little time after, amongst the poor chained men I found some of my own nation, which in a small degree gave ease to my mind. . . .

The Middle Passage was a nightmare he could never shake off.

The stench of the hold while we were on the coast was so intolerably loathsome, that it was dangerous to remain there for any time. . . . The closeness of the place, and the heat of the climate, added to the number in the ship, which was so crowded that each had scarcely room to turn himself, almost suffocated us. This produced copious perspirations, so that the air soon became unfit for respiration, from a variety of loathsome smells, and brought on a sickness among the slaves, of which many died. . . . This wretched situation was again aggravated by the galling of the chains, now become insupportable, and the filth of the necessary tubs, into which the children often fell. . . .

The experience decimated the boy, he wanted to die, and had to be force-fed with a whip. He had "never seen among any people such instances of brutal cruelty."

There was slavery, of course, in his own country, he later reflected, but the differences were crucial. When the traders passed through his village, "Sometimes indeed we sold slaves to them, but they were only prisoners of war, or such among us as had been convicted of kidnapping, or adultery, and some other crimes which we esteemed heinous. . . ."

When a trader wants slaves he applied to a chief for them and tempts him with his wares. It is not extraordinary if on this occasion he yields to the temptation with as little firmness, and accepts the price of his fellow creatures liberty with as little reluctance as the enlightened merchant. Accordingly he falls on his neighbors and a desperate battle ensues. If he prevails and takes prisoners, he gratifies his avarice by selling them; but if his party be vanquished and he falls into the hands of the enemy, he is put to death . . . no ransom can save him. . . . The spoils were divided according to the merit of the warriors. Those prisoners which were not sold or redeemed we kept as slaves: but how different was their condition from that of the slaves in the West Indies! With us they do no more work than other members of the community, even their master; their food, clothing and lodging were nearly the same as theirs, (except that they were not permitted to eat with

those who were freeborn), and there was scarce any other difference between them. . . .   Some of these slaves have even slaves under them as their
own property and for their own use. . . .

Arriving at Bridge-Town, Barbados, he was "conducted immediately to
the merchant's yard, where we were all pent up together like so many sheep
in a fold." A few days later, at the auction, he began to understand the
slavemasters' strategy of divide and rule: "I remember . . . there were several
brothers, who in the sale were sold in different lots." Their "cries at part-
ing" moved him, thirty years later, to cry out:

O, ye nominal Christians! might not an African ask you, learned you this
from your God, who says unto you, Do unto all men as you would men
should do unto you? Is it not enough that we are torn from our country
and friends, to toil for your luxury and lust of gain? . . .   Are the dearest
friends and relations, now rendered more dear by their separation from
their kindred, still to be parted from each other, and thus prevented from
cheering the gloom of slavery with the small comfort of being together and
mingling their sufferings and sorrows?

Shipped to a Virginia plantation, "constantly grieving and pining, and
wishing for death," he was summoned from the fields to the big house one
hot day and ordered to fan his master. What he saw in the kitchen turned
his stomach: "A black woman slave . . . was cooking the dinner, and the
poor creature was cruelly loaded with various kinds of iron machines; she
had one particularly on her head, which locked her mouth so fast that she
could scarcely speak; and could not eat nor drink. . . ." This contrivance
was called "the iron muzzle."

One day a lieutenant in the royal navy by the name of Pascal, visiting
Virginia, purchased him for thirty sterling pounds, and gave him a new
name, Gustavus Vassa. His life for the next few years as the lieutenant's
slave opened up new vistas for the precocious lad. He stayed from time to
time in the houses of the lieutenant's friends, went to school at odd moments and gathered the knowledge that would later help him as shipping
clerk and navigator, and began to think about Christian religion, and got
himself baptized. With Pascal, he served in the expedition against Louis-
bourg and in the maneuvers of Admiral Boscawen in the Mediterranean
during the Seven Years War. When the British sailed from Halifax to Cape
Breton, he remembered, "We had the good and gallant General Wolfe on
board our ship, whose affability made him highly esteemed and beloved by
all the men. He often honoured me, as well as other boys, with marks of
his notice, and saved me once a flogging for the fighting with a young
gentleman."

But at the end of the war, Pascal, who had promised to free his intrepid
servant, betrayed and sold him to James Doran, master of the *Sally*, on his
way to the West Indies. For the next three years, from 1763 to 1766,
Equiano had the bitter chance to observe and analyze the nature of bondage in the Caribbean.

At Montserrat, Captain Doran sold the eighteen-year-old youth to "Mr.
Robert King, a Quaker, and the first merchant in the place," who promised

to send him to school in order to improve his arithmetic and train him as a clerk. Equiano's portrait of this tight-fisted Quaker dealer in all sorts of goods, including black flesh and blood—he was no John Woolman or Anthony Benezet—is a small masterpiece.

Mr. King dealt in all manner of merchandises, and kept from one to six clerks. He loaded many vessels in a year; particularly to Philadelphia, where he was born, and was connected with a great mercantile house in that city. He had besides many vessels and droggers, of different sizes, which used to go about the island; and others, to collect rum, sugar, and other goods. I understood boats very well . . . and this hard work . . . in the sugar seasons used to be my constant employment. I have rowed the boat, and slaved at the oars, from one hour to sixteen in the twenty-four. . . .

And as he toiled to enrich his master, he observed the misery of his brother slaves. As bad as King was, others were worse:

In going about the different estates on the island, I had all the opportunity I could wish for to see the dreadful usage of the poor men; usage that reconciled me to my situation, and made me bless God for the hands into which I had fallen.

Indeed, King had found a good thing in Equiano:

There was scarcely any part of his business, or household affairs, in which I was not occasionally engaged. I often supplied the place of a clerk, in receiving and delivering cargoes to the ships in tending stores, and delivering goods: and besides this, I used to shave and dress my master when convenient, and take care of his horse. . . . I worked likewise on board of different vessels of his . . . and saved him, as he used to acknowledge, above a hundred pounds a year.

Longing to purchase his liberty, cruising the islands, he began trading in small articles to amass the sum that King would demand; but at times, the inhumanity of white to black in the islands nearly drove him berserk.

The reader cannot but judge of the irksomeness of this situation to a mind like mine, in being daily exposed to new hardships and imposition, after having seen many better days, and been as it were, in a state of freedom and plenty; added to which, every part of the world I had hitherto been in seemed to me a paradise in comparison of the West-Indies.

Equiano was never a Gabriel Prosser or Nat Turner—indeed, in his earlier years, while he strove stubbornly for his own individual freedom, there is, at times, in his *Narrative* a certain fatalism in his thinking about the possibility of general emancipation.

My mind was . . . hourly replete with inventions and thoughts of being freed, And, if possible, by honest and honourable means; for I always remembered the old adage . . . that "Honesty is the best policy;" [from Poor Richard?] And likewise that other golden precept—"To do unto all men as I would they should do unto me." However, as I was from early years a predestinarian, I thought whatever fate had determined must ever come to pass, and therefore, if ever it were my lot to be freed nothing could prevent me, although I should at present see no means or hope to obtain my freedom; on the other hand if it were my fate not to be freed I never should be so, and all my endeavours for that purpose would be fruitless. In the midst of these thoughts I therefore looked up with prayers anxiously to God for my liberty; and at the same time used every honest means, and did all that was possible on my part to obtain it.

Yet, even as he "became master of a few pounds" of freedom money, "dishonest" means were not entirely excluded.

I determined to make every exertion to obtain my freedom and to return to Old England. For this purpose I thought a knowledge of navigation might be of use to me; for, though I did not intend to run away unless I should be ill used; yet, in such a case, if I understood navigation, I might attempt my escape in our sloop, which was one of the swiftest sailing vessels in the West Indies, and I could be at no loss for hands to join me . . . but this, as I said, was only to be in the event of my meeting with any ill usage. I therefore employed the mate of our vessel to teach me navigation, for which I agreed to give him twenty-four dollars. . . .

Yet, in the Caribbean, helplessly enough, a black seaman who was a slave might find himself ferrying his manacled brothers from market to market. Thus, at the end of 1764, Equiano's captain sailed for South Carolina with "a lead of new slaves"—"live cargo," they were called—and a little later "took slaves on board for St. Estatia, and from thence to Georgia." Back in Montserrat, "we took in, as usual, some of the poor oppressed natives of Africa," and "set off again for Georgia and Charles Town."

   In Savannah, he had a narrow escape. One Sunday night, as he exchanged pleasantries with a few black friends,

it happened that their Master, one Doctor Perkins, who was a very severe and cruel man, came in drunk; and not liking to see any strange negroes in his yard, he and a ruffian of a white man, he had in his service, beset me in an instant, and both of them struck me with the first weapons they could get hold of. I cried out as long as I could for help and mercy; but, though I gave a good account of myself. . . .   They beat and mangled me in a shameful manner, leaving me near dead. I lost so much blood from the wounds I received, that I lay quite motionless, and was so benumbed that I could not feel anything for many hours. Early in the morning they took me away to the jail.

In Philadelphia—a heaven compared with Savannah—where all Friends were not of Robert King's caliber, he sold his own goods "chiefly to the Quakers," who "always appeared to be a very honest discreet sort of people, and never attempted to impose" on him. It was there that he heard the inspired George Whitefield preach: "When I got into the church I saw this pious man exhorting the people with the greatest fervour and earnestness, and sweating as much as I ever did in slavery on Montserrat beach."

   At last, during the summer of 1766, the great day dawned. Equiano, just twenty-one, with forty pounds in his pocket to buy himself free, shamed his unwilling master into keeping his promise—King was forced to admit that he had been clearing one hundred pounds a year on his slave's labor—and then take him on as a free "able-bodied sailor at thirty-six shillings per month." Although Equiano was overjoyed to return to his "original free

African state," he had few illusions about the good life for a black freeman in America. Even in Philadelphia,

were it not for the benevolence of the Quakers in that city many of the sable race who now breathe the air of liberty would, I believe, be groaning indeed under some planter's chains. . . . Hitherto, I had thought only slavery dreadful, but the state of a free negro appeared to me now equally so at least, and in some respects even worse, for they live in constant alarm for their liberty; and this is but nominal, for they are universally insulted and plundered without the possibility of redress. . . .

"In this situation," he asked, "is it surprising that slaves, when mildly treated, should prefer even the misery of slavery to such a mockery of freedom?"

Farther south, in Georgia, the situation of the free black was even more perilous. During the summer of his liberation, on a Savannah street, the slave of a merchant, egged on by his owner, insulted him. When he dealt the slave a blow, the merchant threatened to have him "flogged all round the town." There is no fatalism in Equiano's reaction.

There was a free black man, a carpenter, that I knew, who, for asking a gentleman that he worked for for the money he had earned, was put into gaol; and afterwards this oppressed man was sent from Georgia, with false accusations, of an intention to set the gentleman's house on fire, and run away with his slaves.

He would not allow himself to be flogged.

I dreaded of all things, the thoughts of being striped as I never in my life had the marks of violence of that kind. At that instant a rage seized my soul, and for a little I determined to resist the first man that should offer to lay violent hands on me, or basely use me without a trial; for I would sooner die like a free man, than suffer myself to be scourged by the hands of ruffians, and my blood drawn like a slave.

By good luck he foiled his torturers, but swore never to go back to Savannah: "I thus took a final leave of Georgia; for the treatment I had received in it disgusted me very much against the place."

The West Indies were even more intolerable. The young black mariner had been building a reputation in the islands for his seamanship. On a voyage from Georgia, the captain had died during a storm; the mate proved himself a bungler; and Equiano had to navigate the vessel back to Montserrat. "Many were surprised," he notes with pride, "when they heard of my conducting the sloop into the port, and I now obtained a new appelation, and was called Captain." Yet this was scant compensation for the systematic white brutality of the Caribbean. Returning to Georgia with a cargo of slaves in January of 1767, an ignorant captain wrecked the boat on the shoals of the Bahamas:

The captain immediately ordered the hatches to be nailed down on the slaves in the hold, where there were about twenty, all of whom must unavoidably have perished if he had been obeyed. . . . I asked him why? He said that every one would endeavour to get into the boat, which was but small, and thereby we should be drowned; for it would not have carried above ten at the most. I could no longer restrain my emotion and I told him he deserved drowning for not knowing how to navigate the vessel . . .

the hatches were not nailed down. . . .

"I was disgusted with the West Indies," he concludes, "and thought I never should be entirely free until I left them."

Equiano's acute observations of slavery in the Caribbean are an important source for the historical study of the system in its nuances of depravity. The quality of his outraged commentary may be judged by gathering a few of his passages on an aspect of the institution that interested him deeply—the miscegenation of black and white in the West Indies. Working on the vessels of his Quaker master, Robert King, he was "often a witness to cruelties of every kind, which were exercised" on his "unhappy fellow slaves."

I used frequently to have different cargoes of new negroes in my care for sale; and it was almost a constant practice with our clerks, and other whites, to commit violent depredations on the chastity of the female slaves; and these I was, though with reluctance, obliged to submit to at all times, being unable to help them. . . . I have known our mates to commit these acts most shamefully, to the disgrace, not of Christians only, but of men. I have even known them gratify their brutal passions with females not ten years old; and these abominations some of them practised to such scandalous excess, that one of our captains discharged the mate and others on that account.

As against the literal rape of Africa—

Yet in Montserrat I have seen a negro man staked to the ground, and cut most shockingly, and then his ears cut off bit by bit, because he had been connected with a white woman who was a common prostitute: as if it were no crime in the whites to rob an innocent African girl of her virtue, but most heinous in a black man only to gratify a passion of nature, where the temptation was offered by one of a different colour, though the most abandoned woman of her species.

For killing his own slave, whatever the reason, a law enacted by the Assembly of Barbados fined the murderer the sum of fifteen pounds.

Mr. James Tobin . . . gives an account of a French planter of his acquaintance in the island of Martinique who showed him many mulattoes working in the fields like beasts of burden, and he told Mr. Tobin they were all the produce of his own loins! And I myself have known similar instances. Pray, reader, are these sons and daughters of the French planter less his children by being gotten on a black woman? And what must be the virtue of those legislators and the feelings of those fathers, who estimate the lives of their sons, however begotten, at no more than fifteen pounds. . . .

"But is not the slave trade," he asks, "entirely a war with the heart of man?" And then, a little later, an instance of the absurd: "While I was in . . . St. Kitt's, a very curious imposition on human nature took place: A white man wanted to marry in the church a free black woman that had land and slaves in Montserrat, but the clergyman told him it was against the law of the place to marry a white and a black in the church. . . . The man then asked to be married on the water, to which the parson consented, and the two lovers went in one boat and the parson and clerk in another, and thus the ceremony was performed."

When, in January of 1767, Equiano climbed aboard the *Andromache,* bound for London, there were sad partings with black friends, but no regrets.

I had free dances, as they are called, with some of countrymen, previous to my setting off. . . . With a light heart I bade Montserrat farewell . . . and with it I bade adieu to the sound of the cruel whip, and all other dreadful instruments of torture; adieu to the offensive sight of the violated chastity of the sable female, which has too often accosted my eyes; adieu to oppressions, although to me less severe than most of my countrymen. . . .

So, a year after he had bought himself free, Olaudah Equiano quit America once and for all, as he then thought, to take up another kind of life in a more liberal place. But, now and then, as if driven by an anthropologist's zeal to add fresh data to his case, he would return to the land of the "cruel whip." In the spring of 1771, he shipped as a steward on a vessel bound for Madeira and Barbados—"once more to try my fortune in the West Indies"—and, in the winter, he voyaged to Jamaica, "a very fine large island, well peopled," where he was intrigued by the persistence of African mores.

When I came to Kingston, I was surprised to see the number of Africans who were assembled together on Sundays; particularly at a large commodious place, called Spring Path. Here each different nation of Africa meet and dance after the manner of their own country. They still retain most of their native costumes: they bury their dead, and put victuals, pipes and tobacco, and other things, in the grave with the corpse, in the same manner as in Africa.

But Jamaica, "the most considerable of the West Indian islands," was, as usual, a "scene of roguery."

I saw many cruel punishments inflicted on the slaves in the short time I stayed there. In particular I was present when a poor fellow was tied up and kept hanging by the wrists at some distance from the ground, and then some half hundred weights were fixed to his ankles, in which posture he was flogged unmercifully. There were also, as I heard, two different masters noted for cruelty on the island, who had staked up two negroes naked, and in two hours the vermin stung them to death.

London was a world of absorbing interest to Equiano—he learned the art of the hairdresser, mastered the French horn, went to night school, and in the daytime assisted the scientist, Dr. Charles Irving, "so celebrated for his successful experiments in making sea water fresh."

Displaced so early from his own culture, baptized without conviction, there was a hunger within him to settle the large philosophical questions for his peace of mind. Searching for religious light, he sat and listened in a variety of churches. Neither Quaker, nor Catholic, nor Jew had an answer that gladdened his heart. "I really thought the Turks were in a safer way of salvation than my neighbours," he felt at one point, and "I determined at last to set out for Turkey, and there to end my days." When the Calvinist-Methodists seemed to offer the best solution to the knottiest question in his mind—"the difference between human works and free election"—he ended his soul searching, joined the fellowship of Westminster Chapel, composed twenty-eight quatrains of "Miscellaneous Verses" on the "benefits of Christianity," reminiscent of Jupiter Hammon's, and printed them in the pages of the *Narrative*.

He was still a struggling member of the black poor of London, and the cupboard was often bare. From time to time, he "thought it best, therefore, to try the sea again in quest" of bread—a quest which he did not resist, for he was "still of a roving disposition, and desirous of seeing as many different parts of the world" as he could. Curious to see the East, he signed up as an able seaman on a Turkeyman headed for Smyrna. The ancient splendor, cheap wine, luscious fruits, and the women with veiled faces—some of them "out of curiosity uncovered them to look at me"—delighted him, but it was the racial openness of the Turks, who treated him "always with great civility," that fascinated the African observer.

In general I believe they are fond of black people; and several of them gave me pressing invitations to stay amongst them. . . . I was surprised to see how the Greeks are, in some measure, kept under by the Turks, as the negroes are in the West-Indies by the white people.

There were voyages, also as seaman or steward, to other parts of the Mediterranean, to Genoa, where everything pleased, except that all the "grandeur" was in his "eyes disgraced by the galley slaves, whose condition both there and in other parts of Italy is truly piteous and wretched." Later, in Portugal and Spain, the convert who had struggled for an acceptable Christian doctrine, was tempted by the Church of Rome. At the bull ring in Cádiz, he encountered a Father Vincent, to whom he expressed his dislike of the sport as a "great scandal of Christianity and morals."

I had frequent contests about religion with the reverend father. . . . In his zeal for my conversion, he solicited me to go to one of the universities in Spain, and declared that I would have my education free; and told me, if I got myself made a priest, I might in time become even pope; and that Pope Benedict was a black man. As I was ever desirous of learning, I paused for some time upon this temptation . . . we parted without conviction on either side.

A voyage westward, to the Mosquito Shore of Honduras and Nicaragua, stemming from his missionary zeal to convert "four Musquito Indians, who were Chiefs in their own country, and were brought here by some English traders for some selfish ends," opened up other insights into the ways of the world. One of the Indians, a youth of eighteen, was the king of Mosquitia's son, in whom he took a special interest, tutoring him at sea in English and scripture via "Fox's Martyrology with cuts." The whole dubious enterprise, a child of Dr. Irving's brain, which involved the cultivation of a plantation hacked out of the wilderness with slave labor, turned out to be a fiasco, except perhaps in the opportunity it gave the African to record and analyze a new array of data on comparative racial and social systems. "The natives," he wrote, "are well made and warlike; and they particularly boast of never having been conquered by the Spaniards." These unchristian Indians seemed to him "to be singular, in point of honesty, above any other nation I was ever amongst." Living under an open shed, with all their goods, "we slept in safety . . . if we were to lie in that manner in Europe we should have our throats cut at first sight." Fed up with the drunken debauched white colonizers, he finally managed to slip off; his only regret, the part he played in the recruitment of blacks to man the plantation: "All my poor countrymen, the slaves, when they heard of my leaving them, were very sorry, as I had always treated them with care and affection, and did every thing I could to comfort the poor creatures, and render their condition easy."

It was on the trip back to England that Equiano, in a casual paragraph, makes his single reference to the American Revolution: "We had many very heavy gales of wind in our passage; in the course of which no material incident occurred, except that an American privateer, falling in with the fleet, was captured and set fire to by his Majesty's ship the Squirrel."

There was even a voyage to the Arctic. Back home in London after the Mosquito debacle, "now tired of the sea," he returned to his job with Irving, the purifier of seawater. But when the good doctor, the following spring, invited by Constantine Phipps to join him in an expedition to seek a "north-east passage" to the Orient, suggested that his black assistant come along, "roused by the sound of fame, to seek new adventures, and find, towards the north pole . . . a passage to India," Equiano was happy to accept the offer. During the four-month adventure his main task on the H. M. sloop-of-war *Race Horse* was to turn salt water into fresh with Irving's machine, but at times when the floes crushed the wooden ships, he felt, with the rest, that his end would be an icy grave. He never reached India—had he looked forward to observing a new code of race and morality in that fabulous place?—but, with Dr. Irving, he felt glad that they had sailed nearer to the Pole "than any navigator had ever ventured before."

The anti-slavery activity carried on by Equiano in England during the 1780s as a leading representative of the African Diaspora, culminating with the publication of the *Narrative* at the end of the decade, was the crowning achievement of his life. His mind seems to have been set on going to Africa either as an explorer for the African Association or as a Christian missionary "in hope of doing good, if possible," among his countrymen." Sponsored by influential friends, he sought ordination by the Lord Bishop of London—"your memorialist is a native of Africa, and has a knowledge of the manners and customs of the inhabitants of that country"—but "from scruples of delicacy," he reported, the bishop "declined to ordain me."

As the effort to halt the slave trade gathered strength, Equiano emerged as London's chief black abolitionist. When, in September 1781, the notorious Captain Luke Collingwood, master of the *Zong*, transporting 440 slaves from Africa to Jamaica, jettisoned almost a third of the sick and dying in order to collect their insurance, it was Equiano who initiated the movement that made the atrocity on the *Zong* an international *cause célèbre*. "Gustavus Vassa called on me with an account of 132 Negroes being thrown alive into the sea from on board an English slave ship," Granville Sharp recorded in his journal, and later Sharp demanded that the Admiralty act quickly on the case—"having been earnestly solicited and called upon by a poor negro for my assistance to avenge the blood of his slaughtered countrymen."

Equiano's thirst to see new places was not easily slaked, and even in the midst of organizing the anti-slavery cause he planned excursions at home and abroad. For awhile he served a nobleman in the Dorsetshire militia encamped at Coxheath; and in 1783, "from motives of curiosity," he toured eight counties of Wales. The land seemed to burn his feet; he "thought of visiting old ocean again;" and in the spring of 1785, he embarked as a steward on a ship sailing to Philadelphia:

I was very glad to see this favorite old town once more; and my pleasure was much increased in seeing the worthy Quakers freeing and easing the burthens of many of my oppressed African brethren. It rejoiced my heart when one of these friendly people took me to see a free-school they had erected for every denomination of black people. . . .

In October, back in London, "accompanied by some of the Africans," he presented an "address of thanks," for their abolitionist labors to the Friends of the Grace-Church-Court in Lombard Street on behalf of "the poor, opressed, needy and much degraded Negroes"—a "captivated . . . people."

In 1786, another opportunity to go to Africa turned up. "On my return to London in August," he wrote,

I was very agreeably surprised to find that the benevolence of government had adopted the plan of some philanthropic individuals to send the Africans from hence to their native quarter; and that some vessels were then engaged to carry them to Sierra Leona . . . a select committee of gentlemen for the black poor . . . sent for me . . . they seemed to think me qualified to superintend part of the undertaking, they asked me to go with the black poor to Africa. . . . I expressed some difficulties on the account of the slave dealers, as I would certainly oppose their traffic in the human species by every means in my power.

But once again nothing came of his high hopes. Appointed commissary of stores for the black poor going to Africa, he became enmeshed in a web of white duplicity and negligence. The controversy was hot, and Equiano did not mince words. Some of the black poor feared a British plot to lead them back into chains, and Ottobah Cugoano, a Fanti and former slave in London, expressed his doubt in print. *In the Public Advertiser* for 1787, Equiano exposed the "great villains" who "mean to serve (or use) the blacks the same as they do in the West Indies," while his opponents accused him of "advancing falsehoods as deeply black as his jetty face," of inciting blacks to mutiny—quoting the Reverend Fraser, one of Equiano's "villians," who charged him with urging the settlers to boycott his sermons "for no other reason whatever than that I am *white*."

As Paul Edwards, a recent commentator has noted, the authorities finally vindicated Equiano and awarded him fifty pounds for his services: "On the whole, Equiano appears to have been in the right, and to have been dismissed as a troublemaker because he was not prepared to turn a blind eye to corrupt procedures, and the neglect of the black settlers. "Equiano's worst crime appears to have been his anxiety to see that justice was done to his own people. . . ."

Although he did not get to Africa, the fiasco did not blunt his zeal "to assist in the cause" of his "much injured countrymen," and the *Narrative* comes to an end in 1788 with his petition to the Queen "in behalf of my African brethren."

I do not solicit your royal pity for my own distress; my sufferings, although numerous, are in a measure forgotten. I supplicate your Majesty's compassion for millions of my African countrymen who groan under the lash of tyranny in the West Indies. . . . [I] implore your interposition with your royal consort, in favour of the wretched Africans, that . . . a period may now be put to their misery—and that they may be raised from the condition of brutes, to which they are at present degraded, to the rights and situation of freemen. . . ."

"May the time come—at least the speculation to me is pleasing," is his final word, "when the sable people shall gratefully commemorate the auspicious era of extensive freedom."

The *Interesting Narrative* came off the press in 1789 when Equiano was forty-four, and although the writer had only another eight years to live, he had the joy of its quick and solid success on both sides of the ocean. During the spring of 1792, *The Gentleman's Magazine* of London carried a notice of the marriage of "Gustavus Vassa, the African, well known as the champion and advocate for procuring the suppression of the slave trade" to a Miss Cullen of Ely. The same magazine recorded his death in London on April 31, 1797. In his last moments, he was visited by his friend and co-worker, the great Granville Sharp, with whom he had petitioned king and Parliament. Some years later, Sharp's niece, Jemima, avidly reading the *Narrative,* asked her uncle about the character of its author. "He was a sober, honest man," Sharp replied—"and I went to see him when he lay upon his death bed, and had lost his voice so that he could only whisper. . . ." Of course, Olaudah Equiano, whose book imaged forth a real African during the era of the American Revolution, would never lose his voice.

PART V ☞

Eleven

Against

the

Odds

In white America of the independence time, it was hard for talented black men and women—slave or free—to rise tall out of the swamp of racism, to forge ahead fulfilling all their powers. Looking backward, it seems almost incredible that more than a few from Attucks and Banneker to Wheatley and Equiano, managed to carve their names—and sometimes their faces—on the great shield of Afro-American history. The odds against them were great. Yet what of the others, the tens of thousands, north and south, who lived through that time, slaving in the fields and kitchens, working as farm-hands and woodcutters, drovers and waggoners, as craftsmen in shops and forges, the men of the sea, the whalemen and the sealmen—the breathless runaways, the brave women, doubly oppressed—must not the plain folk also be counted as part of the black presence in the time of the American Revolution?

Of late, diggers into the black American past have been exhuming hitherto forgotten figures who emerged as men and women of mark in their hour and place—individuals whose lives disclose a great deal about the voiceless masses from which they arose. The historian assembles the image with more or less success from hints and scraps—an epitaph on a weathered tombtone, a paragraph hidden in a county history, a stained marriage rec-ord, a last will and testament, a strain of folklore that is nearly true. Here are a few of these modest lives picked from many—five women and six men, eleven against the odds in a white world they never made.

LUCY TERRY PRINCE:
VERMONT ADVOCATE AND POET

Lucy Terry Prince, who, like Phillis Wheatley, was stolen from Africa as a child, was one of the most remarkable women of her time. Like Phillis, she was a poet, but only a single poem of her making remains to delight us. What is known of her life would suggest a body of verse that, to our loss, has not survived.

Lucy first appears in the record as the slave of Ebenezer Wells in Deerfield, Massachusetts. She was baptized at the age of five in the summer of 1735 during the revival known as the "Great Awakening" and nine years later admitted to the "fellowship of the church." When she was sixteen, a war party of Indians attacked the frontier town and the massacre, which she could not forget, stirred her later to write a rough-hewn ballad on the bloody tragedy.

> August 'twas the twenty-fifth,
> Seventeen hundred forty-six;
> The Indians did in ambush lay,
> Some very valiant men to slay,
> The names of whom I'll not leave out.
> Samuel Allen like a hero fout,
> And though he was so brave and bold,
> His face no more shall we behold.
> Eleazer Hawks was killed outright,
> Before he had time to fight,—
> Before he did the Indians see,
> Was shot and killed immediately.
> Oliver Amsden he was slain,
> Which caused his friends much grief and pain.
> Simeon Amsden they found dead,
> Not many rods distant from his head.
> Adonijah Gillett we do hear
> Did lose his life which was so dear.
> John Sadler fled across the water,
> And thus escaped the dreadful slaughter.
> Eunice Allen see the Indians coming,
> And hopes to save herself by running,
> And had not her petticoats stopped her,
> The awful creatures had not catched her,
> Nor tommy hawked her on her head,
> And left her on the ground for dead.
> Young Samuel Allen, Oh lack-a-day!
> Was taken and carried to Canada.

"Bars Fight"—"Bars" was a colonial word for meadow—which got into print for the first time a century later, was handed down in the oral memory of Deerfield people. As late as 1893, an old woman of the town remembered another version of the ballad that began with the lines:

'Twas nigh unto Sam Dickinson's mill,
The Indians there five men did kill.

On May 17, 1756, Lucy Terry married Abijah Prince, a free black, twice her age who owned land and paid taxes in a nearby town. They lived in Deerfield in a house near a brook, still called Bijah's Brook, and began to raise a family. "One of the most noteworthy characters in the early history of Deerfield was a colored woman, known as 'Luce Bijah,' " wrote Josiah Gilbert Holland, Emily Dickinson's close friend, who in 1855 printed Lucy's poem for the first time in his *History of Western Massachusetts*. "She was the slave of Ebenezer Wells, and was noted for her wit and shrewdness. Her house was the constant resort of the boys, to hear her talk."

Meanwhile Abijah was looking elsewhere for a permanent home. When Deacon Samuel Field left him a one-hundred acre lot in Guilford, Vermont, the Princes, in the 1760s, moved north.

Guilford, with its two thousand citizens, as Martha Wright has pointed out, was an unusual village, a kind of Concord in Vermont. It was busy with its farms, brickyards, tanneries, quarries, and potasheries, but it kept its schools open all the year and paid its teachers well. The villagers owned pianos, melodeons, and other musical instruments, and in 1790 the Guilford Social Library boasted a circulation of three hundred volumes. Townspeople were proud of writers like Royall Tyler, the playwright, and Henry Denison, the poet, who lived among them. It was an ambience in which a woman like Lucy Prince, with her gift of pen and tongue, might find congenial.

Life was not all smooth sailing in Guilford. In 1785, Lucy first showed her mettle in standing up for her rights in a public forum. When the Princes were threatened with violence by their white neighbors, the Noyses, she personally appeared before the governor's council and asked for protection. The council found in her favor and ordered the selectmen of Guilford to defend the black family.

By this time, there were six children: Cesar, Festus, Drucilla, Tatnai, Durexa, and Abijah, Jr. She was eager that at least one of her sons might have a good education, and she applied for his admission to Williams College. "He was rejected on account of his race," wrote George Sheldon, the historian of Deerfield. "The indignant mother pressed her claim before the trustees in an earnest and eloquent speech of three hours, quoting an abundance of law and Gospel, chapter and verse, in support of it, but all in vain. The name of no son of Lucy Prince graces the catalogue of Williams College." What could she expect? In 1834, a dozen years after she had passed away, when the Debating Society of that college argued the question, "Ought the New England colleges to graduate people of colour?" it was the negative that won the day.

Before the trustees of Williams College, Lucy had lost her case; but, somewhat later, before the Supreme Court of the United States, she triumphed with éclat. This time, the issue was an attempt of one Colonel Eli Bronson to steal a lot that the Princes owned on the Batten Kill in Sunderland, not far from the house of Ethan Allen. Lawsuits followed. Sheldon is once again the source of the tradition.

The town at length took the matter up, and finally it reached the Supreme Court of the United States, where, we may suppose, Col. Bronson met a Waterloo defeat, and Luce Bijah gained a national reputation. The Court was presided over by Hon. Samuel Chase of Maryland. Col. Bronson employed two leading lawyers of Vermont, Stephen R. Bradley and Royall Tyler, the wit and poet, and afterwards chief justice of the state. Isaac Tichenor, later governor of Vermont, managed the case of Abijah and Lucy. He drew the pleadings, and our Lucy argued the case at length before the court. Justice Chase said that Lucy made a better argument than he had heard from any lawyer at the Vermont bar.

There is not much more to tell. When the War of Independence broke out, Cesar and Festus, the two oldest sons, went down to Massachusetts and enlisted in the army. Cesar perhaps fought with the Green Mountain Boys. Festus, a gifted musician, who could play a number of instruments, after the peace, married a white woman and farmed in Sunderland. Durexa had a reputation as a poet, although some thought she was insane. Abijah died in 1794. In 1803, Lucy went to Sunderland to live, and in her extreme old age rode horseback back and forth to Bennington eighteen miles away. As long as she lived, she made an annual pilgrimage over the Green Mountains to visit Abijah's grave. She died at Sunderland, ninety-one years old.

ALICE: PIONEER OF PHILADELPHIA

All knowledge of Alice is on a few pages of a curious volume, a mélange of a hundred sketches of *Eccentric Biography; or, Memoirs of Remarkable Female Characters, Ancient and Modern,* printed by Isaiah Thomas in 1803. Arranged alphabetically, Alice and her portrait [figure 89] came first, followed by "Arc, Joan of."

Alice was born a slave in Philadelphia in 1686, of parents shipped from Barbados, and lived in that city until she was ten. Then her master moved to Dunk's Ferry, where she continued to the end of her days. Like du Sable at Chicago, she knew the site of a great city when it was primeval forest; like Yarrow Mamout she lived so long that she became a kind of oral historian, a repository of the memory of things. When Jefferson wrote the Declaration, she still had a quarter century to go. Here is her story, slightly abridged.

She remembered the ground on which Philadelphia stands, when it was a wilderness, and when the Indians [its chief inhabitants] hunted wild game in the woods, while the panther, the wolf, and the beasts of the forest were prowling about the wigwams and cabins in which they lived. Being a sensible intelligent woman, and having a good memory, which she retained to the last, she would often make judicious remarks on the population and improvements of the city and country; hence her conversation became peculiarly interesting, especially to the immediate descendants of the first settlers, of whose ancestors she often related acceptable anecdotes. She remembered William Penn, the proprietor of Pennsylvania, Thomas Story, James Logan, and several other distinguished characters of that day. During a short visit which she paid to Philadelphia last fall, many respectable persons called to see her, who were all pleased with her innocent cheerfulness, and that dignified deportment, for which (though a slave and uninstructed) she was ever remarkable. In observing the increase of the city, she pointed out the house next to the episcopal church, to the southward, in Second street, as the first brick building that was erected in it. . . . The first church, she said, was a small frame that stood where the present building stands, the ceiling of which she could reach with her hands from the floor. She was a worthy member of the episcopal society, and attended their public worship as long as she lived . . . she has often been met on horseback, in a full gallop, to church, at the age of 95 years. The veneration she had for the bible induced her to lament that she was not able to read it; but the deficiency was in part supplied by the kindness of many of her friends, who, at her request, would read it to her, when she would listen with great attention, and often make pertinent remarks. She was temperate in her living, and so careful to keep to the truth, that her veracity was never questioned; her honesty also was unimpeached, for such was her master's con-

212

fidence in it, that she was trusted at all times to receive the ferriage money, for upwards of forty years. This extraordinary woman retained her hearing to the end of her life, but her sight began to fail gradually in her ninety-sixth year, without any visible cause than from old age. At one hundred she became blind . . . she would frequently row herself out into the middle of the stream, from which she seldom returned without a handsome supply of fish for her master's table. — About the one hundred and second year of her age, her sight returned. . . .   Before she died, her hair became perfectly white, and the last of her teeth dropt sound from her head at the age of 116 years. At this age she died (1802) at Bristol, in Pennsylvania.

89. Alice. Frontispiece illustration from
*Eccentric Biography; or Memoirs of
Remarkable Female Characters, Ancient and
Modern*, 1803. Yale University Library.

BELINDA OF BOSTON: "MARKED
WITH THE FURROWS OF TIME"

On February 4, 1783, "Belinda an Affrican," at three score and ten, submitted to the general court a personal plea, signed with her mark, full of pain and anger. It is possible that Phillis Wheatley or Prince Hall listened carefully as she poured out her grief, and then edited her words into the formal language of a petition. Even so, her own anguished voice, speaking for many sisters and brothers forgotten by the Revolution, pierces through the rhetoric of the times, as she begins with her childhood memories of Africa.

Seventy years have rolled away, since she on the banks of the Rio da Volta, received her existance—the mountains Covered with Spicy forests, the valleys loaded with the richest fruits, spontaneously produced; joined to that happy temperature of air which excludes excess, would have yielded her the most compleat felicity, had not her Mind received early impressions of the cruelty of men, whose faces were like the moon, and whose Bows and Arrows were like the Thunder and the lightning of the Clouds. The idea of these, the most dreadful of all Enemies, filled her Infant slumbers with horror . . . before she had twelve years injoyed the fragrance of her native groves . . . even when she, in a sacred grove, with each hand in that of a tender Parent, was paying her devotions to the great *Orisa* who made all things—an armed band of white men, driving many of her Country-men in Chains, rushed into the hallowed shades—could the Tears, the sighs, and supplications, bursting from tortured parental affection, have blunted the keen edge of avarice, she might have been rescued from agony, which many of her Countrys Children have felt, but which none hath ever yet described. She cannot forget the horror of the slave ship—"three hundred Affricans in chains, suffering the most excruciating torments, and some of them rejoicing that the pangs of death came like balm to their wounds."

And then America! alas! how unlike the Land where she received her being! . . . she learned to catch the ideas, marked by the sounds of language, only to know that her doom was slavery, from which death alone was to emancipate her.—What did it avail her, that the walls of her Lord were hung with Splendor . . . fifty years her faithful hands have been compelled to ignoble Servitude for the benefit of an Isaac Royall, untill, as if Nations must be agitated, and the world convulsed, for the preservation of that freedom, which the almighty father intended for *all* the human Race, the present war Commenced.

Isaac Royall has fled, and aged Belinda, who slaved her whole life to increase his estate, is free at last—to starve:

The face of your Petitioner, is now marked with the furrows of time, and her frame feebly bending under the oppression of years, while she, by the Laws of the Land, is denied the enjoyment of one morsel of that immense wealth, a part whereof hath been accumulated by her own industry, and the whole augmented by her servitude.

She asks for minimal justice:

Wherefore, casting herself at the feet of your honours . . . she prays that such allowance may be made her, out of the estate of colonel Royall, as will prevent her, and her more infirm daughter, from misery in the greatest extreme, and scatter comfort over the short and downward path of their lives. . . .

Four years later, a Philadelphia magazine, *The American Museum,* put the manuscript into print. There is no record of a response by the general court.

ELIZABETH FREEMAN

AND THE BILL OF RIGHTS

"A woman once lived in Massachusetts," wrote Harriet Martineau in 1838, "whose name ought to be preserved in all histories of the State...."

Mum Bett, whose real name was Elizabeth Freeman, was born, it is supposed, about 1742. Her parents were native Africans.... At an early age she was purchased, with her sister . . . by Colonel Ashley, of Sheffield, Massachusetts. The lady of the mansion, in a fit of passion, one day struck at Mum Bett's sister with a heated kitchen shovel. Mum Bett interposed her arm and received the blow, the scar of which she bore to the day of her death.

She "resented the insult and outrage," left the house of her master, and refused to return.

Colonel Ashley appealed to the law for the recovery of his slave. Mum Bett called on Mr. Sedgwick, and asked him if she could not claim her liberty under the law. He inquired what could put such an idea into her head. She replied that the "Bill of Rights" said that all were born free and equal, and that, as she was not a dumb beast, she was certainly one of the nation.

When people later asked her how she learned the doctrine on which she based her case, she replied, "By keepin' still and mindin' things."

But what did she mean, she was asked, by keeping still and minding things? Why, for instance, (she replied), when she was waiting at table, she heard gentlemen talking over the Bill of Rights and the new constitution of Massachusetts; and in all they said she never heard but that all people were born free and equal, and she thought long about it, and resolved she would try whether she did not come in among them.

Theodore Sedgwick, of nearby Stockbridge, a young lawyer and future senator with anti-slavery ideas, who would later befriend Agrippa Hull, listened carefully to the angry black woman and took her case. Thus did Elizabeth Freeman inaugurate her historic suit against Colonel John Ashley, wealthy landowner and merchant. Sedgwick argued the case before the county court in the town of Great Barrington, the birthplace of another champion of freedom. When the jury set Elizabeth free—and ordered the colonel to pay her thirty shillings damages—the legal fact was established that a Bill of Rights, in Massachusetts at least, had indeed abolished slavery.

In 1781, towards the end of the war, when all this took place, Elizabeth Freeman was a widow nearing forty with a young daughter—her husband had fallen on a battlefield of the Revolution. Colonel Ashley pleaded with her to return to his home and work for wages. She refused. In gratitude to the lawyer who had fought for her freedom, she stayed on with the Sedgwicks as housekeeper for many years. Her courage in defending their home from foraging Shaysites was legendary in the Berkshires. Eventually, she departed from the Sedgwicks and set up house with her daughter.

Two years after her death, in a lecture delivered at the Stockbridge Lyceum, in which he urged the abolition of slavery in the "Cause of Man," Theodore Sedgwick cited as his prime example, Elizabeth Freeman, well known to all in his audience.

If there could be a practical refutation of the imagined superiority of our race to hers, the life and character of this woman would afford that refutation . . . she had nothing of the submissive or subdued character, which succumbs to superior force. . . . On the contrary, without ever claiming superiority, she uniformly . . . obtained an ascendency over all those with whom she was associated in service. . . . Even in her humble station, she had, when occasion required it, an air of command which conferred a degree of dignity. . . . She claimed no distinction; but it was yielded to her from her superior experience, energy, skill, and sagacity.

In later life, she was in great demand as nurse and midwife: "Here she had no competitor. . . . When a child, wailing in the arms of its mother, heard her steps on the stairway, or approaching the door, it ceased to cry." Sedgwick had never known anyone of greater natural endowments.

This woman, by her extreme industry and economy, supported a large family. . . . She could neither read nor write; yet her conversation was instructive, and her society was much sought. She received many visits at her own house, and very frequently received and accepted invitations to pass considerable intervals of time in the families of her friends.

Elizabeth Freeman lived to a ripe old age, through the Revolution and the War of 1812, surrounded by her grandchildren and great-grandchildren. In her last will and testament, she bequeathed to her daughter a black silk gown, gift of her African father, and a "short gown" that her African mother had worn. In 1811, when she was almost seventy, young Susan Sedgwick lovingly painted her portrait in watercolors on a piece of ivory (color plate 7, following page 84). Another Sedgwick, Catherine, the famous novelist, for whom she had cared as a child, wrote a piece about her in 1853, recalling that the words that had inspired her to fight for her freedom came directly from the Declaration of Independence. In the Sedgwick family plot of the old burial ground in Stockbridge, she rests next to Catherine. A plain stone marks her grave, with the following inscription:

ELIZABETH FREEMAN
known by the name of
MUMBET
died Dec. 28, 1829
Her supposed age was 85 years.
Born a Slave

to which might be added: "She struck the death blow of slavery in Massachusetts."

YARROW MAMOUT:

MARYLAND MUSLIM

Just how many African Muslims sweated as slaves in Christian America is a question that scholars have not yet settled. Ben-Ali, a young student in the western Sudan, had the misfortune to find himself on a slave ship bound for America in an early year of the nineteenth century, and in the Georgia State Library there is a manuscript in his fine Arabic hand consisting of long excerpts from the *Risalah,* a well-known text of the Malikite school of Mohammedan law dealing with the ritual of ablutions and the call to prayer. Half a century later in the same state, another Muslim, dubbed London by his master, wrote out in Arabic a phonetic transcription of the four Gospels and several hymns. In the early 1730s, the celebrated Job Ben Solomon, Prince of Boudou in the land of Futa—who knew the whole Koran by heart—spent two years in Maryland as a slave, until a letter that he wrote to his father in purest Arabic came to the attention of Sir Hans Sloane, the linguist of Oxford University, and led to his freedom and an African throne.

Still another black Muslim who had been kidnapped in Africa and sold as a slave in Maryland, long before Job Ben Solomon, was Yarrow Mamout, who bought his own freedom, lived through the Revolution, acquired property, never gave up his religion, and lived to be over a hundred years old. One winter day in the year 1819, the artist Charles Willson Peale—whose son Raphaelle had painted Absalom Jones—visiting Washington to record the visages of American worthies for his Baltimore Museum, rode over to Georgetown to do the centenarian's portrait [color plate 6, following page 84]. In his diary for that day, the only source for the life of Yarrow Mamout, he wrote at length:

I spent the whole day and not only painted a good likeness of him, but also the drapery and background—However to finish it more completely I engaged him to set the next day—and early in the morning went to see some of the family who had knowledge of him for many years & whose Ancestors had purchased him from the ship that brought him from Africa. A Mr. Bell in a Bank directed me to an ancient widow who had set him free—on making inquiry of this Lady about his age, for he told me that he would be 134 years old in next March, I found that he counted 12 moons to the year, and that he was 35 years old when he was first brought to America by Captn Dow — But the widow Bell told me that it was a practice in former times when slaves was brought into the Country, they were valued by a committee who estimated their age and she thought that he had been sold as 14 years or thereabout, yet he might be a little older —

That at the decease of Mr Bell he became the property of her husband—that Yarrow was always an industrious hard working man and had served them faithfully for many years, and her Husband intending to build a large House in Georgetown, told Yarrow if he would be very industrious in Making the Bricks for that House and out houses, that when he had made all the Bricks, that he would set him free. Yarrow completed his task, but his master died before he began the House, and the widow knowing the design of her Husband, told Yarrow that as he had performed his duty, that she had made the necessary papers to set him free & now he was made free. Yarrow made a great many Bows thanking his mistress and said that [if] ever mistress wanted work done, Yarrow would work for her . . . after Yarrow obtained his freedom he worked hard and saved his money until he got 100$ which [he] put into an old gentlemans hands to keep for him—that person died and Yarrow lost his money—however it did not dispirit him, for he still worked as before and raised another 100$ which he put into the care of a young merchant in Georgetown, and Yarrow said young man no die—but this merchant became a Bankrupt and thus Yarrow mett a 2d heavy loss—yet not dispirited he worked & saved a 3d sum amounting to 200$, some friend to Yarrow advised him to Buy bank stock in the Columbia Bank—this advice Yarrow thought good for he said Bank no die—and he was amongst the first who contributed to that Bank about 26 years past. . . .

Yarrow owns a House and lotts and is known by most of the Inhabitants of Georgetown & particularly by the Boys who are often teazing him which he takes in good humour. It appears to me that the good temper of the man has contributed considerably to longevity. Yarrow has been noted for sobriety & a cheerfull conduct, he professes to be a Mahometan, and is often seen & heard in the Streets singing Praises to God—and conversing with him he said man is no good unless his religion come from the heart.   he said never stole one penny in his life—yet he seems delighted to sport with those in company, pretending that he would steal something—The Butchers in the Market can always find a bit of meat to give to Yarrow—sometimes he will pretend to steal a piece of meat and put it into the Basket of some gentleman, and then say me no tell if you give me half —

The acquaintances of him often banter him about eating Bacon and drinking Whiskey—but Yarrow says it is no good to eat Hog—& drink whiskey is very bad.

I retouched his Portrait the morning after his first setting to mark what rinkles & lines to characterize better his Portrait. . . .

It is said that Peale was interested in Yarrow Mamout only because he was a specimen of healthy, cheerful old age, but something more is caught forever in the portrait. The face of the venerable black Muslim is shrewd, sad, witty, cynical. He has seen a lot in his long life.

VENTURE SMITH:

COLONIAL JOHN HENRY

"I was born at Dukandarra, in Guinea, about the year 1729," related old Venture Smith of Haddam Neck, Connecticut, to Elisha Niles, school teacher and Revolutionary veteran.

My father's name was Saungm Furro, Prince of the tribe of Dukandarra. My father had three wives. Polygamy was not uncommon in that country, especially among the rich, as every man was allowed to keep as many wives as he could maintain. By his first wife he had three children. The eldest of them was myself, named by my father, Broteer. . . . I descended from a very large, tall and stout race of being, much larger than the generality of people in other parts of the globe. . . .

Like Olaudah Equiano, he was an early victim of the African slave trade. At the age of eight, one of two hundred and sixty blacks canoed from "the castle" to a Rhode Island slaver, a steward bought him, as a private speculation, for four gallons of rum and a piece of calico, and renamed him "Venture." A quarter of the cargo perished in the Middle Passage to Barbados. His third owner gave him a surname—thus Broteer, son of a Guinea prince, became Venture Smith, New England slave.

The *Narrative of the Life and Adventures of Venture, a Native of Africa, But Resident above Sixty Years in the United States of America, Related by Himself* is an epic of heroic labor and of Bunyanesque strength that became a myth. Venture Smith, who according to tradition, was straight and tall, weighed over three hundred pounds and measured six feet around the waist, was a New England John Henry who swung his ax to break his chains.

But there is no humor in the tale of this black Bunyan. Venture Smith was no ring-tailed roarer who told tall tales. At nine, he carded wool and pounded corn for the poultry, and for the next dozen years worked day and night for his master while he hungered for freedom and planned to win it one way or another. He was abused. One day his master's son ordered him "very arrogantly" to drop what he was doing and take on another task.

I replied to him that my master had given me so much to perform that day, and that I must faithfully complete it in that time. He then broke out into a great rage, snatched a pitchfork and went to lay me over the head therewith, but I as soon got another and defended myself with it. . . . He immediately called some people. . . . and ordered them to take his hair rope and come and bind me with it. They all tried to bind me, but in vain, though there were three assistants in number.

Later, when Venture felt it was useless further to resist, he was taken "to a gallows made for the purpose of hanging cattle on" and suspended there-from for an hour.

At twenty-two, he married Meg, another slave on the farm, and with three indentured whites stole his master's boat, stocked it with food, and at midnight, "mutually confederated not to betray or desert one another on pain of death," steered for Montauk Point and the Gulf of Mexico. But the conspirators fell out, and the plan aborted. When Venture defended Meg from being beaten by her mistress, she turned her frenzy on him: "She took down her horse whip, and while she was glutting her fury with it, I reached out my great black hand, raised it up and received the blows of the whip on it which were designed for my head. Then I immediately com-mitted the whip to the devouring fire." This was not the end. In revenge, his master clubbed him on the head from behind, and later, with a brother, ambushed him on horseback as he walked down a lonely road. "I became enraged at this and immediately turned them both under me, laid one of them across the other, and stamped them both with my feet. . . ." The two whites summoned help to manacle his hands and padlock his legs with a large oxchain: after a few days "my master asked me with contemptuous hard names whether I had not better be freed from my chains and go to work. I answered him 'No,' 'Well, then,' said he, 'I will send you to the West Indies, or banish you. . . .' I answered him, 'I crossed the waters to come here and I am willing to cross them to return.' "

This giant black man, who would suffer no insult, was a problem for owners who profited by his sinews: "One time my master sent me two miles after a barrel of molasses, and ordered me to carry it on my shoulders. [He did.] When I lived with Capt. George Mumford, only to try my strength I took upon my knees a tierce of salt containing seven bushels, and carried it two or three rods. Of this fact there are several eye witnesses now living."

Meanwhile he toiled and scraped to hoard enough to buy his freedom. He managed to put away "two johannes, three old Spanish dollars, and two thousands of coppers . . . by cleaning gentlemen's shoes and drawing-boots, by catching muskrats and minks, raising potatoes and carrots . . . by fishing in the night," and Meg contributed five pounds. Through a free black friend, he acquired a piece of land and in two years farmed ten pounds out of it. A new master allowed him to hire himself out once in a while and keep part of his earnings. One fall and winter, he worked on Long Island: "In that six months' time I cut and corded four hundred cords of wood, besides threshing out seventy-five bushels of grain. . . . At night I lay on the hearth, with one coverlet over and another under me." In 1765, his master finally liberated him for "seventy-one pounds two shillings." He was thirty-six years old: "I had already been sold three different times, made considerable money with seemingly nothing to derive it from, had been cheated out of a large sum of money, lost much by misfortunes and paid an enormous sum for my freedom."

Although he was now free, his wife and children were still slaves. He settled on Long Island, where he performed prodigies of labor, while he lived like a Spartan, to pile up the dollars to free them. His hired axe toppled grove after grove. He purchased Meg for forty pounds (and "thereby prevented having another child to buy, as she was pregnant") and his daughter Hannah for forty-four, paid four hundred dollars to liberate his sons, Solomon and Cuff, and redeemed from slavery three black friends. (Solomon died soon after of scurvy on a whaleship; Cuff enlisted in the East Haddam militia and fought in the army of the Revolution.) He never stopped. Chartering a thirty-ton sloop, he took on a crew and plied the wood trade to Rhode Island, fished with set-nets and pots for eels and lobsters, shipped out on a seven-month whaling voyage, and raised cart-loads of watermelons for market.

When he was forty-seven, he sold out and moved back to Connecticut, bought land, built a house, and hired two black farmhands. When one of them defaulted on a debt, he procured a warrant and carried him on his shoulders two miles to court. As time went on, he acquired "boats, canoes and vessels, not less than twenty." His enormous labor paid off, but being black he had to work three times as hard as white for the same returns. There was heartache. Fleeced by a Captain Elisha Hart of Saybrook, he found that justice was hard to come by.

I applied to several gentlemen for counsel in this affair, and they advised me, as my adversary was rich, and threatened to carry the matter from court to court till it would cost me more than the first damages would be,—to pay the sum and submit to the injury, which I accordingly did, and he has often since insultingly taunted me with my unmerited misfortune. Such a proceeding as this committed on a defenceless stranger, almost worn out in the hard service of the world, without any foundation in reason or justice, whatever it may be called in a Christian land, would in my native country have been branded as a crime equal to highway robbery. But Captain Hart was a *white gentleman,* and I a *poor African,* therefore it was *all right, and good enough for the black dog.*

When his *Narrative* was printed in New London in 1798, he said in it:
I am sixty-nine years old. . . . My strength which was once equal if not superior to any man whom I have ever seen, is now enfeebled so that life is a burden, and it is with fatigue that I can walk a couple of miles, stooping over my staff. . . . But amidst all griefs and pains, I have many consolations; Meg the wife of my youth, whom I married for love and bought with my money, is still alive. My freedom is a privilege which nothing can equal.

A village historian, over a century later, repeated a pleasant story of his wedding day:
It is related of Venture that on the occasion of his marriage he threw a rope over the house of his master, where they were living, and had his wife go to the opposite side of the house and pull on the rope hanging there while he remained and pulled on his end of it. After both had tugged at it awhile in vain, he called her to his side of the house and by their united effort the rope was drawn over to themselves with ease.

He then explained the object lesson: "If we pull in life against each other we shall fail, but if we pull together we shall succeed."

The strength and skill of Venture Smith were talked about in Connecticut and Long Island for a hundred years after his death. Stories about this folk work-hero passed into tradition with variation of all kinds. One old-timer remembered that when Venture lifted the great tierce of sale, his brogan shoes burst off his feet. Another recalled that a "noted wrestler tried his skill in wrestling with Venture, but found he might as well try to remove a tree." He was too heavy to ride on a horse's back, so used a two-wheeled cart. "Sometimes his horse did not behave well, and then, Venture would put one hand in front of his horse's forelegs and one hand behind them and jounce the fore parts of the horse up and down a few times and remark, 'There!' The horse would usually behave well after such a jouncing."

Venture's axe was almost always a part of the tale. It was reported that this axe weighed nine pounds and that he never raised it higher than his head—said he didn't believe in chopping air. He could cut up nine cords in a day and often paddled his canoe forty-five miles across Long Island Sound and back to chop wood and bring back clams. Once, when he was old and blind, and had to be led by his grandchildren, he moved a loaded scow stuck high up on the beach. "Venture said, 'Lead me down. True, I am blind, but I can give you a lift.' The timbers fairly cracked as his great hands touched the scow. She swept into the water like a bird on the wing." Another tradition has it that, after his sight failed, when he bought oxen, he seized each ox by its hind legs and raised it up to estimate it weight.

Borne down by age and illness, Venture Smith died on September 19, 1805, in his seventy-seventh year. Like an epic warrior, his body was conveyed in a boat across the Cove and carried three miles by four men, two white and two black, to the burial ground of the First Congregational Church. As they arrived at the cemetery, one of the black pallbearers, crushed by the weight of the bier, exclaimed: "Durned great Negro! Ought to have quartered him and gone four times. It makes the gravel stones crack under my feet." On the brown-stone slab that marks his grave, next to his wife Meg's, is the inscription: "Sacred to the Memory of Venture Smith, African. Though the son of a King, he was kidnapped and sold as a slave, but by his industry he acquired money to purchase his freedom."

MOSES SASH: "A CAPTAIN & ONE
OF SHAISES COUNCILL"

When debt-ridden farmers led by the Revolutionary veteran, Captain Daniel Shays, arose in western Massachusetts during the winter of 1786-87, Prince Hall in Boston pledged the support of his lodge of black Masons in the crushing of the rebellion. Whatever Hall's real reasons may have been, Governor Bowdoin rejected the offer. It is doubtful that more than a few black troops marched west to suppress this "little rebellion" that so alarmed the men of "wealth and talent" of the state. Were there Afro-Americans who stood with Shays? There is record of at least one black veteran of the Revolution who fought in the uprising and possibly served as an officer in a section of the guerilla army.

At the time of the uprising, Moses Sash of Worthington was thirty-two years old. Ten years earlier, like Shays, he had enlisted in the Continental Army and at the end of the war had trudged home from West Point to resume the old life. The documents describe him as farmer and laborer; five feet, eight inches high; complexion, black; hair, wool.

Among the records of the supreme judicial court of Massachusetts there is a crumbling packet of grand jury indictments, naming thirty-two traitorous rebels, variously denominated yeoman, husbandman, tanner, tradesman, laborer. Moses Sash is the only black man of the group, the only laborer, and the only rebel to have two indictments leveled against him.

The first of the indictments reads as follows:

The jurors of the Commonwealth of Massachusetts upon their oath present that Moses Sash of Worthington . . . a negro man & Labourer being a disorderly, riotous & seditious person & minding & contriving as much as in him lay unlawfully by force of arms to stir up promote incite & maintain riots mobs tumults insurrections in this Commonwealth & to disturb impede & prevent the Government of the same & the due administration of justice in the same, & to prevent the Courts of justice from sitting as by Law appointed for that purpose & to promote disquiets, uneasiness, jealousies, animosities & seditions in the minds of the Citizens of this Commonwealth on the twentieth day of January in the year of our Lord Seventeen hundred & eighty seven & on divers other days & times as well before as since that time at Worthington . . . unlawfully & seditiously with force & arms did advise persuade invite incourage & procure divers persons . . . of this Commonwealth by force of arms to oppose this Commonwealth & the Government thereof & riotously to join themselves to a great number of riotous seditious persons with force & arms thus opposing this commonwealth & the Government thereof as aforesaid & the due administration of justice in the same, and in pursuance of his wicked seditious purposes aforesaid unlawfully & seditiously, did procure guns, bayonets, pistols, swords, gunpowder, bullets, blankets & provisions & other warlike instruments offensive & defensive & other warlike supplies, & did cause & procure them to be carried & conveyed to the riotous & seditious persons as aforesaid in evil example to others to offend in like manner against the peace of the Commonwealth aforesaid & dignity of the same.

Thus, Moses Sash, in January 20, 1787, as a participant in an insurrectionary demonstration called by a rebel convention, had tried to stop the courts from foreclosing mortgages and jailing debtors in "the due administration of justice." Five days later, in fact, he would flee with Shays after government mortars had scattered the rebels from Arsenal Hill in Springfield. As Bowdoin's general pursued the insurgents through Chicopee and South Hadley, Shays rallied his band on two hills in Pelham, sending out parties to forage for food and guns. Thus, the second indictment against Sash, who on January 30, "fraudulently, unlawfully & feloniously two guns to the value of five pounds of certain persons to the jurors unknown with force and arms did steal away."

Eventually, the new governor, John Hancock, pardoned almost all the insurgents, leaders, and followers. On the back of the first indictment against Moses Sash are the words: "a Captain & one of Shaises Councill." It is the only indictment of the packet so endorsed. Thus far, the archives have not yielded any further data to account for the high place of this black private of the first Revolution in the second revolution of Daniel Shays.

AMOS AND VIOLATE FORTUNE: FIRST CITIZENS OF NEW HAMPSHIRE

On January 28, 1796, at the parsonage of a small town in New Hampshire, a meeting was held "for the purpose of forming a Collection of Usefull books to be called the Social Library in Jaffrey." Among the twenty-two charter members present that day was venerable Amos Fortune, a free black man and one of the more literate citizens of the town, who, as a boy, had been purchased from a Yankee slave dealer and had served as a chattel for half a century.

Where he got the name of Fortune no one knows. It was in Boston, possibly, during his youthful years, that he learned to read and write and picked up the craft of bookbinding. As a slave in Woburn, Massachusetts, he learned the art of the tanner from his master, Ichabod Richardson. For nearly forty years Fortune slaved for Richardson until, in the year 1770, he was permitted to buy himself free. Sixty years old, he now began to live. He was a master tanner and business was good. He paid his church and town taxes regularly and in 1774 purchased a half-acre on the Wilmington Road. When he was sixty-eight, tired of being a bachelor, he bought and wedded Lydia Somerset in nearby Lexington, where the war had started a few years earlier. When Lydia died a few months after the marriage he bought and wedded Violate Baldwin, who would outlive him by a year.

In 1781, for reasons unknown, the Fortunes moved to Jaffrey, New Hampshire. There he set up his tannery and again he prospered. After a time, he took in apprentices, black and white—a white doctor sent him his son to learn tanning, as well as reading and writing. He joined the church, became one of the first citizens of Jaffrey.

There were a few other free black families in Jaffrey, but none had done as well as the Fortunes. Amos reached out to them. He knew enough law to act as an attorney for a brother in distress, and he took into his household two black girls who became part of the family.

In 1796, after he had paid in his three dollars as a founding member of the Social Library—a dollar and a half was a good day's pay at the time— he began to rebind the books in the collection, using his own fine leather, which is still soft and warm.

Five years later, at the age of ninety-one, Amos died. In his will he left everything to Violate except for a few pieces of furniture and a foot-wheel loom that went "to Celyndia Fortune, my adopted daughter." The final item of the will reveals the public benefactor: if there is any money left after Violate's death, it is to be used "to give a handsome present...to the Church of Christ in this town, and the remaining part . . . a present for the Support of the School. . . ." The church acquired a silver communion service; the fund he bequeathed to the school is still used for annual prizes.

Another item in Amos Fortune's will reveals his pride in a long life well-lived: "I order my executor after my decease and after the decease of . . .

90 and 91. Gravestones of Amos and Violate Fortune. Fiberglass facsimiles of originals in Jaffrey, New Hampshire. Smithsonian Institution, Office of Exhibits.

my beloved wife that handsome grave Stones be erected to each of us if there is any estate left for that purpose." The "handsome grave Stones" stand today in the churchyard behind the Meeting House in Jaffrey. Carved on the gray slate, beneath the urn and willow, are two epitaphs that Amos himself perhaps composed:

SACRED
to the memory of
Amos Fortune,
who was born free in
Africa, a slave in America
he purchased liberty,
professed Christianity,
lived reputably, and
died hopefully.
Nov. 17, 1801,
AET. 91

SACRED
to the memory of
Violate,
by sale the slave of
Amos Fortune, by Marri-
age his wife, by her
fidelity his friend and
solace, she died his widow
Sept. 13, 1802
AET. 73

JOHN JACK AND CASEY THE RUNAWAY: TWO CONCORD SLAVES

In Concord, Massachusetts, not far from Emerson's "rude bridge," John Jack, former slave of Benjamin Barron, a shoemaker, built a cabin in 1761, after he had purchased his freedom. At the same time, he asked lawyer Daniel Bliss to draw up his will, leaving everything after burial expenses to his wife, Violet. John Jack died two years before the shot was fired heard round the world, and Daniel Bliss, later a Tory expatriate, write the epitaph carved on the tombstone, which a London newspaper printed as an "ironic comment" on the claims of the Sons of Liberty. When the original gravestone wore away, the lawyers of Concord in 1830 replaced it with a replica [figure 92].

The abolitionist, Henery David Thoreau, curious about Concord's ancient history, records another black man of Concord who lived in the Revolutionary time, an African slave named Casey, who also loved liberty. He was about twenty "when stolen from Africa; left a wife and one child there," wrote Thoreau in his journal in 1858. One day his master's son "threw snowballs at him . . .and finally C., who was chopping in the yard, threw his axe at him. . . ." Master "said he was an ugly nigger and he must put him in jail." Casey ran away, "pursued by his neighbors, and hid himself in the river up to his neck till nightfall" and then "cleared far away, enlisted, and was freed as a soldier after the war." Casey "used to say that he went home to Africa in the night and came back again in the morning; i.e., he dreamed of home. . . ."

No doubt John Jack knew Casey, the runaway slave. Did they talk together about their dreams of Africa?

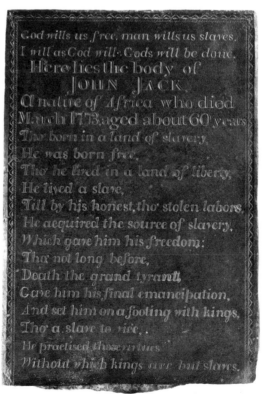

92. Gravestone of John Jack. Fiberglass facsimile of original in Concord, New Hampshire. Smithsonian Institution, Office of Exhibits.

PART VI

The Incomplete Revolution

Toward the end of June in 1852, the seventy-sixth year of the American Republic, papers and placards in Rochester, New York, carried the news that Frederick Douglass would deliver a Fourth of July oration in Corinthian Hall. The address was one of the profoundest utterances of his career [figure 93]. His great voice soared out of the hall to assail the ears of all white America.

Fellow citizens, why am I called upon to speak here today? What have I, or those I represent, to do with your national independence? Are the great principles of political freedom and of natural justice, embodied in that Declaration of Independence, extended to us? and am I, therefore, called upon to bring our humble offering to the national altar, and to confess the benefits and express devout gratitude for the blessings resulting from your independence to us?

☞ Suppose, now, it is the twenty-fourth birthday of the United States of America, the Fourth of July of 1800—the year Nat Turner was born and Gabriel Prosser was hanged. Suppose, also, the place is Philadelphia, the hall Richard Allen's Bethel Church—and Absalom Jones is addressing a black congregation on the meaning of the Fourth of July.

Three years earlier, four worried runaways from North Carolina, working and hiding out in Philadelphia, had come to him with their anguish. What could they do to escape the clutches of that terrible law—the Fugitive Slave Act—that Congress had passed and President Washington had signed in the year 1793 [figure 94]? The Reverend Jones listened and pondered, and then took up his quill. It was time for a decisive thrust. Days passed as he put the items of the indictment into their proper order. The result was that four black men submitted to the "President, Senate, and House of Representatives" of the United States an historic petition on the rights of Afro-Americans—the first that the Congress would be forced to consider.

As Jones framed the document, it began with a statement of the case.

Being of African descent, late inhabitants and natives of North Carolina, to you only, under God, can we apply with any hope of effect, for redress of our grievances, having been compelled to leave the State wherein we had a right of residence, as freemen liberated under the hand and seal of humane and conscientious masters, the validity of which act of justice, in restoring us to our native right of freedom, was confirmed by judgment of the Superior Court of North Carolina . . . yet, not long after this decision, a law of that State was enacted, under which men of cruel disposition, and void of just principle, received countenance and authority in violently seizing, imprisoning, and selling into slavery, such as had been so emancipated; whereby we were reduced to the necessity of separating from some of our nearest and most tender connexions, and of seeking refuge in such parts of the Union where more regard is paid to the public declaration in favor of liberty and the common right of man, several hundred, under our circumstances, having in consequence of the said law, been hunted day and

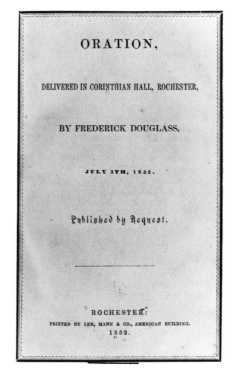

ORATION,

DELIVERED IN CORINTHIAN HALL, ROCHESTER,

BY FREDERICK DOUGLASS,

JULY 5TH, 1852.

Published by Request.

ROCHESTER:
PRINTED BY LEE, MANN & CO., AMERICAN BUILDING.
1852.

93. *Oration, Delivered in Corinthian Hall, Rochester, by Frederick Douglass, July 5th, 1852.* Rochester, 1852. Library of Congress.

231

SECOND CONGRESS

OF THE

UNITED STATES:

At the Second Session, begun and held at the City of PHILADELPHIA, in
the State of Pennsylvania, on Monday, the fifth of November,
one thousand seven hundred and ninety-two.

An ACT *respecting Fugitives from Justice, and Persons escaping from the Service of their Masters.*

Sec. 1. BE it enacted by the Senate and House of Representatives of the United States of America in Congress assembled, That whenever the executive authority of any state in the union, or of either of the territories north-west or south of the river Ohio, shall demand any person as a fugitive from justice, of the executive authority of any such state or territory to which such person shall have fled, and shall moreover produce the copy of an indictment found, or an affidavit made before a magistrate of any state or territory as aforesaid, charging the person so demanded, with having committed treason, felony or other crime, certified as authentic by the governor or chief magistrate of the state or territory from whence the person so charged, fled, it shall be the duty of the executive authority of the state or territory to which such person shall have fled, to cause him or her to be arrested and secured, and notice of the arrest to be given to the executive authority making such demand, or to the agent of such authority appointed to receive the fugitive, and to cause the fugitive to be delivered to such agent when he shall appear : But if no such agent shall appear within six months from the time of the arrest, the prisoner may be discharged. And all costs or expenses incurred in the apprehending, securing, and transmitting such fugitive to the state or territory making such demand, shall be paid by such state or territory.

Sec. 2. *And be it further enacted,* That any agent, appointed as aforesaid, who shall receive the fugitive into his custody, shall be empowered to transport him or her to the state or territory from which he or she shall have fled. And if any person or persons shall by force set at liberty, or rescue the fugitive from such agent while transporting, as aforesaid, the person or persons so offending shall, on conviction, be fined not exceeding five hundred dollars, and be imprisoned not exceeding one year.

Sec. 3. *And be it also enacted,* That when a person held to labour in any of the United States, or in either of the territories on the north-west or south of the river Ohio, under the laws thereof, shall escape into any other of the said states or territory, the person to whom such labour or service may be due, his agent or attorney, is hereby empowered to seize or arrest such fugitive from labour, and to take him or her before any judge of the circuit or district courts of the United States, residing or being within the state, or before any magistrate of a county, city or town corporate, wherein such seizure or arrest shall be made, and upon proof to the satisfaction of such judge or magistrate, either by oral testimony or affidavit taken before and certified by a magistrate of any such state or territory, that the person so seized or arrested, doth, under the laws of the state or territory from which he or she fled, owe service or labour to the person claiming him or her, it shall be the duty of such judge or magistrate to give a certificate thereof to such claimant, his agent or attorney, which shall be sufficient warrant for removing the said fugitive from labour, to the state or territory from which he or she fled.

Sec. 4. *And be it further enacted,* That any person who shall knowingly and willingly obstruct or hinder such claimant, his agent or attorney in so seizing or arresting such fugitive from labour, or shall rescue such fugitive from such claimant, his agent or attorney when so arrested pursuant to the authority herein given or declared ; or shall harbour or conceal such person after notice that he or she was a fugitive from labour, as aforesaid, shall, for either of the said offences, forfeit and pay the sum of five hundred dollars. Which penalty may be recovered by and for the benefit of such claimant, by action of debt, in any court proper to try the same ; saving moreover to the person claiming such labour or service, his right of action for or on account of the said injuries or either of them.

JONATHAN TRUMBULL, *Speaker of the*
House of Representatives.
JOHN ADAMS, *Vice-President of the United*
States, and President of the Senate.

APPROVED, February twelfth, 1793.
G°: WASHINGTON, *President of the United States.*

94. The Fugitive Slave Act, approved by George Washington, February 12, 1793.
Library of Congress.

night, like beasts of the forest, by armed men with dogs, and made a prey of as free and lawful plunder.

Then, with painstaking care, Jones wrote out their individual stories in exact detail.

I, Jupiter Nicholson, of Perquimans County, N.C., after being set free by my master, Thomas Nicholson, and having been about two years employed as a seaman in the service of Zachary Nickson, on coming on shore, was pursued by men with dogs and arms; but was favored to escape by night to Virginia, with my wife, who was manumitted by Gabriel Cosand, where I resided about four years in the town of Portsmouth, chiefly employed in sawing boards and scantling; from thence I removed with my wife to Philadelphia, where I have been employed, at times, by water, working along shore, or sawing wood. . . .

I, Jacob Nicholson, also of North Carolina, being set free by my master, Joseph Nicholson, but continuing to live with him till, being pursued night and day, I was obliged to leave my abode, sleep in the woods, and stacks in the fields, &c, to escape the hands of violent men. . . .

I, Joe Albert, manumitted by Benjamin Albertson . . . we were night and day hunted by men armed with guns, swords and pistols, accompanied with mastiff dogs. . . . After binding me with my hands behind me, and a rope around my arms and body, they took me about four miles to Hartford prison, where I lay four weeks . . . with the assistance of a fellow-prisoner (a white man) I made my escape and for three dollars was conveyed, with my wife, by a humane person, in a covered wagon by night, to Virginia. . . . On being advised to move northward, I came with my wife to Philadelphia, where I have labored for a livelihood upwards of two years, in Summer mostly, along shore in vessels and stores, and sawing wood in the Winter.

I, Thomas Pritchet . . . built myself a house, cleared a sufficient spot of woodland to produce ten bushels of corn . . . this I was obliged to leave . . . being threatened by Holland Lockwood . . . that if I would not come and serve him, he would apprehend me, and send me to the West Indies; Enoch Ralph also threatening to send me to jail, and sell me for the good of the country; being thus in jeopardy, I left my little farm, with my small stock and utensils, and my corn standing, and escaped by night into Virginia, where shipping myself for Boston . . . but my mind being distressed on account of the situation of my wife and children, I returned to Norfolk in Virginia, with a hope of at least seeing them, if I could not obtain their freedom; but finding I was advertised in the newspaper, twenty dollars the reward for apprehending me, my dangerous situation obliged me to leave Virginia, disappointed of seeing my wife and children, coming to Philadelphia, where I resided in the employment of a waiter upward of two years.

Now, Jones broadened the plea:

We beseech your impartial attention to our hard condition, not only with respect to our personal sufferings, as freemen, but as a class of that people who, distinguished by color, are therefore with a degrading partiality, considered by many, even of those in eminent stations, as unentitled to that public justice and protection which is the great object of government. . . .

If, notwithstanding all that has been publicly avowed as essential principles respecting the extent of human right to freedom . . . we cannot claim the privilege of representation in your councils, yet we trust we may address you as fellow-men, who, under God, the sovereign Ruler of the Universe, are intrusted with the distribution of justice, for the terror of evil-doers, the encouragement and protection of the innocent, not doubting that you are men of liberal minds . . . who can admit that black people (servile as their condition generally is throughout this Continent) have natural affections, social and domestic attachments and sensibilities. . . .

He was now ready for his essential point, the final question, the meaning of the Revolution:

the unconstitutional bondage in which multitudes of our fellows in complexion are held, is to us a subject sorrowfully affecting; for we cannot conceive this condition (more especially those who have been emancipated and tasted the sweets of liberty, and again reduced to slavery by kidnappers and man-stealers) to be less afflicting or deplorable than the situation of citizens of the United States, captured and enslaved through the unrighteous policy prevalent in Algiers. . . . May we not be allowed to consider this stretch of power, morally and politically, a Governmental defect, if not a direct violation of the declared fundamental principles of the Constitution; and finally, is not some remedy for an evil of such magnitude highly worthy of the deep inquiry and unfeigned zeal of the supreme Legislative body of a free and enlightened people?

Could black men get a hearing in "the supreme Legislative body of a free and enlightened people?" News of the debate drifted back to Absalom Jones as he waited for Congress to act. Representative John Swanwick of Pennsylvania had sponsored the petition, but Blount of North Carolina would have none of it. Swanwick was eloquent: he was "surprised at the gentleman from North Carolina desiring to reject this petition; he could not have thought . . . that the gentleman was so far from acknowledging the rights of man, as to prevent any class of men from petitioning."

The subject of their petition had a claim to the attention of the House. They state they were freed from slavery, but they were much injured under a law of the United States . . . their case was very hard. He animadverted on the atrocity of that reward of ten dollars offered for one of them if taken alive, but that fifty should be given if found dead, and no questions asked. . . . Horrid reward! Could gentlemen hear it and not shudder?

Blount did not shudder, but merely remarked that Swanwick was "mistaken in calling the petitioners free men," while James Madison "thought this case had no claim on their attention," and another representative pointed out that "the practice of a former time, in a similar case, was, that the petition was sealed up and sent back to the petitioners, not being allowed even to remain on the files of the office . . . to encourage slaves to petition the House . . . would tend to spread an alarm throughout the Southern States; it would act as an 'entering-wedge,' whose consequences could not be foreseen."

☛ Now, three years later, as Absalom Jones climbs into the pulpit, built by his friend, Richard Allen, with his own hands, he recalls that Congress had given short shrift to that first black petition. On the lapel of his clerical broadcloth is pinned a handsome medallion of basalt and jasper, which shows a slave in chains asking the question, "Am I Not a Man and a Brother?" [figure 95]. The cameo was the work of Josiah Wedgwood, the English abolitionist and potter, executed for the London Society for the Abolition of Slavery, and he had sent over a package of them to Benjamin Franklin in Philadelphia to be distributed to advocates of the anti-slavery cause. "I have seen in their countenances," wrote the elderly Franklin to Wedgwood during the spring of 1787 [figure 96], "such Mark of being affected by contemplating the Figure of the Suppliant (which is admirably executed) that I am persuaded it may have an Effect equal to that of the best written Pamphlet in procuring favour to those oppressed People."

95. "Am I Not A Man And A Brother?" Black basalt on white jasper medallion by Josiah Wedgwood, 1787. The Buten Museum of Wedgwood.

Beginning his Fourth of July oration, it is possible that Absalom Jones pointed to the medallion on his lapel as he thanked God for all the benefits the Revolution had conferred on the black people of the still new Nation. It was heartening to note that among white folk of property and standing —Franklin was one of them—societies for the abolition of bondage, formed in a number of states, were working to do away with the slave trade and slavery, boycotting the products of slave labor, buying slaves free, founding schools for black children. Six years earlier, in 1794, ten of these state societies, including Maryland and Virginia, had held their first national convention not far from Bethel.

As for the institution of slavery itself, the struggle for liberty and equality had indeed raised sharply in many a patriot breast the question of whether the spirit of seventy-six was broad enough to encompass black as well as white. Progress had been made, at least in those states where slaves were fewest. Pennsylvania had led off, and the legislatures and courts of Connecticut, Rhode Island, Massachusetts, New Hampshire, and New York were putting an end to the evil system. Of New England's 13,000 blacks, three-quarters were free, and in Massachusetts and Vermont there were no slaves at all. In New York, New Jersey, and Pennsylvania, of their 50,000 blacks, more than a quarter no longer wore chains. And, on the frontier, Congress had banned slavery forever in the territory of the Northwest.

Then, too, the soil of independence had proved fertile for the planting of black churches, for the bringing forth of black genius—warriors, preachers, writers, organizers, scientists, captains, colonizers, educators, and others. Could it not be said, with some justice, that it was only with the

Sir,   Philad. May 15. 1787.

I received the Letter you did me
the honour of writing to me the 29th of
Feby past, with your valuable Presents of
Cameos, which I am distributing among
my Friends, in whose Countenances I have
seen such Marks of being affected by contemplating the Figure of the Suppliant, (which
is admirably executed) that I am persuaded
it may have an Effect equal to that of the
best written Pamphlet, in procuring Favour
to those oppressed People.   Please to accept
my hearty Thanks; and believe me to be, with
great Esteem, Sir,
                              Your most obedient Servant
                                          B Franklin

J. Wedgwood Esqr

96. Letter from Benjamin Franklin to Josiah Wedgwood, May 15, 1787.
Library of Congress.

Revolution that black men and women in America began to see themselves for the first time as a People?

He paused on the question, while the congregation waited, and then went on.

All this was well and good, perhaps a ray of hope for the future. But it was only half the story. It was only six months before, on Christmas Day, in a mood of anger and despair, that he had been moved to formulate a second petition to the Congress of the United States, this time signed by seventy-odd black freemen [figure 97], including Richard Allen and himself. Would it be appropriate for him now, as the second half of his oration for the Fourth of July, to read that petition aloud? The black heads nodded, and he began:

To the President, Senate, and House of Representatives of the United States—

The petition of the People of Colour, Freemen within the City and Suburbs of Philadelphia: —

Humbly Sheweth,

That thankful to God our Creator and the Government under which we live, for the blessing and benefit extended to us in the enjoyment of our natural right to Liberty, and the protection of our Persons and property from the oppression and violence which so great a number of like colour and National Descent are subjected; We feel ourselves bound from a sense of these blessings to continue our respective allotments and to lead honest and peaceable lives, rendering due submission to the Laws, and exciting and encouraging each other thereto, agreeable to the uniform advice of our real friends of every denomination. — Yet, while we feel impressed with grateful sensations for the Providential favours we ourselves enjoy, We cannot be insensible of the conditions of our afflicted Brethren, suffering under curious circumstances in different parts of these States; but deeply sympathizing with them. We are incited by a sense of Social duty and humbly conceive ourselves authorized to address and petition you in their behalf, believing them to be objects of representations in your public Councils, in common with ourselves and every other class of Citizens within the Jurisdiction of the United States, according to the declared design of the present Constitution formed by the General Convention and ratified in the different States, as set forth in the preamble thereto in the following words—vix—"We the People of the United States in order to form a more perfect union, establish Justice, insure domestick tranquility, provide for the Common Defence, and to secure the blessings of Liberty to ourselves and posterity, do ordain &c."—We apprehend this solemn Compact is violated by a trade carried on in clandestine manner to the Coast of Guinea, and another equally wicked practised openly by Citizens of some of the Southern States upon the waters of Maryland and Delaware: Men sufficiently callous as to qualify for the brutal purpose, are employed in kidnapping those of our Brethren that are free, and purchasing others of such as claim a property in them; thus these poor helpless victims like droves of Cattle are seized, fettered, and hurried into places provided for this most

Philadelphia 30th of December 1799 —

97. Signers of the petition to the Congress of the United States, December 30, 1799, including Absalom Jones and Richard Allen. National Archives.

horrid traffic, such as dark cellars and garrets, as is notorious at Northurst, Chester-town, Eastown, and divers other places;—After a sufficient number is obtained, they are forced on board vessels, crouded under hatches, and without the least commiseration, left to deplore the sad separation of the dearest ties in nature, husband from wife, and Parents from children thus pocket'd together they are transported to Georgia and other places and there inhumanly exposed to sale: Can any Commerce, trade, or transaction, so detestably shock the feelings of Man, or degrade the dignity of his nature equal to this, and how increasingly is the evil aggravated when practised in a Land, high in profession of the benign doctrines of our blessed Lord who taught his followers to do unto others as they would they should do unto them!——Your petitioners desire not to enlarge the volumes [that] might be filled with the sufferings of this grossly abused class of the human species (700,000 of whom it is said are now in unconditional bondage in these United States.) but, conscious of the rectitude of our motives in a concern so nearly affecting us, and so essentially interesting to [the] welfare of this Country, we cannot but address you as Guardians of our Civil rights, and Patrons of equal and National Liberty, hoping you will view the subject in an impartial and unprejudiced Light.——We do not wish for the immediate emancipation of all, knowing that the degraded state of many and their want of education, would greatly disqualify for such a change; but humbly desire you may exert every means in your power to undo the heavy burdens, and prepare the way for the oppressed to go free, that every yoke may be broken.

The Law not long since enacted by Congress called the Fugitive Bill, is, in its execution found to be attended with circumstances peculiarly hard and distressing for many of our afflicted Brethren in order to avoid the barbarities wantonly exercised upon them, or thro fear of being carried off by those Men-stealers, have been forced to seek refuge by flight; they are then hunted by armed Men, and under colour of this law, cruelly treated, shot, or brought back in chains to those who have no just claim upon them.

In the Constitution, and the Fugitive bill, no mention is made of Black people or Slaves—therefore if the Bill of Rights, or the declaration of Congress are of any validity, we beseech that as we are *men,* we may be admitted to partake of the Liberties and unalienable Rights therein held forth— firmly believing that the extending of Justice and equity to all Classes would be a means of drawing down the blessing of Heaven upon this Land, for the Peace and Prosperity of which, and the real happiness of every member of the Community, we fervently pray——

Absalom Jones had ended his oration, there was no applause, and the congregation filed out of the church. The suppliant slave on Franklin's medallion was still in chains, and to his imploring question, "Am I Not a Man and a Brother?" the Revolution could hardly reply with a thundering yes.

That same summer, a tall, twenty-four-year-old slave by the name of Gabriel, born in the year of the Declaration, the property of one Prosser in Jefferson's Virginia, tried to organize a few thousands of his fellows to strike for their freedom. The plan failed. In the autumn, Gabriel and about thirty-five of his brothers were sent to the gallows. Gabriel would not talk. James Monroe, then governor of Virginia, questioned him, but he "seemed to have made up his mind to die, and to have resolved to say but little on the subject of the conspiracy." At the trial, one of the conspirators testified that "he was present when Gabriel was appointed General. . . . That none were to be spared of the whites except Quakers, Methodists, and French people," and that he and a friend had intended "to purchase a piece of silk for a flag, on which they would have written 'death or Liberty'. . . ." Another defendant declared that he "had nothing more to offer than what General Washington would have had to offer, had he been taken by the British and put to trial by them. I have adventured my life in endeavouring to obtain the liberty of my countrymen, and am a willing sacrifice to their cause. . . ."

☞ "Are the great principles of political freedom and of natural justice, embodied in that Declaration of Independence extended to us?"—a half-century has passed and Frederick Douglass [figure 98], on the Fourth of July, goes on to answer his question.

Would to God, both for your sakes and ours, that an affirmative answer could be truthfully returned to these questions! Then would my task be light, and my burden easy and delightful. For *who* is there so cold, that a nation's sympathy could not warm him? . . . Who so stolid and selfish, that would not give his voice to swell the hallelujahs of a nation's jubilee, when the chains of servitude had been torn from his limbs? I am not that man. In a case like that, the dumb might eloquently speak, and the "lame man leap as an hart."

But such is not the state of the case. I say it with a sad sense of the disparity between us. I am not included within the pale of this glorious anniversary! Your high independence only reveals the immeasurable distance between us. The blessings in which you, this day, rejoice, are not enjoyed in common.—The rich inheritance of justice, liberty, prosperity and independence, bequeathed by your fathers, is shared by you, not by me. The sunlight that brought light and healing to you, has brought stripes and death to me. This Fourth of July is *yours,* not *mine. You* may rejoice, *I* must mourn. To drag a man in fetters into the grand illuminated temple of liberty, and call upon him to join you in joyous anthems, were inhuman mockery and sacrilegious irony. . . .

What, to the American slave, is your 4th of July? I answer; a day that reveals to him, more than all other days in the year, the gross injustice and cruelty to which he is the constant victim. To him, your celebration is a sham; your boasted liberty, an unholy license; your national greatness, swelling vanity; your sounds of rejoicing are empty and heartless; your denunciation of tyrants, brass fronted impudence; your shouts of liberty and equality, hollow mockery; your prayers and hymns, your sermons and thanksgivings, with all your religious parade and solemnity, are, to Him, mere bombast, fraud, deception, impiety, and hypocrisy—a thin veil to cover up crimes which would disgrace a nation of savages. There is not a nation on the earth guilty of practices more shocking and bloody than are the people of the United States, at this very hour.

Three years later, six years before the Civil War, at the close of his path-breaking volume on *The Colored Patriots of the American Revolution,* the black historian, William C. Nell, would view the historic event as incomplete.

The Revolution of 1776, and the subsequent struggles in our nation's history, aided, in honorable proportion, by colored Americans, have (sad, but true, confession) yet left the necessity for a second revolution, no less sublime than that of regenerating public sentiment in favor of Universal Brotherhood. To this glorious consummation, all, of every complexion, sect, sex and condition, can add their mite, and so nourish the tree of liberty, that all may be enabled to pluck fruit from its bending branches; and, in that degree to which colored Americans may labor to hasten the day, they will prove valid their claim to the title, " Patriots of the Second Revolution."

98. Frederick Douglass. J. W. Hurn. Undated photograph. Library of Congress.

Catalog

of

the

Exhibition

1. Liberty Displaying the Arts and Sciences
Samuel Jennings (active in Philadelphia 1787 to ca. 1792)
Oil on canvas, 1792
60¼ x 73
Lent by Library Company of Philadelphia
Figure 1

2. *The Colored Patriots of the American Revolution*
by William C. Nell
Boston, 1855
Lent by Library of Congress, Rare Books Division
Figure 2

3. *Service of Colored Americans in the Wars of 1776 and 1812*
by William C. Nell
Boston, 1851
Lent by Howard University Library

4. *The Loyalty and Devotion of Colored Americans in the Revolution and the War of 1812*
by William Lloyd Garrison
Boston, 1861
Lent by Library of Congress, Rare Books Division

5. Advertisement, William Brown of Framingham, Massachusetts, for his runaway slave, "Crispas"
Boston Gazette, October 2, 1750
From original in Massachusetts Historical Society
Figure 4

6. "The Bloody Massacre perpetrated in King Street, Boston, on 5 March 1770, by a party of the 29th Regiment"
Paul Revere (1735-1818)
Line engraving, State II, 1770
9⅝ x 8⅝
National Gallery of Art, Rosenwald Collection
Figure 3

7. Broadside, "An account of a late Military Massacre at Boston, or the consequences of quartering troops in a populous well-regulated town, taken from the *Boston Gazette,* March 12, 1770"
Engraved and printed by Paul Revere
19 x 15⅜
From original in The New-York Historical Society

8. Diagram of the Boston Massacre, drawn for use in the subsequent trial
Paul Revere (1735-1818)
Ink on paper, 1770
8¼ x 13
From original in Boston Public Library, Mellen Chamberlain Autograph Collection
Figure 5

9. Verdict of the coroner's jury upon the body of Michael Johnson [Crispus Attucks]
March 6, 1770
12¼ x 7⅝
Lent by The Bostonian Society

10. *The Trial of William Weems, James Hartegan . . . for the murder of Crispus Attucks . . .*
Boston, 1770
Lent by Williston Memorial Library, Mount Holyoke College, South Hadley, Massachusetts

11. Entry from diary of John Adams, July 1773: Letter of Adams (pseudonym "Chrispus Attucks") to Governor Thomas Hutchinson
From original in Massachusetts Historical Society
Figure 6

12. "The Boston Massacre . . . Commemorative Festival in Faneuil Hall," with speeches by William C. Nell, Dr. John Rock, Theodore Weld, and Wendell Philips
The Liberator, March 12, 1858
From original in Library of Congress

13. Letter, Frederick Douglass to the Citizens' Committee
October 5, 1888
10½ x 8, four pages
Lent by Library of Congress, Manuscripts Division

Only the last page of this letter is in Douglass's hand. The first three are written by the second Mrs. Douglass.

14. *A Memorial of Crispus Attucks, Samuel Maverick, James Caldwell, Samuel Gray, and Patrick Carr*
The Boston City Council
Boston, 1889
Lent by Library of Congress, Rare Books Division

Account of the ceremonies for the unveiling of the monument dedicated to those who fell in the Boston Massacre.

15. *The Appendix: Or, Some Observations on the Expediency of the Petition of the Africans*
by "A Lover of Constitutional Liberty"
Boston, 1773
Lent by Library of Congress, Rare Books Division

16. Broadside, circular letter sent "in behalf of our fellow slaves in this province, and by order of their Committee" to each member of the Massachusetts House of Representatives
Boston, April 20, 1773

10½ x 7½

Lent by The New-York Historical Society

Figure 7

17. Petition "in behalf of all thous who by divine Permission are held in a state of slavery, within the bowels of a free country" to Governor Thomas Hutchinson and the Massachusetts House of Representatives
June 1773

Collections of the Massachusetts Historical Society, vol. III, 5th series, Boston, 1877

Original manuscript unlocated

18. "The Petition of a Grate Number of Blacks of this Province" to Governor Thomas Gage and the Massachusetts General Court
May 25, 1774

Collections of the Massachusetts Historical Society, vol. III, 5th series, Boston, 1877

Original manuscript unlocated

19. "The Petition . . . in behalf of all those . . . held in a State of *Slavery* within the Bowels of a Free Country" to Governor Thomas Gage and the Massachusetts House of Representatives
June 1774

Collections of the Massachusetts Historical Society, vol. III, 5th series, Boston, 1877

Original manuscript unlocated

20. Letter, Abigail Adams to John Adams expressing her concern over slavery
September 22, 1774

12⅛ x 7⅜

Lent by Massachusetts Historical Society

21a. The Battle of Lexington

21b. A View of the Town of Concord

21c. The Engagement at the North Bridge in Concord

21d. A View of the South Part of Lexington
Amos Doolittle (1754-1832) after Ralph Earl

Line engravings, 1775

13 x 17½

Lent by Albany Institute of History and Art

22. "Payroll for the Tenth Company in the 38th Regiment of Foot in the Service of the united colonies and commanded by a Colonell Loammi Baldwin, Esq., for the month of August, 1775"

From original in Massachusetts Archives

23. Broadside, "A List of Names of the Provincials who were killed and wounded . . . at Concord"

18 x 8

Facsimile reprint of original published by S. G. Drake, Boston, 1775

Lent by Library of Congress, Rare Books Division

24. *West Cambridge on the Nineteenth of April, 1775*
by Samuel Abbot Smith
Boston, 1864

Lent by Library of Congress

25. Broadside, "A Bloody Butchery, By the British troops: or the Runaway Fight of the Regulars"
1775

21 x 16⅛

Lent by Massachusetts Historical Society

Figure 8

26. Lt. Grosvenor and his Negro Servant Peter Salem
John Trumbull (1756-1843)

Oil on panel, 1786

20¹¹⁄₁₆ x 17⅜

Lent by Yale University Art Gallery, The Mabel Brady Garvan Collection

Color plate 1

27. The Battle of Bunker Hill
James Mitan (1776-1822) after John Trumbull

Engraving, 1801

23½ x 29½

Lent by The Metropolitan Museum of Art, Bequest of Charles Allen Munn, 1924

Figure 11

28. French Charleville musket

45-inch barrel

Lent by The National Museum of History and Technology, Military History Division, Smithsonian Institution

Figure 10

29. Recommendation of Salem Poor for his bravery "in the late Battle at Charlestown"
December 5, 1775

From original in Massachusetts Archives

30. "Return of Captain Benjamin Lock's Company in the 37th Regiment of Foot in the Continental Army commanded by Lt. Colo. William Bond" [containing the names of Cuff Whitemore (a Negro), Isaiah Bayoman (a Mulatto), and Job Potamia (a Negro)]
October 6, 1777

From original in Massachusetts Archives

Figure 9

31. Certification of William Florey's (Flora) service in the 15th Virginia Regiment
July 16, 1806
8 x 7⅜
Lent by Virginia State Library
Figure 12

32. Certification of William Flora's service in the 16th Virginia Regiment
May 30, 1806
5⅜ x 8¼
Lent by Virginia State Library

33. "The Battle of Great Bridge"
Virginia Historical Register and Literary Companion, vol. VI, 1853
Lent by Virginia Historical Society

34. Draft of the Declaration of Independence written by Thomas Jefferson with corrections by Benjamin Franklin and John Adams. This includes a passage, later deleted, on the slave trade.
Facsimile reprint of original in Library of Congress
Figure 13

35. Petition, "A Great Number of Negroes who are detained in a state of Slavery, in the Bowels of a free and Christian Country," to the Massachusetts General Court, January 13, 1777
From original in Massachusetts Archives
Figure 14

36. Petition of Prime, Prince, and others of Stratford and Fairfield, Connecticut, to the General Assembly of Connecticut
May 4, 1779
9 x 7¼
Lent by Connecticut State Library
Figure 15

37. Petition of blacks of Portsmouth, New Hampshire
November 12, 1779
From original in New Hampshire Archives

38. George Washington
John Trumbull (1756-1843)
Oil on canvas, 1780
36 x 28
Lent by The Metropolitan Museum of Art, Bequest of Charles Allen Munn, 1924
Figure 17

39. Le Général Washington
Noel le Mire (1724-1801) after a painting by Jean-Baptiste Le Paon
Engraving, not dated
21½ x 15½
Lent by Library of Congress, Prints and Photographs Division
Figure 16

40. The British Surrendering their Arms to General Washington after their defeat at Yorktown in Virginia, 1781
John Francis Renault (active in United States ca. 1795-ca. 1819)
Engraving, 1819
25½ x 35
Lent by Library of Congress, Prints and Photographs Division

41. The Washington Family
Edward Savage (1761-1817)
Engraving, 1798, after his 1796 painting
19 x 25
Lent by Mr. and Mrs. John Philip Pierce, Jr., Alexandria, Virginia
Figure 18

42. Excerpt from the last will and testament of George Washington, respecting William Lee
From original in Fairfax County Courthouse, Virginia
Photograph courtesy of Library of Congress
Figure 19

43. James Armistead Lafayette
John B. Martin (1797-1857)
Oil on canvas, ca. 1824
26½ x 24½
Lent by The Valentine Museum, Richmond
Color plate 2

44. Engraving of the Marquis de Lafayette's original certificate of November 21, 1784, commending James Armistead Lafayette for his service during the Revolutionary War, with portrait after John B. Martin
Artist and date unknown
11 x 8½
Lent by Virginia Historical Society
Figure 21

45. Lafayette at Yorktown
Jean-Baptiste Le Paon (1738-1785)
Oil on canvas, 1783
49½ x 40
Lent by Lafayette College, Easton, Pennsylvania
Figure 20

46. "An Act to Emancipate James, A Negro Slave, the Property of William Armistead, Gentleman"
The Statutes at Large: Being a Collection of All the Laws of Virginia, vol. 12, p. 380-381
William W. Hening, editor
Richmond, 1823
Lent by Library of Congress, Law Division

47. Commemorative medal, unveiling of Daniel Chester French's Lafayette Memorial (1915-1917) in Prospect Park, Brooklyn, New York

Augustus Lukeman (1872-1935)

Bronze, 1918

2 x 2⁷/₁₆

Lent by The National Museum of History and Technology, Division of Numismatics, Smithsonian Institution

48. Agrippa Hull

Unidentified artist

Oil on canvas, 1848

28¼ x 26

Lent by Historical Room, Stockbridge Library, Stockbridge, Massachusetts

Color plate 3

49. Affidavit, Revolutionary War record of Agrippa Hull
June 12, 1828

13 x 8⅛

Lent by National Archives

50. Letter, Charles Sedgwick and Agrippa Hull to Richard Rush, acting secretary of state
June 12, 1828

13 x 8⅛

Lent by National Archives

Figure 22

51. "The Black Men of the Revolution and War of 1812" by John Greenleaf Whittier
The National Era, July 22, 1847

From original in Library of Congress

52. Costumer de L'Armé Américaine en 1782

Watercolor drawing in the revolutionary journal of Baron Ludwig Von Closen, 1780-1783

From original destroyed by fire in 1921; photograph courtesy Library of Congress

Figure 23

53. The Revolutionary Journal of Baron Ludwig von Closen 1780-1783; entries for July 4, 1781 and July 9, 1781

A 1905 French transcript of the original manuscript destroyed by fire in 1921

Lent by Library of Congress, Manuscripts Division

54. Letter, Colonel Peter Horry to General Nathanael Greene explaining that lack of Negro laborers handicapped American military operations
June 28, 1781

7¼ x 9½

Lent by William L. Clements Library, University of Michigan, Ann Arbor. Nathanael Greene Papers

55. The Battle of Cowpens

William Ranney (1813-1857)

Oil on canvas, 1845

36 x 46

From original owned by Mr. Frederick Donhauser, Stony River, Alaska

Figure 24

56. Excerpt from the payroll of Simsbury, Connecticut, soldiers in the Continental Army "Zechery Prince, Now Ded, Rec'd His Freedom"
April 10, 1779

12¾ x 15

Lent by Connecticut State Library

Figure 25

57. Honorable discharge of Oliver Cromwell signed by George Washington
June 5, 1783

13 x 10

Lent by National Archives

Figure 30

58. *The Battle of Groton Heights*
by William Wallace Harris and Charles Allyn
New London, Connecticut, 1882

Lent by Library of Congress

59. Bronze placque commemorating the death of Major William Montgomery while leading the British attack on Fort Griswold. Jordan Freeman, with spear, is portrayed at left

From original in Fort Griswold State Park, Groton, Connecticut

60. Tablet with names of Jordan Freeman and Lambo Latham on Memorial Gateway to Old Fort Griswold, Groton, Connecticut

Photograph courtesy of Fort Griswold State Park

61. Washington's Passage of the Delaware

Thomas Sully (1783-1872)

Oil on canvas, 1819

146½ x 207

From original in Museum of Fine Arts, Boston

Figure 27

62. Washington Crossing the Delaware

Paul Girardet (?–?) after Emanuel Leutze

Engraving, proof before title, not dated

22⅜ x 38⅛

Lent by The New York Public Library, Astor, Lenox and Tilden Foundations, Prints Division

Figure 28

63. Land grant of 112 acres to Austin Dabney

Acts of the General Assembly of the State of Georgia
Milledgeville, 1821

Lent by Library of Congress

64. *Sketches of Some of the First Settlers of Upper Georgia, of the Cherokees, and the author* (including Austin Dabney)
by George R. Gilmer
New York, 1855

Lent by Library of Congress, Rare Books Division

65. Land grant of 250 acres in Washington County, Georgia, to Austin Dabney

From unlocated original

66. Letter from Colonel George Muter regarding the guns saved by Jupiter during the enemy's siege of Richmond
March 29, 1781

5⅜ x 8

Lent by Virginia State Library

Figure 26

67. Obituary of Hector
Norristown Free Press, Norristown, Pennsylvania, January 15, 1834

Lent by Historical Society of Montgomery County, Norristown, Pennsylvania

68. Manumission of Quaco
Records of the State of Rhode Island and Providence Plantations in New England, vol. IX, p. 509, 510
John R. Bartlett, editor
Providence, 1864

From original in Library of Congress

69. *Biography of Revolutionary Heroes; Containing the Life of Brig. Gen'l William Barton . . .*
by Mrs. Catherine Williams
Providence, 1839

Smith College Library, Northampton, Massachusetts

70. *Military Journal of the American Revolution*
by James Thatcher, M.D.
Hartford, 1862

From original in Library of Congress

71. "The Capture of Prescott"
Manufacturers and Farmer's Journal, June 25, 1835, Providence, Rhode Island

From original in The Rhode Island Historical Society

72. Obituary of Prince (Jack Sisson)
Providence Gazette, November 3, 1821

From original in The Rhode Island Historical Society

73. "An Act for the Manumission of a Negro named Saul. (Passed, November 13, 1792)"
The Statutes at Large: Being a Collection of All the Laws of Virginia, vol. XXII, p. 619
William W. Hening, editor
Richmond, 1821

Lent by Library of Congress, Law Division

74. "An Ordinance for Enfranchising a Negro Woman and her Child;" (The deceased slave, Antigua's reward for "services which he has performed for the State" was the freedom of his wife and child)
Statutes at Large of South Carolina, vol. IV, p. 545
Charleston, 1838

Lent by Library of Congress

75. "Memoir of General John Cropper of Accomack County, Virginia"
by Barton Wise
Proceedings of the Virginia Historical Society at the Annual Meeting Held December 21-22, 1891
Richmond, 1892

Lent by Virginia Historical Society

76. Letter (author's copy), George Washington to Major Henry Lee concerning Washington's grant of "1000 dols. promised the negro pilots"
July 26, 1779

12¼ x 8

Lent by Library of Congress, Manuscript Division

77. "The Schooner Liberty" with commendation of slaves [Harry and Cupid], "courageous patriots"
Virginia Historical Register and Literary Advertiser, vol. I, 1848, p. 80

Lent by Library of Congress

78. Unidentified gentleman, possibly James Forten

Unidentified artist

Watercolor on paper

From original in The Historical Society of Pennsylvania

Figure 29

79. "An act for the purchase and manumitting negro Caesar [Tarrant] (Passed the 14th of November, 1789)"
The Statutes At Large; Being a Collection of All the Laws of Virginia, vol. XIII, p. 102
William W. Hening, editor
Richmond 1821

Lent by Library of Congress, Law Division

80. "The Schooner Patriot"–"Captain" Mark Starlins, "The Noble African"
Virginia Historical Register and Literary Advertiser, vol. I, 1848, pp. 129–131

Lent by Library of Congress

81. Petition of Lucretia Pritchett for reimbursement for the loss of her slave Minny "who behaved with uncommon bravery in an engagement with a piratical tender, and was killed by the enemy in attempting to board her."
June 15 and 26, 1776

Proceedings of the Convention of Delegates for the Counties and Corporations in the Colony of Virginia, Held at Richmond Town, in the County of Henrico on the 20th of March, 1775
Richmond, 1816

Lent by Library of Congress, Law Division

82. Death notice of Caesar Hodgson in logbook of the United States ship of war, *Ranger,* captained by John Paul Jones
February 25, 1780

Photostat copy in National Archives of original in possession of The Rosenbach Company, New York, 1933

83. Entry from the diary of William Pynchon of Salem, June 1781-December 1781 (August 13, 1781) regarding Titus

6¼ x 8½

Lent by Massachusetts Historical Society

84. "An act manumitting two negro men slaves [Jack Knight and William Boush] belonging to the Commonwealth (passed 30 October, 1789)"

The Statutes at Large; Being a Collection of All the Laws of Virginia, vol. XIII, 103
Wm. Hening, editor
Richmond, 1821

Lent by Library of Congress, Law Division

85. Speech of Representative William Eustis of Massachusetts to the House, December 12, 1820

The Debates and Proceedings of the Congress of the United States
Sixteenth Congress, Second Session, comprising the period from November 13, 1820, to March 3, 1821
Washington, 1855

Lent by Library of Congress, Law Division

86. "Return of Freemen Inlisted during the War in First Rhode Island Battalion Commanded by Col. C. Green"

6½ x 8⅛

Lent by The Rhode Island Historical Society

Figure 31

87. *Travels in North America in the Years 1780-1781-1782 translated from the French* . . . p. 454 [mentioning the blacks in the Rhode Island Regiment]
by Francois Jean Marquis de Chastellux
London, 1787

Lent by Library of Congress

88. Flag presented by John Hancock to the "Bucks of America"
Silk, 40½ x 62¼

Lent by Massachusetts Historical Society

Figure 32

89. Henri Christophe
Richard Evans (1784-1871)
Oil on canvas, ca. 1818

35½ x 26½

Formerly in the collection of the late Sir Bruce S. Ingram, London; present whereabouts unknown

Figure 34

90. "An Account of the Battle of Savannah, dated Charlestown, October 20, 1779"
New Jersey Gazette, December 8, 1779

From original in Library of Congress

91. "Precis des Opérations de L'Escadre du Roi, Commandée par le Comte d'Estaing"
Paris Gazette, January 7, 1780

From original in Library of Congress

92. Jean-Baptiste Belley, deputy to the Versailles Convention
Anne Louis Girodet de Roucy-Trioson, 1797

Oil on canvas

From original in Musée National du Château de Versailles

Figure 33

93. *How the Black St. Domingo Legion Saved the Patriot Army in the Siege of Savannah, 1799*
by T. G. Steward

Occasional Papers, no. 5, The American Negro Academy, Washington, D.C. 1899

Lent by Howard University, Moorland Collection

94. Broadside, Proclamation of John Murray, Earl of Dunmore, in defense of His Majesty's cause, printed aboard H.M.S. *William*
November 7, 1775

17 x 10¾

Lent by Tracy W. McGregor Library, University of Virginia, Charlottesville

Figure 35

95. Broadside, Williamsburg Proclamation of John Murray, Earl of Dunmore, reprinted under the direction of Patrick Henry
November 7, 1775

12¼ x 7⅝

Lent by Tracy W. McGregor Library, University of Virginia, Charlottesville

96. Broadside, A Circular letter from Patrick Henry sent with copies of the Dunmore Proclamation
November 20, 1775

6¼ x 9½

Lent by Library of Congress, Rare Books Division

97. Reply to the Dunmore Proclamation, probably written by Patrick Henry, advising slaves not to join the British
Purdie's *Virginia Gazette,* November 24, 1775

From original in Library of Congress

98. Broadside, the Virginia Convention's Declaration of policy in response to the Dunmore Proclamation
December 14, 1775

From original in John Carter Brown Library, Providence

Figure 36

99. Sir Henry Clinton's "Philipsburg Proclamation" concerning use of Negroes in the British army in the hand of Lord Rawdon, Clinton's aide-de-camp
June 30, 1779

7¼ x 9

Lent by William L. Clements Library, University of Michigan, Ann Arbor, Sir Henry Clinton Papers

100. New Year Greetings from the Black Pioneers to General Clinton
January 1, 1781
12¼ x 7¾
Lent by William L. Clements Library, University of Michigan, Ann Arbor, Sir Henry Clinton Papers

101. Broadside, "Observations on the Slaves, and the Indented Servants, inlisted in the Army, and in the Navy of the United States"
16½ x 10¼
Lent by Library of Congress, Rare Books Division
Figure 37

102. Report that Dunmore's black regiment, which made up a large part of his army, wore the inscription "Liberty to Slaves" on their breasts
Maryland Gazette, December 14, 1775
Lent by Maryland Historical Society

103. "The King of England's Soldiers"
A History of Georgia, from its First Discovery by Europeans to the Adoption of the Present Constitution in MDCCXCVIII
by Rev. William Bacon Stevens
Philadelphia, 1859
Lent by Library of Congress

104. Report of Tye being fatally wounded while leading an attack on the home of Captain Joshua Huddy
Pennsylvania Packet, Philadelphia, October 3, 1780
From original in Library of Congress

105. "Extract of a letter from Monmouth County, Pennsylvania, June 12, 1780" regarding Tye
Pennsylvania Gazette and Weekly Advertiser, June 21, 1780
From original in Library of Congress
Figure 38

106. Letter, Colonel W. Malcolm to Major General William Heath regarding Peck, a Tory spy
December 7, 1776
From original in Massachusetts Historical Society

107. Excerpt from John Andre's report of intelligence before May 12, 1780, referring to Duncan, "a Negro who ran away from his master in Charlestown"
From original in Clements Library, University of Michigan, Ann Arbor

108. Christopher Gadsden to William Moultrie, July 1, 1776, regarding Sampson
Memoirs of the American Revolution, So Far as it Related to the States of North and South Carolina, and Georgia, vol. I
by William Moultrie
New York, 1802
Lent by Library of Congress

109. Letter, Mann Page to Thomas Jefferson, enclosing court proceedings against a slave, Billy, accused of treason
May 13, 1781
8½ x 6½,   13⅛ x 8⅛,   9¼ x 7¾
Lent by Virginia State Library

110. List of the names of the Negroes [Black Pioneers] belonging to Captain Martin's Company . . .
not dated
7½ x 12¼
Lent by William L. Clements Library, University of Michigan, Ann Arbor, Sir Henry Clinton Papers

111. "A Return of the Company of Black Pioneers Commanded by Col. Allen Steward 13 of September 1783"
From original in Public Records Office, London
Photograph courtesy of Colonial Williamsburg
Figure 39

112. The Petition of Thomas Peters to William Wyndham Grenville, "one of his Majesty's Principal Secretaries of State"
From original in the British Public Records Office, London

113. Letter, Colonel John Simpson to Colonel Richard Cogdell, July 15, 1775, regarding slave conspiracy in North Carolina
Colonial Records of North Carolina, vol. X, pp. 94-95
William L. Saunders, editor
Raleigh, 1886-1890
From original in North Carolina State Department of History and Archives

114. Letter, Henry Laurens to Colonel Stephen Bull concerning the "Rebellious Negroes Upon Tybee Island, South Carolina"
March 16, 1776
From original in the Laurens Papers, South Carolina Historical Society

115. The First African Baptist Church of Savannah, photograph, ca. 1880
The First African Baptist Church of North America
by Edgar Garfield Thomas
Savannah, 1925
Lent by Library of Congress
Figure 41

116. Portrait of Andrew Bryan from stained glass window of First African Baptist Church, Savannah, Georgia
Figure 40

117. *The Baptist Annual Register for 1790, 1791, 1792, and part of 1793*
by John Rippon
London, 1793
Lent by Library of Congress

118. Richard Allen
Unidentified artist
Pastel and chalk, 1784
15½ x 12½
Lent by Mrs. Dorothy Porter, Washington, D.C.
Color plate 4

119. Reverend Richard Allen, Bishop of the First African Methodist Episcopal Church
P. S. Duval
Lithograph, not dated
9⅜ x 6
Lent by Free Library of Philadelphia, Frederick Lewis Collection

120. Reverend Richard Allen
Published by J. Dainty
Stipple engraving, 1813
11½ x 8⅜
Lent by Library Company of Philadelphia
Figure 46

121. Absalom Jones
Raphaelle Peale (1774-1825)
Oil on paper, 1810
34½ x 29¼
On indefinite loan to the National Portrait Gallery from The Wilmington Society of the Fine Arts, Delaware Art Museum
Color plate 5

122. Liverpoolware jug with portrait silhouette of Absalom Jones
ca. 1808
9⅛ high
Lent by National Portrait Gallery, Gift of Sidney Kaplan
Figure 49

123. The African Episcopal Church of St. Thomas
W. L. Breton
Lithograph, June 1829
15⅛ x 21⅜
Lent by The Historical Society of Pennsylvania
Figure 47

124. Pulpit, constructed and used by Richard Allen
height, 40½ x width, 30½ x length, 71
Lent by Mother Bethel, African Methodist Episcopal Church, Philadelphia
Figure 43

125. *A Narrative of the Proceedings of the Black People, During the Late Awful Calamity in Philadelphia, in the Year 1793: and A Refutation of some Censures Thrown Upon Them in some late Publications*
by Absalom Jones and Richard Allen
Philadelphia, 1794
Lent by Library of Congress, Rare Books Division
Figure 42

126. *The Life, Experiences and Gospel Labors of the Rt. Rev. Richard Allen, written by Himself*
by Richard Allen
Philadelphia, 1793
Lent by Library Company of Philadelphia
Figure 50

127. *The Doctrines and Disciplines of the African Methodist Episcopal Church*
by Richard Allen and Jacob Tapisco
Philadelphia, 1817
Lent by Allegheny College, Meadville, Pennsylvania

128. *A Thanksgiving Sermon, preached January 1, 1808, . . . On Account of The Abolition of the African Slave Trade*
by Absalom Jones
Philadelphia, 1808
Lent by The Historical Society of Pennsylvania
Figure 48

129. *A Sermon Preached before the General Assembly of the Presbyterian Church . . . May 23, 1803*
by Henry Kollock
Philadelphia, 1803
Lent by Princeton University Archives

130. The First Methodist Episcopal Church in America. Erected AD 1768 on Golden Hill (now John Street), City of New York
Joseph B. Smith (1798-1876)
Watercolor, 1817
Lent by Museum of the City of New York, J. Insley Blair Collection
Figure 44

131. Peter Williams
Unidentified artist
Oil on canvas, ca. 1815
25 x 20¼
Lent by The New-York Historical Society
Figure 45

132. *A Narrative of the Lord's Wonderful Dealings with John Marrant, a Black*
Rev. William Aldridge, editor
London, 1785
Lent by Library of Congress, Rare Books Division
Figure 51

133. Review of *A Narrative of the Lord's Dealings with John Marrant*
Monthly Review, vol. LXXIII (November 1785), London
Lent by Amherst College Library

134. *A Sermon Preached on the 24th Day of June 1789 . . . at the Request of . . . Grand Master, Prince Hall . . . of the African Lodge of Free and Accepted Masons . . . in Boston, by the Reverend Brother Marrant, Chaplain*
Boston, 1789
Lent by American Antiquarian Society
Figure 52

135. *A Narrative of the Life of John Marrant of New York*
Rev. William Aldridge, editor
Leeds, 1813
Lent by Library of Congress, Rare Books Division

136. Portrait of the Reverend Lemuel Haynes, frontispiece
Sketches of the Life and Character of the Reverend Lemuel Haynes, A.M.
by Timothy Mather Cooley
New York, 1837

Lent by Library of Congress

Figure 53

137. Reverend Lemuel Haynes in the Pulpit
Unidentified artist
Papier-mâché tray, ca. 1800-1820
25 11/16 x 20 15/16

Lent by Museum of Art, Rhode Island School of Design, Lucy Truman Aldrich Collection

Color plate 8

138. "A Muster Roll of the Minutemen that Marched from Granville ye 29th Apr 1775" including the name Lemuel Haynes
From original in Massachusetts Archives

139. *The Nature and Importance of True Republicanism With a Few Suggestions Favorable to Independence. A Discourse, Delivered at Rutland, Vermont, . . . the Fourth of July, 1801*
by Lemuel Haynes
Rutland, 1801

Lent by Library of Congress, Rare Books Division

Figure 54

140. *Universal Salvation: A very ancient doctrine; with some Account of the Life and Character of its Author*
by Lemuel Haynes
Boston, 1814

Lent by Library of Congress

141. *Mystery Developed; or, Russell Colvin, (Supposed to be Murdered,) in Full Life: and Stephen and Jesse Born, (His Convicted Murderers,) Rescued from Ignominious Death by Wonderful Discoveries*
by Lemuel Haynes
Hartford, 1814

Lent by Library of Congress, Rare Books Division

142. *An Oration upon the Moral and Political Evil of Slavery . . . July 4, 1791*
by George Buchanan
Baltimore, 1793

Lent by Cornell University Library

143. *An Enquiry Concerning the Intellectual and Moral Faculties, and Literature of Negroes: followed with an Account of the Life and Works of Fifteen Negroes & Mulattoes, Distinguished in Science, Literature and the Arts*
by Henri Grégoire, translated by D. B. Warden
Brooklyn, 1810

Lent by Library of Congress, Rare Books Division

144. Letter, Benjamin Banneker to George Ellicott
October 13, 1789
13 1/8 x 8 3/8

Lent by Maryland Historical Society

Figure 55

145. Letter, Benjamin Banneker to Thomas Jefferson
August 19, 1791
17 3/8 x 11 1/4

Lent by Massachusetts Historical Society

146. Letter (draft), Thomas Jefferson to Benjamin Banneker
August 30, 1791

From original in Library of Congress, Manuscript Division

147. Letter, James McHenry to William Goddard and James Angell regarding Banneker and his almanac, August 20, 1791
Benjamin Banneker's Pennsylvania, Delaware, Maryland and Virginia Almanack and Ephemeris For the Year of our Lord 1792
Baltimore, 1792

Lent by Maryland Historical Society

148. Benjamin Rush's peace plan including a proposal for a cabinet office of secretary of peace
Banneker's Almanack and Ephemeris for the Year of our Lord 1793
Philadelphia, 1793

Lent by Library of Congress, Rare Books Division

Figure 56

149. Portrait of Benjamin Banneker, frontispiece
Benjamin Banneker's Pennsylvania, Delaware, Maryland, and Virginia Almanac, for the Year of our Lord, 1795
Baltimore, 1795

Lent by Maryland Historical Society

Figure 57

150. Obituary of Benjamin Banneker
Federal Gazette and Baltimore Daily Advertiser, October 28, 1806

From original in Library of Congress

151. Petition of Paul Cuffe and six other negroes of Dartmouth, Massachusetts, to the general court of Massachusetts
March 14, 1780

From original in Massachusetts Archives

Figure 58

152. Compass used by Captain Paul Cuffe
10 x 10 x 6

Lent by New Bedford Whaling Museum, New Bedford, Massachusetts

Figure 59

153. Captain Paul Cuffe
Mason and Maas, after drawing by John Pole
Wood engraving, 1812
7 7/8 x 6 1/8

Lent by Library of Congress, Prints and Photographs Division

Figure 60

154. Letter, James Pemberton to Captain Paul Cuffe, concerning his voyage to Sierra Leone
June 6, 1808
14½ x 9¼
Lent by New Bedford Free Public Library

155. Letter, Captain Paul Cuffe to John James and Alexander Wilson
June 10, 1809
From unlocated original

156. "Memoir of Captain Paul Cuffe"
The Liverpool Mercury, October 4-11, 1811
From original in Library of Congress

157. Congressional act authorizing Captain Paul Cuffe to take cargo to Sierra Leone, January 10, 1814
12⅝ x 7⅞
Lent by National Archives
Figure 61

158. *A Discourse, Delivered on The Death of Capt. Paul Cuffe, Before the New-York African Institution, in the African Methodist Episcopal Zion Church, October 21, 1817*
by Peter Williams, Jun.
New York, 1817
Lent by Library of Congress, Rare Books Division
Figure 62

159. *Memoir of Captain Paul Cuffee, A Man of Colour . . .*
William Alexander, editor
York, England, 1812
Lent by Library of Congress, Rare Books Division

160. Bill of sale of Jean Baptiste Point du Sable's Chicago property, May 1800
From unlocated original; photograph courtesy *Ebony Magazine*
Figure 63

161. An Imaginary View of the Site of Chicago in 1779, showing the Cabin of Jean Baptiste Point De Saible
Frontispiece, *History of Chicago*, vol. I
A. T. Andreas
Chicago, 1884
Library of Congress

162. Bronze plaque commemorating "Site of the First House in Chicago"
Photograph courtesy Chicago Historical Society

163. Certificate of the Pennsylvania Society for Promoting the Abolition of Slavery concerning James Derham, "a practitioner of physic"
American Museum or Universal Magazine, vol. V (1789), pp. 60-62
Lent by Georgetown University Library

Such certificates were published "in order to . . . enable [the Society] to contradict those who assert that the intellecual faculties of the negroes are not capable of improvement equal to the rest of mankind. . . ."

164. "Account of a wonderful talent for arithmetical calculation, in an African slave [Tom Fuller], living in Virginia"
American Museum or Universal Magazine, vol. V (January 1789), pp. 62-63
Lent by Georgetown University Library

165. Obituary of ". . . Negro Tom"
Columbia Centinel, December 29, 1790
From original in Library of Congress
Figure 64

166. "On the general State, Manners, and Character of the Blacks in the United States [including Tom Fuller]"
New Travels in the United States of America . . . 1788
by J. P. Brissot de Warville
London, 1792, p. 287
Lent by Smithsonian Institution Libraries

167. Manuscript poem, "To the University of Cambridge, wrote in 1767" by Phillis Wheatley
7¼ x 12¼
Lent by American Antiquarian Society
Figure 65

168. Manuscript poem, "On the Death of the Rev. Dr. Sewall, 1767" by Phillis Wheatley
12½ x 7¹⁄₁₆
Lent by American Antiquarian Society

169. Broadside, "An Elegiac Poem, On the Death of . . . George Whitefield"
by Phillis Wheatley, 1770
18⅞ x 12⅝
Lent by Library Company of Philadelphia
Figure 66

170. "Recollection."
by Phillis Wheatley, 1772
The London Magazine: or Gentleman's Monthly Intelligencer, March 1772
From original in Library of Congress

171. Portrait of Phillis Wheatley, frontispiece engraving after Scipio Moorhead
Poems on Various Subjects, Religious and Moral
by Phillis Wheatley
London and Boston, 1773
Lent by Library of Congress, Rare Books Division
Figure 68

172. "To S. M. (Scipio Moorhead), A Young African Painter, On Seeing His Works
Poems on Various Subjects . . .
by Phillis Wheatley
London, 1773
Lent by Library of Congress, Rare Books Division
Figure 69

173. Letter, Benjamin Franklin to Jonathan Williams concerning Franklin's visit to Phillis Wheatley
July 7, 1773
12¾ x 7¾
Lent by Library of Congress, Manuscript Division

174. Review of *Poems on Various Subjects, religious and moral*
by Phillis Wheatley
The London Magazine: or Gentleman's Monthly Intelligencer,
September, 1773, p. 456
From original in Library of Congress

175. Letter, Phillis Wheatley to Obour Tanner
March 21, 1774
9½ x 7¾
Lent by Massachusetts Historical Society
Figure 73

176. Letter, John Paul Jones to Hector McNeill concerning "the Celebrated Phillis" Wheatley
not dated
9 x 7
Lent by The Pierpont Morgan Library
Figure 70

177. Letter and poem by Phillis Wheatley presented to George Washington
The Pennsylvania Magazine, April 1776, p. 193
Lent by Historical Society of Pennsylvania
Figure 71

178. Letter, George Washington to Colonel Joseph Reed concerning the poem he received from Phillis Wheatley
February 10, 1776
The Writings of George Washington, vol. 4, pp. 318-323
John C. Fitzpatrick, editor
Washington, D.C., 1931
Lent by Smithsonian Institution Libraries

179. Letter, George Washington to Phillis Wheatley
February 28, 1776
From Varick transcript, Library of Congress, Manuscript Division

180. *Liberty and Peace, A Poem*
by Phillis Wheatley Peters
Boston, 1784
Lent by The New-York Historical Society
Figure 72

181. *An Elegy, Sacred to the Memory of that Great Divine, the Reverend and Learned Dr. Samuel Cooper, who departed this Life December 29, 1783*
by Phillis Wheatley Peters
Boston, 1784
Lent by Massachusetts Historical Society

182. Obituary of Phillis Wheatley
Independent Chronicle, December 9, 1784
From original in Library of Congress

183. "Elegy on the Death of a Late Celebrated Poetess"
by Horatio
The Boston Magazine, December 1784, pp. 619-620
Lent by Bowdoin College Library, Brunswick, Maine
Figure 74

184. *Poems on Various Subjects, Religious and Moral*
by Phillis Wheatley
Philadelphia (first American edition), 1786
Lent by Library of Congress, Rare Books Division

185. "On Reading the Poems of Phillis Wheatley, the African Poetess"
by Matilda
New York Magazine, 1796, vol. I, pp. 549-550
Lent by Rutgers University, New Brunswick, New Jersey

186. Broadside, "An Address to Miss Phillis Wheatley"
Jupiter Hammon, August 4, 1778
8¾ x 6
Lent by The Connecticut Historical Society
Figure 75

187. Advertisement of Jupiter Hammon's *An Essay on the Ten Virgins*
Connecticut Courant, December 4, 1779
From original in Library of Congress
Figure 76

188. *A Winter Piece: Being A Serious Exhortation. With A Call To the Unconverted.*
by Jupiter Hammon
Hartford, 1782
Lent by The Connecticut Historical Society

189. *An Evening's Improvement. Showing the Necessity of Beholding the Laws of God. To which is added A Dialogue [in verse] the Kind Master And Dutiful servant*
by Jupiter Hammon
Hartford, 1783
Lent by The New-York Historical Society

190. *An Address to the Negroes in the State of New-York*
by Jupiter Hammon
New York, 1787
Lent by The New-York Historical Society
Figure 77

191. Advertisement of a black portraitist
Massachusetts Gazette (formerly *Boston Newsletter*), January 7, 1773
From original in Library of Congress
Figure 78

192. Advertisement by artist John Allwood to "Dispose of His Negro Fellows, Painters . . ."
South Carolina Gazette, March 8, 1773

From original in Charleston Library Society

Figure 79

193. Advertisement for return of a runaway slave, John Frances, "by trade a goldsmith"
Pennsylvania Packet, May 1, 1784

From original in Library of Congress

Figure 80

194. *Rules and Regulations of the Brown Fellowship Society, established at Charleston, South Carolina, 1st November 1790*
Charleston, 1844

Lent by College of Charleston Library

195. *Annals of the First African Church, in the United States of America, Now Styled The African Episcopal Church of St. Thomas*
Reverend William Douglass, editor
Philadelphia, 1862

Oberlin College Library

196. "Constitution of the African Society of Boston"
The Liberator, August, 1832

From original in Library of Congress

197. *Laws of the African Society, Instituted at Boston . . . 1796*
Boston, 1802

Lent by Massachusetts Historical Society

198. *The Sons of Africans: An Essay on Freedom, With Observations on the Origin of Slavery. By A Member of the African Society of Boston*
Boston, 1808

Lent by Library of the Boston Athenaeum

Figure 81

199. Prince Hall's Manumission Paper, April 9, 1770

From original in Price Notarial Records, Library of the Boston Athenaeum

200. Bill of sale for five drumheads from Prince Hall to Colonel Crafts, Regiment of Artillery, Boston, April 24, 1777

From original in Massachusetts Archives

Figure 82

201. "Queries Respecting the Slavery and Emancipation of Negroes in Massachusetts. Proposed by the Hon. Judge Tucker of Virginia, and answered by the Rev. Dr. Belknap"
Collections of the Massachusetts Historical Society, Boston, 1795

Lent by Smithsonian Institution Libraries

202. Petition of "African Blacks," signed by Prince Hall and others, to the Massachusetts General Court, January 4, 1787

From original in Massachusetts Archives

Figure 83

203. Petition of a "great Number of Blacks freemen," protesting against the kidnapping and sale of free Negroes, signed by Prince Hall and others, to the Massachusetts General Court, February 27, 1788

A Documentary History of the Negro People in the United States, vol. I (1951), pp. 20-21
Herbert Aptheker, editor

Original document unlocated

204. Petition of "a great number of blacks," for equal educational facilities signed by Prince Hall and others, to the Massachusetts General Court, October 17, 1787

A Documentary History of the Negro People in the United States, vol. I (1951), pp. 19-20
Herbert Aptheker, editor

Original document unlocated

205. *Charge Delivered to the Brethren of the African Lodge on the 25th of June, 1792 . . . in Charlestown*
by Prince Hall
Boston, 1792

Lent by Library of Congress, Rare Books Division

Figure 84

206. *A Charge Delivered to the African Lodge, June 24, 1797 . . . at Menotomy*
by Prince Hall
Boston, 1797

Lent by Library of Congress, Rare Books Division

Figure 85

207. *Constitution and Rules to Be Observed and Kept by the Friendly Society of St. Thomas's African Church of Philadelphia*
Philadelphia, 1797

Lent by Library Company of Philadelphia

Figure 86

208. Gustavus Vassa or Olaudah Equiano

Unidentified artist

Engraving, not dated

8¾ x 5⅜

Lent by The New-York Historical Society

Figure 87

209. *The Interesting Narrative of the Life of Olaudah Equiano, or Gustavus Vassa, the African, Written by Himself*
London, 1789, 2 vols.

Lent by Duke University Library, Durham, North Carolina

210. *The Interesting Narrative of the Life of Olaudah Equiano, or Gustavus Vassa, the African, Written by Himself*

New York (first American edition), 1791

Lent by Howard University, Washington, D.C.

Figure 88

211. *The Interesting Narrative . . . To which are added Poems on Various Subjects, by Phillis Wheatley*
Halifax, 1813

Lent by Library of Congress

212. " 'Luce Bijah,' slave of Ebenezer Wells"
History of Western Massachusetts
by Josiah Gilbert Holland
Springfield, 1855 (vol. II), pp. 359-360
Lent by Library of Congress

213. "Alice"
Eccentric Biography; or Memoirs of Remarkable Female Characters, Ancient and Modern
by Isaiah Thomas, Jr.
1804
Lent by Yale University Library
Figure 89

214. "Petition of an African Slave, to the Legislature of Massachusetts"
by Belinda
American Museum or Universal Magazine, vol. I, 1787, pp. 463-464
Lent by Georgetown University Library

215. Elizabeth Freeman
Susan Sedgwick (ca. 1789-1867)
Watercolor on ivory, 1811
4⅝ x 3⅞
Lent by Massachusetts Historical Society
Color plate 7

216. *The Practicability of the Abolition of Slavery: A Lecture, delivered at the Lyceum in Stockbridge, Massachusetts, February, 1831*
by Theodore Sedgwick
New York, 1831
Lent by Library of Congress

217. Yarrow Mamout
Charles Willson Peale (1741-1827)
Oil on canvas, 1819
24 x 20
Lent by Historical Society of Pennsylvania
Color plate 6

218. Diary of Charles Willson Peale, entry concerning Yarrow Mamout
1818-1819
Lent by American Philosophical Society Library

219. *Narrative of the Life and Adventures of Venture, A Native of Africa, But Resident above Sixty Years in the United States of America; Related by Himself*
(First printing, 1798)
Lent by Library of Congress, Rare Books Division

220. Indictment of Moses Sash, "a negro man & labourer" by the Supreme Judicial Court of Massachusetts, Northampton, April 9, 1787
From original in the office of the clerk of the Supreme Judicial Court for Suffolk County, Massachusetts

221. Gravestones of Amos and Violate Fortune
Fiberglass facsimiles of originals in Jaffrey, New Hampshire
Lent by Smithsonian Institution
Figures 90 and 91

222. Freedom papers of Amos Fortune
From original in Jaffrey Public Library, Jaffrey, New Hampshire

223. Gravestone of John Jack
Fiberglass facsimile of original in Concord, Massachusetts
Lent by Smithsonian Institution
Figure 92

224. Inscription on John Jack's tombstone
Boston Weekly Magazine, February 1805
Lent by Enoch Pratt Free Library, Baltimore

225. Medallion: "Am I Not A Man and a Brother?"
Josiah Wedgwood
Black basalt on white jasper, 1787
1¾₆ x 1⅛
Lent by The Buten Museum of Wedgwood, Merion, Pennsylvania
Figure 95

226. Letter, Benjamin Franklin to Josiah Wedgwood
May 15, 1787
11 x 14
Lent by Library of Congress, Manuscripts Division
Figure 96

227. Broadside, "An Act respecting Fugitives from Justice, and Persons' escaping from the Services of their Masters, February 1793"
12½ x 7¹³⁄₁₆
Lent by Library of Congress, Rare Books Division
Figure 94

228. The earliest black petition to Congress, January 30, 1797
The Debates and Proceedings in the Congress of the United States; Fourth Congress-Second Session (December 5, 1796 to March 3, 1797)
Washington, 1849, pp. 2015-2018

229. Affidavits of service for William Brown, powder monkey aboard the United States frigate *Constellation,* during the quasi-war with France, 1798-1800
9 February, 1799, and 2 February, 1800
From original in National Archives

230. A View of the American Frigate, *Constellation,* capturing the French National Frigate, *L'Insurgente,* within sight of Basseterre, February 9th, 1799
John Fairburn
Aquatint, October 1, 1800
14¼ x 18¼
Lent by United States Naval Academy Museum

231. Letter, Charles Lee, secretary of state ad interim, to Don Raymon de Castro, governor of Puerto Rico, on behalf of Moses Armstead, a prisoner of war
May 16, 1800
From original in National Archives

232. Documents relating to the trial and execution of Gabriel, October 1800
12¼ x 7½
Lent by Virginia State Library

233. Petition of Absalom Jones and others for repeal of the Fugitive Slave Law, to the House of Representatives, December 30, 1799
15½ x 9⅜
Lent by National Archives
Figure 9 7

234. *Oration, Delivered in Corinthian Hall, Rochester . . . July 5, 1852*
by Frederick Douglass
Rochester, 1852
Lent by Library of Congress
Figure 9 3

235. Frederick Douglass
J. W. Hurn, Philadelphia
Photograph, not dated
From original in Library of Congress
Figure 98